The Re-Forming
Tradition

THE PRESBYTERIAN PRESENCE:
THE TWENTIETH-CENTURY EXPERIENCE

Series Editors

Milton J Coalter

John M. Mulder

Louis B. Weeks

The Re-Forming Tradition: Presbyterians and Mainstream Protestantism

By
Milton J Coalter
John M. Mulder
Louis B. Weeks

Westminster/John Knox Press
Louisville, Kentucky

Book design by Gene Harris

First edition

This book is printed on acid-free paper that meets the American National Standards Institute Z39.48 standard. ∞

Published by Westminster/John Knox Press
Louisville, Kentucky

PRINTED IN THE UNITED STATES OF AMERICA
9 8 7 6 5 4 3 2 1

Library of Congress Cataloging-in-Publication Data

Coalter, Milton J.
  The re-forming tradition : Presbyterians and mainstream
Protestantism / by Milton J. Coalter, John M. Mulder, Louis B. Weeks
— 1st ed.
      p.   cm. — (The Presbyterian presence)
  Includes bibliographical references and index.
  ISBN 0-664-25299-0 (alk. paper)

  1. Presbyterian Church—United States—History—20th century.
2. United States—Church history—20th century. I. Mulder, John M.,
1946–   . II. Weeks, Louis B., 1941–   . III. Title. IV. Title:
Reforming tradition. V. Series.
BX8937.C63   1992
285′.1—dc20   91-45552

For
Lin, Martha Claire, and Siram
Mary, Aaron, and Cora
Carolyn, Lou, Lillian, and Sid

Contents

Series Foreword

This series, "The Presbyterian Presence: The Twentieth-Century Experience," is the product of a significant research project analyzing American Presbyterianism in this century. Funded by the Lilly Endowment and based at Louisville Presbyterian Theological Seminary, the project is part of a broader research effort that analyzes the history of mainstream Protestantism. By analyzing American Presbyterianism as a case study, we hope not only to chronicle its fate in the twentieth century but also to illumine larger patterns of religious change in mainstream Protestantism and in American religious and cultural life.

This case study of American Presbyterianism and the broader research on mainstream Protestantism arise out of an epochal change in American religion that has occurred during the twentieth century. Mainstream American Protestantism refers to those churches that emerged from the American Revolution as the dominant Protestant bodies and were highly influential in shaping American religion and culture during the nineteenth century. It includes the Presbyterians, Episcopalians, Methodists, Congregationalists (now the United Church of Christ), Disciples, and American or northern Baptists.

In this century, these churches have been displaced—religiously and culturally—to a significant degree. All have suffered severe membership losses since the 1960s. All have experienced significant theological tensions and shifts in emphasis. All are characterized by problems in their organization as institutions. And yet they remain influential voices in the spectrum of American religion and retain an enduring vitality in the face of a massive reconfiguration of American religious life.

The result is a complex phenomenon that is not easily described. Some would say the term "mainstream" or "mainline" is itself suspect and embodies ethnocentric and elitist assumptions. What characterized American religious history, they argue, was its diversity and its pluralism. Some groups may have believed they were religiously or culturally dominant, but the historical reality is much more pluralistic. Others would maintain that if there was a "mainstream," it no longer exists. Still others would propose that the mainstream itself has changed. The denominations of the evangelical awakening of the nineteenth century have been replaced by the evangelical churches of the late twentieth century—Southern Baptist, charismatic, Pentecostal.

Some propose that the term "mainline" or "mainstream" should be dropped in favor of talking about "liberal" Protestantism, but such a change presents additional problems. Like "evangelical," the term "liberal" is an extremely vague word to describe a set of Christian beliefs, values, and behavior. Furthermore, virtually all the "mainstream" churches contain large numbers of people who would describe themselves as either evangelical or liberal, thus making it very difficult to generalize about them as a denomination.

Despite the debates about terminology and the categories for analyzing American Protestantism, there is general agreement that American culture and American Protestantism of the late twentieth century are very different from what they were in the late nineteenth century. What has changed is the religious and cultural impact of American

Protestantism. A study of American Presbyterianism is a good lens for examining that change, for in spite of their relatively small numbers, Presbyterians are, or were, quintessential mainstreamers, exerting a great deal of influence because of their economic, social, educational, and cultural advantages.

When did the change occur? In a pioneering article written more than fifty years ago, Arthur M. Schlesinger, Sr., pointed to the period from 1875 to 1900 as "a critical period" in American religion. In particular, American Protestants confronted the external challenges of immigration, industrialization, and urbanization and the internal challenges posed by Darwinism, biblical criticism, history of religions, and the new social sciences.[1] Robert T. Handy has maintained that the 1920s witnessed a "religious depression." The result was a "second disestablishment" of American Protestantism. When the churches lost legal establishment in the U.S. Constitution, they attempted to "Christianize" American culture.[2] But by the 1920s, it was clear that both legal and cultural establishment had been rejected. Sydney Ahlstrom points to the 1960s as the time when American religion and culture took a "radical turn" and the "Puritan culture" of the United States was shattered.[3] Wade Clark Roof and William McKinney build on Ahlstrom's argument, proposing that the 1960s and 1970s represent a "third disestablishment," in which mainstream churches lost their religious dominance.[4]

These diverse interpretations underscore the fact that the crises of mainstream Protestantism did not appear suddenly and that the developments within one tradition— American Presbyterianism—are mirrored in other denominations as well. While some of our studies reach back into the late nineteenth century, most of our studies focus on the period after the fundamentalist controversy within Presbyterianism during the 1920s and 1930s. For a variety of reasons, that became a watershed for Presbyterians and ushered in the twentieth century.

The value of this substantial Presbyterian case study can be seen from at least two perspectives. First, this research is designed to write a chapter in the history of American religion and culture. It is the story of the attempt of one tradition—its people and its institutions—to respond to the crosscurrents of the twentieth century. Second, it is an attempt to illumine the problems and predicaments of American Presbyterianism so that its members and leaders might better understand the past as a resource for its future direction.

The series title was carefully chosen. Presence is more than passive existence, and it connotes the landmark that we hope these groups of studies provide for comparing the equally important pilgrimages of other mainline Protestant denominations through the past century. Missiologists have characterized the Christian responsibility as one of "profound presence" in the world, patterned on the presence of God in providence, in the incarnation, and in the work of the Holy Spirit. In the words of missionary and theologian John V. Taylor, Christians "stand" in the world in the name of Christ to be "really and totally present . . . in the present."[5]

Has the Presbyterian presence declined into mere existence? Have the commitments of Presbyterians degenerated into lifeless obligations? What forces have informed, transformed, or deformed our distinctive presence within the Christian community and the society? And can changes in Presbyterianism invigorate their continued yearnings to represent Christ in the world today? These are the questions posed in the series and the queries addressed by the Caldwell Lectures at Louisville Seminary from quite different perspectives.

More than sixty researchers, plus students at Louisville Seminary and generous colleagues in seminaries, colleges, and universities throughout the United States, have cooperated in the research on American Presbyterianism. Many are historians, but others are sociologists, economists, musicians, theologians, pastors, and lay people. What has excited us as a research team was the opportunity of working on a fascinating historical problem with critical implications for the Presbyterian Church and mainstream Protestantism. Animating our work and conversations was the hope that this research might make a difference, that it might help one church and a broader Christian tradition understand the problems more clearly so that their witness might be more faithful. It is with this hope that we issue this series, "The Presbyterian Presence: The Twentieth-Century Experience."

Milton J Coalter
John M. Mulder
Louis B. Weeks

Acknowledgments

This is the last volume in the series, "The Presbyterian Presence." It represents the culmination of five years of research, supported by a grant from the Lilly Endowment.

As the directors of this project, we have incurred many debts. We are very grateful to the more than 60 researchers who participated in this program. Their work, published in the previous six volumes, is the foundation for our own summary of the findings in this book.

We are also indebted to the community of Louisville Presbyterian Theological Seminary for its support and encouragement throughout this endeavor. The Board of Trustees, Alumni/ae Board of Directors, faculty, administrators, staff, and students supported us in producing each volume, and several offered suggestions for improving our work. We are especially appreciative to the staff of our offices—Elna Amaral, Dana Cormack, Beverly Hourigan, Kem Longino, and Jean Newman—who kept us organized amid the mountain of paper the project generated. We also thank Michael Barram for his invaluable assistance in tracking down materials for the text and endnotes. In addition, the faculty and staff of Western Theological Seminary provided an hospitable environment for writing and research during several summers.

The entire project would not have been possible without the initiative and inspiration of Robert Wood Lynn, formerly Senior Vice President for Religion of the Lilly Endowment. His commitment to research and his interest in mainstream Protestantism have reshaped the understanding of American religion and American Protestantism. Upon his retirement in 1989, Craig Dykstra became the Vice President for Religion at the Lilly Endowment, and with his support came the birth of the Louisville Institute for the Study of Protestantism and American Culture at Louisville Seminary. We are very pleased to be working with the Endowment in this broader program of research and leadership education.

Several colleagues graciously agreed to read an earlier draft of this manuscript under considerable time pressure: Wayne Allen, Dorothy Bass, Craig Dykstra, William F. Ekstrom, Clifton Kirkpatrick, James W. Lewis, George M. Marsden, William McKinney, Belle Miller McMaster, Robert Wood Lynn, C. Ellis Nelson, George W. Newlin, Mark Noll, Rick Nutt, Joyce C. Tucker, and Barbara Wheeler. Another group participated in a small conference based on an earlier version of this book: Barbara Z. Barnes, Douglas Brackenridge, Warner Durnell, David Hester, Bradley Longfield, Donald Luidens, Donald McKim, Rick Nutt, Richard Reifsnyder, Dale Soden, and Ronald White. These readers offered helpful criticisms of the book that have improved it considerably.

At the end of this project, we also thank the hundreds of Presbyterians who have listened to our presentations and challenged us with penetrating questions and critiques. This volume has been influenced significantly by that dialogue, and we hope it is the occasion for additional reflection and conversation about the past and future of American Presbyterianism.

Westminster/John Knox Press and its staff have been extremely valuable partners in this enterprise, and we thank particularly Davis Perkins, the Editorial Director and our editor for this volume.

Our research and writing drew us away from our families over the past five years, and we have undoubtedly taxed their interest and patience. In gratitude for their love, support, and patience, we dedicate this book to them.

Milton J Coalter
John M. Mulder
Louis B. Weeks

Introduction

In 1897, Britain celebrated the sixtieth anniversary of Queen Victoria's reign. Many years later, Arnold J. Toynbee recalled this event which marked the close of the nineteenth century—the *Pax Britannica*—by writing: "I remember watching the Diamond Jubilee Procession myself as a small boy. I remember the atmosphere. It was: Well, here we are on the top of the world, and we have arrived at this peak to stay there—forever!" He continued, "There is, of course, a thing called history, but history is something unpleasant that happens to other people. We are comfortably outside all that. I am sure, if I had been a small boy in New York in 1897 I should have felt the same. Of course, if I had been a small boy in 1897 in the Southern part of the United States, I should not have felt the same; I should then have known from my parents that history had happened to my people in my part of the world."[1]

Most American Presbyterians, like other mainstream Protestants, could have echoed Toynbee's words at the end of the nineteenth century. It was the Protestant century in American history, and they had dominated it. Now they stand at the end of the twentieth century, the

American century, and they know: history has happened to them.

This volume is intended to tell that story. It focuses on one strand of mainstream Protestantism—the Presbyterians—and principally its three major branches in the twentieth century. The Presbyterian Church in the U.S.A. (PCUSA) merged in 1958 with the United Presbyterian Church of North America (UPCNA) to form the United Presbyterian Church in the U.S.A. (UPCUSA). The United Presbyterian Church and the Presbyterian Church in the U.S. (PCUS) reunited in 1983 after 122 years of separation, occasioned by the Civil War, and became the Presbyterian Church (U.S.A.), or PC(USA).

In focusing on Presbyterians in the twentieth century, we hope that careful investigation of their experience might shed light on the broader patterns of change in mainstream Protestantism and American religion and culture.

This volume is the final one in the series, "The Presbyterian Presence: The Twentieth-Century Experience." These seven volumes represent the culmination of five years of work on approximately 50 projects by more than 60 researchers. The work was based at Louisville Presbyterian Theological Seminary and coordinated by the three authors of this book.

The Louisville study is part of a much larger body of research on mainstream Protestantism, nearly all of which has been funded by the Lilly Endowment. In the late 1970s and 1980s, the Endowment began to fund projects that examined the most obvious fact about late twentieth-century mainstream Protestantism—its loss of members. Then followed a number of broader studies by others, including Robert Wuthnow, Wade Clark Roof and William McKinney, and William Hutchison.[2]

The Louisville study on Presbyterians is one of two case studies of denominations funded by Lilly in the late 1980s. The other was based at Christian Theological Seminary in Indianapolis and concentrated on the Disciples of Christ.[3] Thus far, the Louisville study is unquestionably the largest and most exhaustive analysis of any single Protestant denomination in the twentieth century. We hope that studies of other denominations can be illuminated by and complement this work.

Despite the magnitude of the Presbyterian project, we are still painfully aware of its gaps and deficiencies. For example, we know that the baby boomers were critical to both the growth and the decline in American Presbyterianism, but we do not have a study of the changes in youth ministry in twentieth-century American Presbyterianism. We also know that the sharp increase in the divorce rate since the 1960s coincided with steep membership decline. Marriage and family correlate with church membership. But we did not investigate whether divorce correlates with leaving the church. We cite these examples to suggest that good research always stimulates additional interesting questions. We also want to acknowledge that although we have learned much about the Presbyterian experience in the twentieth century, there were many questions we did not but should have asked.

The recent round of research on mainstream Protestantism was initiated largely by Robert Wood Lynn, then Senior Vice President for Religion at the Lilly Endowment. The scholarly community owes him an enormous debt, but even more indebted to him are the mainstream Protestant denominations. Lynn initiated this research in the midst of two fascinating developments. First, since at least the 1960s denominations and particularly mainstream Protestant churches had been seriously neglected in the study of American religion. Denominational history was considered a dry, unimaginative way of investigating the richness of religious life in American culture. Second, in the midst of this scholarly neglect, mainstream Protestant denominations were experiencing massive changes. These transformations puzzled and frightened the denominational leaders, as well as their members, but serious inquiry into them was rarely attempted.

Our thesis is that the current situation for American Presbyterians and mainstream Protestants bears more similarity to the late eighteenth and early nineteenth centuries than it does to the period immediately after World War II. Like the Revolutionary and early national periods of American history, the late twentieth century is an era of the re-forming and redefinition of American Presbyterianism and American religious life. This means that we are living in one of the most significant periods in all of American religious history. The scope and magnitude of the problems are intimidating, but the opportunities for reform and renewal are also exciting and promising.

The basic theme of this volume is the fragmentation of American Presbyterianism in the twentieth century. In surveying the Presbyterian research, Dorothy Bass noted that the studies are characterized by three interpretations. One stresses the impact of secularization. The second argues that what happened to various parts of Presbyterianism was a decline in quality. The third focuses on the fragmentation of its life and witness.[4]

While we employ the secularization and decline of quality interpretations to explain some factors, we believe that fragmentation best explains the historical contours of twentieth-century American Presbyterianism. Its value also lies in its suggestion that the problems of American mainstream Protestantism are not due simply to human mistakes or institutional missteps; rather, the difficulties are part of the broad process of modernization that has shaped so much of twentieth-century American culture. Modernization fragments society. It emphasizes technological production and hierarchical, rational bureaucracies. It specializes information and roles; it makes individuals both autonomous and anonymous to one another. It divides life into discrete segments. People live with "home-less minds."[5]

This book plays a contrapuntal theme, emphasizing on the one hand the forces that were transforming American Presbyterianism and American culture, and on the other hand the specific decisions Presbyterians made that shaped their history and now affect their future. Even where it is clear that various policies or programs were misguided or wrong, they were often initiated as reforms with the best of intentions. History teaches many lessons about the law of unintended consequences.

The Louisville-based research on American Presbyterianism was shaped by one basic assumption. We assumed that the PC(USA) and other mainstream Protestant denominations are in trouble. We approached our subject as a study in pathology. What is going wrong? What is the nature of the problems? What are their origins? We focused on problems, not because we were looking for something or some group to blame for the perilous state of Presbyterianism, but to explain the current malaise of the denomination.

Although this assumption needs to be tested and challenged, it has thus far dominated—with good reason—the research and literature on American Presbyterianism and mainstream Protestantism. What it fails to do is account for the many signs of health in the Presbyterian Church (U.S.A.) and mainstream Protestant denominations, and the next stage in the research should attempt to analyze the examples of vitality and the continuing energy of this tradition—even as American religious life is being re-formed and redefined.

We also encouraged researchers to use particular time parameters for the research—namely, the 1920s to the 1980s. Most but not all of the studies used these chronological limits. The time period was chosen in part for theological reasons, since the 1920s mark an important turning point in the Presbyterian theological confrontation with modernism and modernity. In choosing the 1920s, we were also influenced by Robert T. Handy's suggestion that this decade initiated the erosion of mainstream Protestantism's capacity to shape and mold American culture—a major theme of twentieth-century American religious history.[6]

We have three audiences for this book. One is Presbyterians. For five years we have discussed this research with them, and they significantly altered and expanded the scope of our endeavor. Another audience is academic colleagues who may be interested in this case study to learn more about the changing patterns of American religious life. They helped us immeasurably in the early stages of our research by suggesting topics for research. The research agenda was therefore set by an interesting interplay between the academy and the church. A third audience is other mainstream Protestants and people interested in American religion, and we hope that our analysis will indeed be a case study to illumine the broader context of American religion and culture.

Each of the preceding volumes in "The Presbyterian Presence" series were collections of essays. The first one, *The Presbyterian Predicament*, contains six lectures originally delivered as part of the Caldwell lecture series at Louisville Seminary. It was designed to introduce the themes of the next five books. *The Confessional Mosaic* is a collection of essays focusing on theological changes in American Presbyterianism, a long-neglected subject. *The Mainstream Protestant "Decline"* contains essays that expand and deepen our understanding of the complex patterns of membership growth and decline. *The Pluralistic Vision* examines the changing character of education in American Presbyterianism and its leadership. *The Organizational Revolution* charts the changes in Presbyterianism as denominations and institutions, and several of the essays have original insights into the understudied nature of American religious organizations. *The Diversity of Discipleship* is a volume about Presbyterian mission—its expansion in scope as well as its fragmentation.

The Re-Forming Tradition was designed to be a summary and synthesis of this scholarship. Careful readers of the entire series will see that we do not always agree with every author. We authors are not of one mind either. One of us often accents particular themes to the discomfort of the other two. What follows is our attempt to be faithful to the scholarship as we understand it. We hope that this volume will be both the conclusion to the series and an inviting stimulus to readers to explore more fully and deeply the other six volumes on which it is based.

The outline of the book follows the series. Part I, the first seven chapters, provides an overview of the findings in the study. Chapter 1 is an introduction to broad themes and changes in American religion and culture. These are crucial to understanding the development of American Presbyterianism in the twentieth century. Chapter 2 discusses the most obvious sign of difficulty in mainstream Protestantism—the loss of membership—and it draws heavily on the volume *The Mainstream Protestant "Decline."* In chapter 3 we turn our attention to the fascinating but vexing organizational problems in American Presbyterian life, and this chapter arises out of *The Organizational Revolution.* Chapter 4 deals with theology, and it contains information and insight from the essays in *The Confessional Mosaic* and *The Pluralistic Vision.* Chapters 5 and 6 deal with the transformation of Presbyterian mission in the twentieth century— evangelism, mission(s), ecumenism, racial ethnic ministries, and social justice. These two chapters draw on several volumes, most notably *The Diversity of Discipleship.* The theme of chapter 7 is education and nurture, and its argument arises primarily from the research in *The Pluralistic Vision.*

The tone and character of this book change in Part II, which includes chapters 8 and 9. From the beginning of our research, Presbyterians were especially insistent that we tell them what could be done about the problems we identified. As historians, we were a bit reluctant to prescribe, but as Presbyterians ourselves, we felt we owed it to the church to offer some conclusions about what we can do to make the re-forming church a reforming church.

Chapter 8, therefore, outlines seven parallel allegiances that are often in conflict in contemporary American Presbyterianism. Accenting one to the exclusion of the others creates imbalances, and we argue that the church is most faithful to the gospel when it can maintain a flexible equilibrium as it strives to meet the needs of the world.

Chapter 9 then turns specific, outlining a five-part agenda for reform in American Presbyterianism. It should be clear that the particular items of that reform agenda are not intended as the entire answer to the problems of American Presbyterians and mainstream Protestants. Furthermore, the proposals for reform are intended as an interim, short-term strategy to renew the life of American Presbyterianism. The concerns were selected because they arose out of our research and because they have been neglected or distorted. Knowing Presbyterians, we have every reason to believe that this agenda for reform will be debated.

In her study *The March of Folly*, Barbara Tuchman concluded: "Mental standstill or stagnation—the maintenance intact by rulers and policy makers of the ideas they started with—is fertile ground for folly. . . . Learning from experience is a faculty almost never practiced."[7] Though she spoke of leaders in governments, she might well have been speaking of those in any human organization—even the church. We firmly believe, however, that the Presbyterian community is capable of rethinking our Christian life together and learning from experience.

A final personal word: This research project was painful for us and for many of our researchers. Its focus on problems made us keenly aware of the diminished strength of American Presbyterianism and mainstream Protestantism. It prompted us to reexamine many deeply held values and commitments. It has been a poignant reminder of the human character of the church's witnesses with their high commitment and flawed vision.

Each of us is a lifelong Presbyterian—an increasingly rare bird these days, as you will see. We write not only as critical historians but also as individuals who love our church and want to see it emerge from its current travail as a fuller and more faithful participant in the global Christian community. Reading about the re-forming of American Presbyterianism could be a depressing experience, but we hope it will not be. Historians are invariably disguised reformers, and we trust that "The Presbyterian Presence" series and *The Re-Forming Tradition* will provide the occasion for reflection, repentance, and reform. We believe that God is not yet finished with the Presbyterian Church (U.S.A.).

I

The Presbyterian Presence:
The Twentieth-Century
Experience

1

Looking Backward:
Religion and American Culture

Theodore Cuyler stepped into the pulpit at the centennial General Assembly of the Presbyterian Church in the U.S.A. in 1888. The commissioners solemnly listened as Cuyler spoke of the church's past and future in his typical careful diction:

> Within the last hundred years the Presbyterian Church has had a remarkable increase. In 1788 there were only seventeen presbyteries, 177 ministers, 419 churches, and not over 20,000 communicants. Today if we combine the columns of both wings, Northern and Southern, there are 270 presbyteries, 6770 ministers, 8672 churches, and 851,000 communicants. . . . Fathers and brethren! Let us rejoice that we have today witnessed this happy commemoration. As we listen to the stroke of that bell which sounds the exit of a century in our annals, let us answer it back with a heartfelt "Hallelujah." The spirits of the mighty dead, whose achievements we have rehearsed, seem to hover around us to join in our songs of thanksgiving. . . . While we shall adore that ineffable and all-glorious NAME that is above every name . . . , we shall not be ashamed to say, "I was, and I am, a PRESBYTERIAN!"[1]

Cuyler had reason to celebrate, for the PCUSA was prospering. He himself served the Lafayette Avenue Presbyte-

rian Church in Brooklyn, a congregation that had called
him as its founding pastor and had subsequently grown to a
membership of 2,320, one of the largest in the entire denomination.

A century later, the Lafayette Avenue Church had dwindled to 162 members served by an interim pastor.

In 1988 the bicentennial General Assembly of the
reunited Presbyterian Church (U.S.A.) gathered in St.
Louis. There were celebrations—colorful wall decorations,
fifteen-foot puppets on parade, a clown in Revolutionary
attire, massed choirs, strong sermons, and a video production of the General Assembly leaders. And yet, the celebration was muted by comparison. Gone was the extravagant
language of 1888; the Presbyterian Church (U.S.A.) had
seen nearly 25 years of membership decline and intense division over doctrine, social and political issues, and church
programs.

Few in 1988 would have declared with Charles L.
Thompson a century before, "Our spectrum holds the best
metal of the old saints, and the living light of today. . . .
Today a hundred colleges flash it forth, and eight thousand
ministers carry it on. It has crossed the continent to the
Pacific, and its arrows of sunrise pierce the Himalayas."[2]

These two General Assemblies, separated by 100 years,
demonstrate the epochal changes that have swept across
American Presbyterianism in the twentieth century. The
transformation has affected other mainstream Protestant
denominations, and it represents a chapter in the continuing kaleidoscopic re-forming of religion and American culture. The changes are in part the story of the churches
themselves, but they are also a helpful prism for viewing
what is happening to American society as a whole.

To understand American Presbyterianism in the twentieth century requires a preliminary analysis of several different though related political, intellectual, economic, and
social trends that distinctly marked the American religious
and cultural landscape. These factors shaped the environment in which churches developed in this country and in
turn were shaped by those churches.

The American Religious Landscape

Mainstream Protestantism confronted a series of disestablishments from legal recognition and cultural and religious dominance during the twentieth century. It was also fractured by internal strife and division. Divided among themselves, conservative and liberal Protestants became adept at identifying and magnifying their differences. The issues they debated were often critical to Christianity itself, but the twentieth-century civil war in American Protestantism rendered the churches increasingly unable to understand and respond to the massive changes occurring in American society.

The Three Disestablishments of Religion in America

The formation of the United States launched this "first new nation" of Western culture as a far-reaching experiment in the relationship of church and state.[3] For fifteen centuries after the emperor Constantine established the Christian faith as the official state religion of the Roman Empire, the ideal in Western Christianity was religious establishment—the union of church and state. The state recognized a particular church and protected it legally. The church gave religious sanction to the state's authority, and the state undergirded the church's spiritual and temporal power.

Most American colonists, including Presbyterians, retained the ideal of the state churches of Europe, but the religious diversity of the colonies made such an Old World transplant impossible. The federal Constitution of 1787 and the Bill of Rights of 1789 embodied the new vision—the secular state guaranteeing religious liberty, with no religious body enjoying preferred status.[4] The vast majority of American Protestants, and especially Presbyterians, supported this move. They strongly advocated the free expression of religious convictions without state interference.[5]

This legal disestablishment was ambiguous, particularly because the political thought of the nation's founders assumed that religion would provide a common moral basis for the experiment of republican government and because Protestants themselves set forth to "Christianize" or "Protestantize" the American people and institutions.[6] Evangelical Protestants sought to mold and shape American culture so that even though no single church was legally recognized, Christian values would still prevail. Having failed to forge a legal establishment, they attempted to forge a cultural establishment.

When combined with the Protestant community's dominance in numbers and in the seats of power, this informal establishment allowed American Protestants to shape the nation's social conscience and religious aspirations well into the twentieth century. Certain denominations within American Protestantism itself exerted more influence than others under this arrangement. Episcopalians, Presbyterians, and Congregationalists enjoyed disproportionate control over positions of cultural power during the eighteenth century.

During the nineteenth century, this colonial mainline gave way to the "upstart sects"—the Methodists and Baptists, who became the two largest Protestant denominations, as well as the Disciples of Christ, who emerged as a typical expression of frontier evangelicalism with "no creed but the Bible." These three denominations plus the Episcopalians, Presbyterians, and Congregationalists comprised an "Evangelical United Front," as it was dubbed during the nineteenth century. Observers now describe them as mainstream, or mainline, or establishment Protestantism and suggest that the Lutherans joined their number in the mid- to late twentieth century.

This reconfiguration of the mainline indicates that Presbyterians lost their leading role as early as the nineteenth century. In other words, the mainline or mainstream is always being redefined.[7] At every point, these terms are controversial and inexact, but they do suggest the power of these denominations to shape and to embody the central currents of American religion and American culture.

Nineteenth-century America was the heyday of evangelical Protestantism and the evangelical united front. In retrospect, the antebellum era was the formative period for what is known as mainstream Protestantism, and most of the institutions, programs, and theological and ethical concerns of these denominations in the twentieth century can be traced to the early nineteenth century.

Evangelicalism was the unifying dynamo that powered the movement, and experimentation flourished. Institutions, practices, and concerns that seem commonplace to American mainstream Protestantism today existed only in nascent form two hundred years ago: the denomination itself, foreign and domestic missionary work, theological seminaries, freewill offerings as the financial infrastructure of denominations, a wide-ranging social and ethical agenda (ranging from racism and feminism to the problems of substance abuse, mainly alcohol, and urban problems), and the early stirrings of theological pluralism. Others like the Sunday school and the benevolent society or parachurch group had not yet appeared in the eighteenth century.

In retrospect, the Protestant attempt to Christianize American culture is noteworthy for several reasons. First, it succeeded to a remarkable degree. By the late nineteenth century, there was a discernible Christian ethos that permeated much of American culture—politics, education, the press, the arts, and even the sciences. For example, as late as the 1890s the New York newspapers still dutifully reported on the sermons preached in many New York churches. Even the U.S. Supreme Court declared in 1892 that the United States was a Christian nation. Therefore, it affirmed, Congress would not pass laws contrary to the Christian faith.[8]

Second, at its best the quest for a Christian America embodied a vision of a humane society which attempted to deal with the forces that undermined the quality of human life. It is easy to identify the naïveté and myopia that characterized so many nineteenth-century Protestant reformers, but it is also difficult to ignore their courage and commitment.

Third, at its worst the attempt to shape American culture

in a Christian image was flawed in its conception of what a Christian society should be. At the zenith of its influence in the late nineteenth and early twentieth centuries, the evangelical Protestant denominations ministered to a culture that countenanced the forced removal of Native Americans from their land and their relocation onto reservations, the codifying of legal segregation of African Americans, urban race riots and lynchings, the height of anti-Catholic resentment, the violent suppression of labor unions, and the stirrings of imperialism in American foreign policy. It is painful to place the rhetoric of those proclaiming a Christian America alongside its reality.

The erosion of the dream of a Christian or Protestant America was accelerated in the twentieth century by two other informal disestablishments. According to Robert Handy, mainstream Protestantism experienced with the rest of the American population a "swift alteration of national mood" following World War I. The "political partisanship and bickering" that defeated America's entry into the League of Nations left many Americans feeling that "their sacrificial support of the war was being betrayed. . . . Postwar periods of inflation and unemployment brought privation and bitterness; there were a number of stormy strikes; [and] racial tension erupted in ugly urban riots." As a result, Handy notes, "there spread across the nation a sense of disillusionment" with idealism and reform that undermined the attraction to mainstream Protestantism's optimistic crusading spirit.[9]

A so-called "new immigration" during the late nineteenth and early twentieth centuries compounded the impact of these developments. Immigrants from southern and eastern Europe as well as Asia entered the United States during this period in numbers never before encountered. A large number of these immigrants were Roman Catholics, Jews, and adherents of Asian religions. Protestants, especially mainstream Protestants, still enjoyed a disproportionate share of social power. But as the sociologist Will Herberg observed in 1955, Protestants could no longer monopolize the definition of what it meant to be religious in

American society. Instead, a coalition of Protestants, Catholics, and Jews served as the major religious formers of the American conscience.[10] In short, this was a religious disestablishment.

Appearances, however, were deceiving. According to Herberg, none of these religious traditions actually wielded cultural power. Rather, this triumvirate of Protestant-Catholic-Jew had become the unwitting agents for the promotion of an "American Way of Life" which was less the Judeo-Christian tradition and more a nationalistic amalgam of cultural pride and an amorphous "faith in faith."[11] The religiosity of the time is represented in President Dwight D. Eisenhower's oft-quoted affirmation: "Our government makes no sense unless it is founded on a deeply felt religious faith—and I don't care what it is."[12]

The turmoil of the 1960s brought a third, cultural disestablishment to mainstream Protestantism. In previous disestablishments, Presbyterians and other mainstream Protestants retained their cultural power in coalitions with other Protestants or Catholics or at least communities within the Judeo-Christian tradition. But the cultural disestablishment of the 1960s and subsequent decades called into question the very propriety of a synthesis of religion and culture. In matters of belief and morality, a new pluralism was born out of dissent in personal and public faith.[13]

The ideal of a Christian America and establishment Protestantism was ultimately doomed by the reality of the secular state and the pluralism of American culture. Only since the mid-twentieth century has the United States grappled with the ambiguous legacy of the Revolutionary era's creation of a secular state. In church-state cases, the lines between the state and churches seem at once clearer and less defined than ever.[14]

American Civil Religion

The theme of the disestablishments of American religion provides one way of understanding the long-term changes in American mainstream Protestantism's status vis-à-vis the state and the culture. The category of civil religion is another interpretive lens that clarifies the sources of mainstream Protestants' aspirations to create a Christian America as well as of their more recent rejection of that project. Students of American culture have hotly debated the character and even existence of a civil religion, but few contest that the intertwining of religious and political imagery and symbolism has been a prominent feature of American history.[15]

At the heart of American civil religion is a belief in God's election of the American people and the United States as a nation commissioned for a unique role in human history. The roots of this idea reach back to the first settlement of New England, when Puritan leaders like John Winthrop described their pilgrim enterprise as the establishment of a godly "city upon a hill" for the whole world to admire and emulate. The spiritual revivals of the First Great Awakening during the 1740s reinforced and embellished the imagery of America as God's new Israel. Jonathan Edwards suggested that the millennial hopes of Christians across the centuries might be realized in North America, and specifically New England. Even Jefferson in the Declaration of Independence invoked this special relationship with God as a justification for revolt against the political power of England. Therefore, it was no accident that preachers during the American Revolution saw George Washington as an "American Joshua . . . raised up by God and divinely formed by a peculiar influence of the Sovereign of the Universe for . . . conducting this people . . . to Liberty and Independence."[16]

The Revolution transformed the early Puritans' errand into a national mission to "reblaze back from America to Europe, Asia and Africa, and illumine the world with TRUTH and LIBERTY."[17] Coupled with the more traditional Christian hope of bringing all humanity to Christ, this vision propelled evangelical Protestant missions during the nineteenth century.

The Civil War completed the merging of Protestant mission and American republican liberty. As Robert Bellah has observed: "In Lincoln's greatest public statements the tradition of American public oratory, infused with biblical imagery and expressed in an almost Puritan 'plain style,' attained a classic form."[18] Later American presidents followed Lincoln's lead by regularly linking God with America's prosperity, destiny, and leadership in the world.

Bellah believes that the events of the 1960s and 1970s shattered the cohesion of the American civil religion. America's confrontation with racism in the civil rights movement, the decline in a sense of national righteousness during the Vietnam war, its erosion of faith in the integrity of leadership during the Watergate crisis, new challenges to sexual morality and gender roles—all these and more have muted, if not destroyed, the self-confident spirit of American civil religion, despite its partial resurgence in the 1980s and early 1990s.

The fate of American civil religion is critical for mainstream Protestants, since they were key formulators and proponents of it. Their theological instincts for seeking the transformation of their culture by implanting Christian principles into its laws and institutions prepared them for the task, and that is one source of their present dilemma in American culture. The claims for America's special place in the world, which American civil religion encouraged, eventually exceeded their Christian roots. During the last century, American civil religion held that the bond between God and the nation could not be severed by either partner. What had been conditional was now automatic and permanent.

American mainstream Protestants' complicity in escalating these pretensions brought them significant criticism during the twentieth century from both within the church and outside it. As American civil religion came under attack, mainstream Protestants attempted to distance themselves from their own offspring and thereby severed one root of their own identity.

By the end of the century, the chastening of American civil religion became also the story of the mainstream Protestants as they too were forced to accommodate to new realities of diminished cultural prominence and political power.

The Divisions of Protestant Evangelicalism

A third landmark trend that has dramatically affected current American religious configurations is the rupture of the evangelical consensus that unified mainstream Protestants into an Evangelical United Front in antebellum America.

Nineteenth-century evangelical Protestantism saw its own share of ecclesiastical schisms, sharp doctrinal debate, and agonizing struggle over ethical issues like slavery. The 1837 schism of the PCUSA into Old and New School organizations, each claiming to be the one true PCUSA, illustrates how bitter and divisive these conflicts could become. Proponents of the PCUSA (Old School) distrusted their PCUSA (New School) opponents' revival techniques as well as the theological emphases of the revivals, which emphasized the free will of individuals to accept or reject the salvation offered by a sovereign God. They likewise questioned the New School's open-armed alliances both with Congregationalists to evangelize the Old Northwest and with other denominations to provide missionaries to the American frontier and to foreign lands through nondenominational benevolent societies.

Nevertheless, in retrospect, an "evangelical united front" did exist in the antebellum period. Even contending groups like Old and New School Presbyterians held more in common than their overt division would indicate. Individuals like Albert Barnes and Ashbel Green, both pastors in prominent Presbyterian congregations in Philadelphia and leaders of opposing sides in the schism, shared a dual concern for the salvation of individuals and the redemption of American society. Both men practiced an austere piety that required strict Sabbath observance not only for church members but also for the Philadelphia public. Both supported ecumenical cooperation, though admittedly to varying degrees. Green, for instance, rejected the 1801 Plan of

Union between Congregationalists and Presbyterians that
the New School supported. But as early as 1790 Green promoted the formal sharing of delegates, with voice but no
vote, between the PCUSA General Assembly and New England Congregationalist associations so that the two communions could sustain constant communication. Barnes
and Green certainly weighted quite differently the compelling influences of the divine and the free will of the individual in conversion experiences. Yet each acknowledged the
critical impact of both factors in the transformation of
souls.[19]

In fact, the severity of their conflict may actually have
been fueled by what they held in common. The Old and
New Schools shared a common faith in the absolute authority of scripture, a trust that the scriptural message was
self-evident to any serious reader, and the conviction that
the moral code encapsulated in the biblical message can
and should be applied rigorously to individual conduct and
to the society at large. These points of evangelical consensus precipitated severe friction between the Old and the
New School, however, when either group found to their
great wonderment that their opponents misunderstood the
gospel's "plain and simple" meaning for personal piety, for
denominational theology or policy, and for public life.

The evangelical consensus that prevailed even among
Old and New School Presbyterian combatants was itself
shattered by an internecine civil war in American Protestantism generally during the late nineteenth and twentieth
centuries. The terms used to describe the antagonists vary
over time—fundamentalists versus modernists, conservatives versus liberals, and so on. One of the distinguishing
characteristics of American Protestantism in the twentieth
century is the fragmentation of the nineteenth-century
evangelical movement and the fractious contention between and among two major orientations in the Protestant
house.

The early signs of the division came in the late nineteenth century. Social forces—immigration, urbanization,
and industrialization—posed dramatic challenges to

American Protestants. New questions were also raised by the rise of Darwinian science, biblical criticism, the new social sciences of sociology and psychology, and the study of the history of religions.[20]

Evangelical Protestants responded differently. One stream, eventually known as liberalism, sought to welcome the changes as signs of progress and the gradual realization of the kingdom of God. Liberals strove to deal with the urgent social and political problems of the new urban nation and to adapt Christianity to the new systems of thought. The latter move, in concert with the appropriation of higher biblical criticism, altered the way liberal Christians would regard the Bible's authority. Increasingly, liberal Christians distinguished between the "chaff" of biblical revelation—that is, its literal story line and traditional ascriptions of authorship—from the "kernel" of spiritual truth expressed in, through, and sometimes even in spite of the culturally conditioned biblical narrative. This new vision of biblical revelation required a deft critique by scholars of the original languages, taking into account the cultural and theological factors that influenced the original authors' descriptions of ancient events. The "plain and simple" meaning of the biblical text, previously assumed to be available to all serious readers, was no longer so plain or simple.

A second stream of evangelical Protestantism, later known as fundamentalism, aggressively opposed theological modernism or liberalism because of the latter's relativism, redefinition of biblical authority, and emphasis on social concerns to the neglect of individual salvation. Fundamentalism resisted as well the cultural trends toward an urban, industrialized, pluralistic America. Fundamentalism was basically reactionary, and it was pessimistic about the prospects for society short of dramatic divine intervention. Fundamentalists insisted that the new theoretical and social challenges of the late nineteenth and early twentieth centuries seriously defaced the simple and self-evident biblical revelation and its implications for human life. They tended to see history in premillennial terms—as a steady deterioration of human history until Christ would return again to inaugurate his thousand-year rule. Liberals, in contrast, were overwhelmingly postmillennial—expecting the progressive realization of the kingdom of God on earth, before Christ's second coming.[21]

Both conservatives and liberals were divided among themselves as well. Early in the twentieth century the Pentecostal movement emerged with its emphasis on the gifts of the Holy Spirit, particularly the ability to speak in tongues. Pentecostalism spawned new denominations, such as the Assemblies of God, and as it infiltrated Protestant denominations it was termed the charismatic movement or charismatic revival.

Liberals were also a diverse lot. Some were politically progressive; others were not. Some found intellectual refuge in science or natural theology; others held to the categories of biblical authority and divine transcendence.

Each side of the spectrum was witheringly critical of likeminded kin as well as devastating in its denunciation of doctrinal obscurantism (the charge against conservatives) or desertion of the Christian faith (the claim against liberals).

The fundamentalist-modernist debate spanned the denominations that comprised the evangelical united front, and the fight was particularly bitter in the Presbyterian Church in the U.S.A. during the 1920s and 1930s. At the center of the debate was the question of how precise the lines would be in defining the nature of Christian doctrine, and the PCUSA resolved the issue by declaring narrow precision to be inappropriate. The PCUSA became, in the words of Lefferts A. Loetscher, "the broadening church."[22]

The reaction of early fundamentalists tended to be separation, withdrawing from their denominations to establish churches of pure doctrine. However, after World War II, a "neo-evangelical" movement arose, and its leaders frequently remained within mainstream Protestant denominations while supporting institutions and programs that appealed to like-minded evangelicals. Billy Graham became the best-known leader of the movement; the founding of the National Association of Evangelicals in 1943 was the first sign of evangelical cooperation; *Christianity Today* became a major journal for evangelical ideas; and Fuller Theological Seminary represented the burgeoning growth of evangelical theological education.[23]

Twentieth-century American Protestantism, especially American Presbyterianism, is impossible to understand without recognizing the impact of this 100-year-old division between conservatives and liberals. It decisively shaped the agendas of denominations, congregations, educational institutions, and leaders. American mainstream Protestants' identity is no longer determined primarily by denominational affiliation. Instead, they are divided across denominational boundaries by their allegiances to a conservative or liberal Christian agenda in theology, piety, and social outlook.[24]

The American Cultural Landscape

At the beginning of the twentieth century, the melancholic Henry Adams declared, "My country in 1900 is something totally different from my own country of 1860. I am wholly a stranger in it. Neither I, nor anyone else, understands it. The turning of a nebula into a star may somewhat resemble the change. All I can see is that it is one of compression, concentration, and consequent development of terrific energy represented not by souls, but by coal and iron and steam." The intellectual change, he noted, was even more dramatic than the social and economic changes that had transformed American society. "In essentials like religion, ethics, philosophy; in history, literature, art; in the concepts of all science, except perhaps mathematics, the American boy of 1854 stood nearer the year 1 than to the year 1900."[25]

If Adams were to survey the changes in American society of the twentieth century, he would be equally baffled and chagrined. What was only in embryonic form emerged in this century with both unimagined creativity and unbelievable destructiveness. Continued migration of the population to urban centers where industry and technology controlled the rhythms of life would provide Americans new freedoms. But it would also further separate public from private life and fragment both spheres into a dizzying array of disconnected associations and loyalties. Immigration would dramatically alter the racial ethnic and religious complexion of the American populace as well as the norms for assimilation into American society. An unprecedented baby boom following World War II would transform traditional American family patterns and cultural mores. The much-prized individualism of the American frontier would mutate into an even more virulent species of personal independence. Both science and higher education would free themselves from their sometimes constricting former associations with religion, but in turn they would spawn a vision of the search for truth that left little space for religious inquiry or transcendent truth.

American Protestantism and American religion were changed by these processes, and the churches confront a very different future in the twentieth century because of them.

The Compartmentalization of America

One of the most pervasive characteristics of a modern society is its division of life into discernible and often discrete segments. The fractures and fissures in American religion and Protestantism reflect similar patterns of fragmentation in American life and social consciousness during the twentieth century. The compartmentalization of American life has drastically rearranged individual lives, social networks, and patterns of affiliation.

In the last century, American society moved from a largely rural, agrarian culture to a predominantly urban, industrialized economy, based on technology. Modern industry and the urban environment have provided the majority of Americans with more expendable income, more control over their immediate environment, more time for leisure, and more goods and services from which to choose. But they have also imposed their own logic on human life.

Individuals behave as isolated units. They relate to one another in the spirit of the technological ethic: what does the
relationship produce?

Relationships are preserved as long as the level of fulfillment is high and the emotional cost is low. The range of
options for career, pleasure, and religion increases. But the
integration of all three becomes even more difficult as communal life splinters into largely segregated compartments
of work, play, and belief. In fact, these three activities stand
as symbols for a host of possible alternatives in each area.
Americans are free today to choose, based on personal preferences, so far as their financial resources will allow.[26]

This freedom and autonomy have been exacerbated by the
anonymity provided by urban settings. Relationships become more complicated and more temporary as allegiances
are stretched thin or divided in disconnected quests for
meaning and human relationships.[27] While social networks
are more plentiful, they are also more transitory and sharply
limited. The strength of people's allegiances to such networks
frequently depends on the urgency of the issue that attracts
them and/or the usefulness of the group to the individual.[28]

A modern urbanized and industrialized society, based on
technology, cannot function without bureaucracies, which
in the twentieth century characterize not only business and
government but religious and other nonprofit organizations
as well. Hailed at the beginning of the century as pioneers
of efficiency, bureaucrats depend on specialized knowledge
and circumscribed responsibility to manage effectively.
The process of bureaucratizing American religious life was
gradual, with both positive and negative results. An incorporated America produced incorporated churches, with
members simultaneously attracted and repelled by the
compartmentalizing of churches and their functions.[29]

The Changing Demographics
of the American Population

The economic prosperity produced by American industrialization and technology literally altered the face of the

American population. Successive waves of immigrants sought their own share of American prosperity. Between 1820 and 1930, the United States received more than 37 million immigrants. A significant number of Asians entered this country between 1870 and 1930. But two waves of Europeans account for most of the 37 million. Until 1890, the majority of immigrants came from northern and western Europe. After 1890, the so-called "new immigration" began from southern and eastern European countries.[30]

The new wave of immigrants included large numbers of Jews and Roman Catholics. It altered the religious balance among Protestants, Catholics, and Jews in America so dramatically that Protestantism gradually and often grudgingly learned to share its cultural power with these other religious communities.

More recent immigration following World War II has continued to bring Europeans to the United States. But even larger contingents of people came, first from the Caribbean and Central and South America, and later from the Pacific and Southeast Asia.[31]

Between 1980 and 1988, the Hispanic population alone grew by birth and immigration from 14,609,000 to 19,887,000. Since World War II, the Roman Catholic Church has grown faster than the Protestant community in part because of this immigration. A higher birthrate among Catholics also contributed to this trend. Before the 1960s, Catholic teachings on birth control encouraged large families, although since then the Catholic birthrate has declined dramatically.[32]

Black and Hispanic Americans are the fastest-growing ethnic communities in the United States. Indeed, projections indicate that by the middle of the twenty-first century the white American population will become a minority within the total U.S. population. Hispanic Americans will likely become the largest single racial ethnic constituency in the nation.[33]

Beyond these dramatic shifts due to immigration, twentieth-century America has witnessed equally momen-

tous migration within its borders. The American population has been moving west since European colonization.
In the twentieth century, specifically, the growth of western and southern states since World War II has had a deci-
sive effect on recent American culture and American
politics. In 1950, 32.2 percent (48.8 million) of the population lived west of the Mississippi, and 21.6 percent
(32.7 million) of the American people resided in the
South. By 1988, the percentage had risen to 38.7 percent
(95.3 million) living in the West and 23.5 percent (57.8
million) residing in the South.[34]

Demographically, the strength of twentieth-century Presbyterianism lies traditionally among Caucasians concentrated in the Northeast and the Midwest. Therefore, the
PC(USA) was not geographically positioned to take best
advantage of the postwar population shift to the West.[35]

In addition to ethnic and geographic changes, a third important demographic transformation in twentieth-century
America has been the baby boom after World War II. The
baby boomers have had an enormous impact on every facet
of American society. Their effect on American Presbyterianism and mainstream Protestantism will be discussed in
chapter 2. But their sheer numbers cannot be overlooked in
describing the changes in American religion and culture.

Scholars disagree about the precise duration of the baby
boom. Some argue that the boundaries are 1945 to 1965.
During those years, 75 million people were born in this
country.[36] Other researchers divide the baby boomers into
two groups. One consists of 47 million infants born between 1943 and 1955; the other is comprised of 62 million
infants born from 1956 to 1970. Births between 1956 and
1970 outnumber by two-to-one the births recorded from
1928 to 1942.[37]

As Wade Clark Roof and William McKinney have maintained, the size of the baby boom generation shifted family
life-cycle patterns by transforming the society's age structure and triggering a "distinctive generational experience
and culture."[38] The baby boomers have left and will continue to leave a mark on American culture and its institu-

tions. By their magnitude in numbers and by their life experiences as they came to adulthood from the 1960s through the 1980s, they represent both an aberration in long-term demography and a powerful source of change.

Cultural Diversity

Demographic change inevitably affects national life. But its effect is magnified many times when it actually alters a nation's identity and redefines how different groups should participate in its collective life. The twentieth century has witnessed the sanctioning of cultural and religious diversity on an unprecedented scale.

It is important to make a distinction here between the terms "diversity" and "pluralism," since they are frequently used interchangeably. In this work, each term has a separate meaning. Diversity is used for the fact that the American population and, to a lesser extent, mainstream Protestantism are heterogeneous in cultures, races, and religious affiliations. Pluralism, on the other hand, refers more narrowly to the variety of ideological perspectives, particularly various theological outlooks and religious practices. This variety may exist within a culture or a religious tradition either simultaneously or across history. While theological pluralism may grow out of diversity, the sanctioning of diversity does not necessarily assure or require the acceptance of theological pluralism.

Differences in culture, race, and theology are nothing new to the United States. In 1741 the Moravian Count Nicholas von Zinzendorf visited Pennsylvania and observed in shock: "All shades of Sectarians exist here down to open infidelity. . . . Besides the English, Swedish, and German Lutherans, and the Scotch, Dutch, and German Reformed, there [are] Arminians, Baptists, Mennonites from Danzig, Arians, Socinians, Schwenckfelders, German Old Dunkers, New Dunkers, New Lights, Inspired Sabbatarians or Seventh Day Baptists, Hermits, Independents, and Free Thinkers."[39] Colonial America set the stage for the religious diversity of twentieth-century America.

The Whig political thought that shaped the American Revolution and the Constitution assumed that religion, especially American Protestantism, would help forge a cultural consensus in which such diversity would be civilized and minimized. The norm for American cultural life during much of American history became the image of the melting pot. In one sense, this image was misleading because it suggested that each group would add something to the ingredients. In fact, minority racial ethnic communities were expected to conform to the majority's recipe for the American character. In both formal and informal ways, the influence of white, Anglo-Saxon Protestants prevailed, sometimes only by recourse to violence. At the same time, minority groups forged their own subcultures to resist being assimilated into the dominant cultural ethos. For example, even in the midst of slavery, African Americans preserved and nourished a diversity of folk cultures from Africa.[40]

In the twentieth century, several factors combined to erode the model of assimilation. The dominant WASP culture itself began fragmenting after World War I. But the most wrenching and far-reaching changes occurred in the 1950s and 1960s. The second emancipation, the civil rights movement, assaulted the legalized discrimination and racism in American society. It unleashed the self-consciousness of African Americans and other racial ethnic minorities, as well as women and other groups who recognized that they were politically, economically, and culturally oppressed.

Second, the meteoric rise of mass media transmitted a world of cultural diversity into American homes, and finally, many members of the huge baby boom generation questioned the moral integrity and superiority of traditional Western culture. The counterculture of the 1960s and 1970s eventually became tame, but it had lasting effects in challenging the dominant cultural consensus and celebrating moral individualism and social diversity.

As the norm of conformity declined, individual expression and autonomy have soared, straining the bonds that unite the culture. In both American politics and religion, programs requiring widespread support can only succeed by appealing to the special interests of diverse groups and individuals.[41]

Individualism

Appeals to American individuals and individualism are, like pluralism, hardly new to these borders. The perceptive nineteenth-century observer Alexis de Tocqueville, who coined the term "individualism," said of this American trait: "Individualism is a mature and calm feeling, which disposes each member of the community to sever himself from the mass of his fellows and to draw apart with his family and his friends, so that after he has thus formed a little circle of his own, he willingly leaves society at large to itself."[42]

Recent research highlights the growth of an even more vigorous strand of individualism in modern American culture. Robert Bellah and his colleagues in *Habits of the Heart* suggest that contemporary Americans find it difficult to commit to relationships or organizations of every sort.[43] In religion, Americans are increasingly selective about choosing their beliefs among a variety of religious traditions and identify with diverse churches and religious institutions at various points in their lives.

The New Age religious movement may be a highly visible example of this trend toward individualism and diverse choices. But Bellah's group of researchers captured a classic example of a radically individualistic understanding of religion in Sheila Larson. During her interview she declared: "I believe in God. I'm not a religious fanatic. I can't remember the last time I went to church. My faith has carried me a long way. It's Sheilaism. Just my own little voice." She described her ethic as follows: "It's just try to love yourself and be gentle with yourself. You know, I guess, take care of each other. I think He would want us to take care of each other."[44]

How common such Sheilas are in American culture is

difficult to determine with any accuracy. But a more mundane, though equally revealing, instance of this individualistic impulse in American religion is provided by a Gallup poll. The vast majority of Americans declare that one should arrive at one's religious beliefs independently of one's church or synagogue.[45]

Science

The fragmentation of life in modern societies has been exacerbated by the phenomenal power of modern science. Particularly during the twentieth century, modern science has improved the quality of human health and opened up new opportunities for both mastery and abuse of the environment. Furthermore, the social sciences have illumined the complexity of the human psyche and the diversity of culture. Science has transformed the way in which twentieth-century Americans conceive of their world and life within it.

Modern science brackets the question of supernatural causes in order to focus on the interaction of natural phenomena. Lesslie Newbigin has argued that this scientific method has led Western cultures to create a new form of orthodoxy. According to Newbigin, post-Enlightenment thought recognizes certain pieces of information as "facts." These bits of data are organized into systems in order to form the "hard" knowledge of the sciences. Factual information can be verified by visual and mechanical observation or at least predicted by statistical probability. Once verified, these "facts" are considered true for all people, in all places, and at all times.[46]

"Facts," however, are different from values, which cannot be proved by the scientific method. Values, therefore, lack the certainty of "fact" and, by implication, are less true. For this reason, it is assumed that values should not be imposed on the larger society and are relegated to the private realm of personal opinion or preference.[47]

The social sciences have also transformed the consciousness of modern Americans. Mainstream Protestant educators were key figures in introducing the new sciences of psychology and sociology into the academy and the church during the late nineteenth and early twentieth centuries. In their idealism, they sought to use the new disciplines to humanize and Christianize society.

The insights of psychology raised new and troubling questions for Christian faith. By emphasizing the dynamics of the unconscious and human personality, psychology seemed to undermine the objective truth of religion and the freedom of the human will. Sociologists also demonstrated the complexity of culture and the tremendous impact of social forces on human life and personality. Coupled with the rise of modern historical methodologies, the social sciences have impressed the modern consciousness with the relativity of human knowledge. What is true in one culture and in one era may not be true in another. What was wrong for one era may be good for another. In stressing the conditional character of all human life, the social sciences both enrich human knowledge and fragment the world and its history.[48]

The new regimen of "public facts–private values" and relative truths does more than bracket the supernatural temporarily for investigative purposes. It restricts the religious search to the privacy of the home and the self or the religious community. The fragmentation wrought by modernization is difficult to overcome by appeals to a moral consensus, since values cannot be imposed on the autonomous individual's will. The power of science in relativizing and privatizing religion and morality in the twentieth century has encouraged that fragmentation. The public square, to use Richard J. Neuhaus's image, is "naked" of moral and especially religious values.[49]

The Modern University

The principal institution for transmitting the ideal of the scientific method has been the modern university, which has transformed all of American education. The modern university embodied the ideal of the power of reason to control nature and improve human life. It sought to establish excellence on the basis of scholarship. Furthermore, the modern university was conceived as independent of the church or religious institutions. As Charles W. Eliot of Harvard announced in 1891, "it is impossible to found a university on the basis of a sect."[50]

Protestants dominated higher education during the colonial period and throughout the nineteenth century, and Presbyterians were heavily involved in this massive educational endeavor. However, two events symbolize the beginning of the Protestant displacement in higher education and its secularization. In 1862, Congress passed the Morrill Act, which launched a network of land-grant colleges and initiated the movement of the government into higher education. Fourteen years later in 1876, Johns Hopkins was founded as the first modern American university. The inaugural ceremonies at Johns Hopkins were indicative of the new ethos of the university: There was no prayer of invocation or benediction.[51]

The secularizing effects of the modern university were not immediately evident. At the turn of the century, about half of American undergraduates still attended church-related institutions. In 1890, 92 percent of 24 state colleges required chapel attendance, and 17 percent still expected church attendance. By 1939, chapel services were still offered in 24 percent of the state colleges and universities. Only eight percent made attendance compulsory, although 57 percent of all state schools covered the cost for religious convocations as well as special chapel speakers, and 40 percent underwrote voluntary religious groups.[52]

But by the early decades of the twentieth century, the center of gravity in American higher education had shifted to public and private institutions, shaped increasingly not by the vision and ideals of the church but by the values and norms of the university.

A case in point is the changes in college and university curricula that followed the Civil War. James Turner has noted that the capstone of the antebellum curriculum was a moral philosophy course normally taught to seniors by the college president. This course tried to give "students an explicit and articulated explanation of the unity of God's truth" by illustrating "how solutions to problems in ethics, political theory, law, psychology, [and] religion all flowed from the divine constitution of nature."[53]

This assumed coherence of all knowledge based on a belief in a divine creator increasingly fell out of favor in academic circles as areas of study became more specialized and as intellectual challenges like Darwinian science posed new questions for traditional Christian theology. By the late nineteenth century, the humanities—particularly the fields of comparative literature, art history, and to a lesser extent, philosophy—were already stepping in to fill the void left by the disappearance of moral philosophy courses. The cement holding together this new curricular pattern was no longer a divine creator but rather the deep truths of great books and art in "liberal culture," meaning the intellectual and moral discoveries of Western, male, elite culture. In the early twentieth century this bonding agent provided a substitute center for higher education's curriculum that was moral and vaguely spiritual, though not clearly Christian.[54] But its cohesive powers have not withstood the test of late-twentieth-century challenges from new participants in higher education whose intellectual and/or social base was neither Western, male, nor elite.

Two other influences in the early part of this century encouraged the shift to a more secularized environment on the university campus.

One was the rise of accrediting bodies, commissioned to bring some standardization of faculty qualifications, curriculum, and institutional support. As a reform movement, accreditation was the educational equivalent of the quest for rational standardization that marked the ethos of an industrialized, modern society. Another influence was the antiecclesiastical slant of new, powerful philanthropic foundations. For example, the Carnegie Foundation insisted that if an educational institution wanted to participate in its pension program (the precursor of TIAA/CREF [Teachers Insurance and Annuity Association/College Retirement Equities Fund], now the largest pension fund in the country), it had to renounce sectarian allegiances and have a certain percentage of faculty with the Ph.D. degree. Similarly, the Rockefellers' General Education Board gave millions to build college endowments but also tried to eliminate from the beneficiaries what they considered to be marginal church-related colleges.[55]

Events after World War II only perpetuated and accentuated these changes. The GI Bill of Rights made higher education accessible to millions more students; the baby boomers swelled the enrollments of colleges and universities. Federal, state, and local governments moved aggressively to establish public institutions or expand existing ones with new tax revenues. Church-related institutions expanded as well, but not to the same degree. The statistics are striking: There were 2.6 million students enrolled in higher education in 1950; 3.6 million in 1960; 8.6 million in 1970; and 12.1 million in 1980.[56]

In 1965, government-sponsored institutions enrolled two-thirds of all undergraduates. Half of the remainder were in church-related institutions, but Roman Catholic colleges claimed the majority of those. By 1987, the federal government estimated that 80 percent of all college students attended public institutions. The cost of higher education grew in staggering proportion to the student population. Total expenditures on higher education grew from a mere $2.2 billion in 1950 to $5.6 billion in 1960, and then mushroomed to $23.4 billion by 1970 and $107.7 billion in 1986.[57]

As the social location of higher education moved from church-related to state institutions, higher education became more secularized. The first form of secularization, according to George Marsden, was methodological in nature. Methodological secularization in its early forms did not deny the existence of the supernatural or the transcendent. It simply argued that critical study of historical and natural phenomena was better served if questions of first cause or ultimate meaning were momentarily set aside. Protestants in higher education did not consider this scientific method antagonistic to their faith claims. In fact, they welcomed it as an ally, for it promised that exploration of creation's infinite variety would only reinforce belief in an equally infinite and complex deity.[58]

Methodological secularization encouraged professionalization and specialization in the modern scholar. Mainstream Protestants participated actively in this effort to investigate with increasing precision discrete pieces of human knowledge. They did not anticipate that the dazzling practical successes of the scientific method might blind the public to the questions of ultimate meaning which the method itself only intended to bracket temporarily.[59]

The technological advances made possible by science spawned ideological secularization—a faith that science alone could explain all of life's questions, including religious ones, given sufficient time and freedom. The ideological secularists regarded religion's subjective allegiance as incompatible with the objective inquiry required by science. Some individuals, inside and outside the academy, came to view theological questions as little more than inadequately formed queries that science would eventually formulate and answer more satisfactorily.[60]

Liberal Protestant theology in the early twentieth century prepared Protestants for this radically new notion. At its heart this theological movement welcomed the new sciences as potentially fruitful contributors to Christian understanding and they attempted to reinterpret Christian faith to address their implications. Its proponents considered themselves reformers, rejecting what they perceived as reactionary Christianity and endorsing the categories of modern thought in order to sustain a vibrant spirituality with real intellectual integrity. They assumed that both public and private education would remain at the least identifiably moral, if not Christian. When political and cultural diversity exploded at mid-century, the effect of methodological and ideological secularization was clear: Protestants had been disestablished as a significant influence in higher education. The authority for American higher education was to be found in the standards of the American university, with its neutrality if not hostility toward questions of religious truth.[61]

The secularization of higher education, fueled by the expansion of public institutions, generated a dramatic change in college-educated people. During the 1950s, Americans with more education expressed about the same level of conventional religious beliefs as those who had not attended college. But between 1957 and 1974 the percentage of college-educated individuals who believed that all or most of society's problems were answered by religion fell 26 points. Among those with a grade school education, it dropped 6 percent.[62]

Robert Wuthnow identifies this division as an "education gap." The gap has spawned speculation that a "new class" emerged during this period. With more college or university education than the general population, the "new class" includes professionals engaged in the burgeoning service sector of the economy. They specialize in the acquisition and management of information rather than the production of goods.[63]

The views of the "new class" contrast sharply with those of the less educated and the college educated of earlier generations, who pursued occupations related to the manufacture and sale of goods. The members of the "new class" express greater "tolerance towards homosexuality, favor legalized abortion, hold egalitarian attitudes towards women, and disapprove of antimiscegenation law." They support taxes for education, Medicare, space exploration, environmental protection, urban improvement, and government welfare. They are more permissive on life-style issues, and they are more likely to describe themselves as religious liberals. As such, they have joined with some educated clergy of their generation to foster social activism in mainstream Protestant denominations.[64]

Much more research needs to explore the effect of higher education on religious belief and behavior, but the secularization of these institutions represents a major shift in American culture. It has profound implications for all churches, especially mainstream Protestant denominations, which have supported and encouraged this process. Just as instruction in public elementary and secondary schools can no longer self-consciously promote religion or encourage religious practice, so also mainstream Protestants can no longer rely on higher education to nurture Christian faith and allegiance. In fact, its secularity often undermines the church.

Conclusion

The trends in American religion and culture outlined in this chapter have encouraged some to explain these changes through theories of secularization. These theories posit some point in the past (usually the medieval period) when religion and public life were so closely intertwined that religion provided the primary justification for society's structures, rules, and values. Under the combined pressures of industrialization and scientific rationalization, secularization theories suggest, society loses its religious identity and purpose.[65]

More recently, scholars have revised the secularization paradigm because it does not square with the modern Western experience. American society has been especially difficult to explain because it both confirms and contradicts the thesis. For example, communal bonds based on familial ties or religious affinities have been seriously frayed. Similarly, a sacred canopy of American Christianity once arched across much of the culture's horizon, offering at least public religious validation of social values and institutions. But religious authority has been dramatically challenged and eroded. On the other hand, Americans' religious beliefs and experience remain remarkably strong at the end of the twentieth century. A recent Gallup poll indicates that a significant majority of Americans believe in a personal God who watches over and judges humanity, a God who performs miracles today, and one before whom individuals will be called in the future to answer for their sins. The vast majority of Americans also affirm the Bible as either the literal or inspired Word of God, and one-third of the population have had a profound religious experience, either sudden or gradual, which has been life changing.[66]

Two variations of secularization theories help explain the contours of American religion and society in the twentieth century. The first emphasizes that American culture is part of a modernization process. The chief effect of modernization on culture is fragmentation. Some parts of the society may become secular; others remain religious. Because American society seems to have become simultaneously more secular and persistently religious in the twentieth century, modernization becomes a helpful category for interpreting the changes that have engulfed American Presbyterians and mainstream Protestants in this century.[67]

A second interpretation is what John F. Wilson calls privatization. The enduring power of religion in the face of secularity is due to a modern society's pressure to make religious belief and behavior a private rather than a public matter. Consequently, even though religious symbols and practices may be less evident in modern America, that does not mean that they have lost their capacity to provide meaning and purpose to individual human life, now expressed in isolation and privacy.[68]

Privatization and secularization help explain some of what has happened to American Presbyterianism and mainstream Protestantism, but the theory of modernization explains more of the complexity of this history. As American culture became more modern, it also fragmented. Since American Presbyterians and mainstream Protestants felt a profound sense of religious and moral stewardship for society and were thereby significantly shaped by its dramatic transformation, their story in the twentieth century is also one of fissures and fragments.

The historian William G. McLoughlin's interpretation of American religion cautions that this perception of fragmentation may be illusive. In *Revivals, Awakenings, and Reform,* McLoughlin argues that American religion and culture pass through periods of intense division and conflict, which he defines as "awakenings." Using the work of Anthony F. C. Wallace, he describes an awakening as a revitalization movement in which basic religious, moral, and social values are questioned and transformed. Two such awakenings occurred in modern America, he argues. The first spanned the period from 1890 to 1920 as Americans adjusted to urbanization, industrialization, and immigration and new intellectual developments in religion and science. The second began in 1960 and may have ended in 1990. During this period American society struggled with profound moral issues regarding race, war, national identity, the environment, sexual behavior, and gender roles. Every awakening both challenges and builds upon the previous awakenings, McLoughlin maintains, and what emerges from it is a revitalized culture with elements of older and new traditions.[69]

It is too soon to assess whether McLoughlin's interpretation of the last three decades is correct. What is evident is that the Presbyterian experience in the twentieth century has been painful because of the fragmenting impact of modernization on its communal life and common confession. For many Presbyterians the turmoil of the twentieth century was captured in the words of William Butler Yeats:

> Turning and turning in the widening gyre
> The falcon cannot hear the falconer;
> Things fall apart; the center cannot hold.[70]

2

Whither the Mainstream Protestants?
Membership Growth and Decline

The most publicized characteristic of mainstream Protestantism in recent years has been its dramatic membership decline. For Presbyterians the story is depressingly familiar. In 1965 the combined membership of the UPCUSA and the PCUS stood at 4.25 million; by 1990 PC(USA) membership had dropped to 2,856,000, reflecting a loss of 1.4 million members and a decline of 33 percent.

The Presbyterian pattern was matched by other mainstream Protestant denominations. Between 1966 and 1988, Presbyterians lost 31 percent of their members. American Baptists experienced no loss but gained only 0.7 percent. The Disciples of Christ lost 43 percent; the Episcopal Church, 28 percent; the United Church of Christ, 20 percent; and the United Methodist Church, 18 percent.[1]

This phenomenon has been the source of a great deal of internal debate within church circles. Some maintain that the decline has been due to the spread of an ill-defined "liberalism" and social activism within the mainstream Protestant denominations. The growth of conservative denominations in the face of mainstream Protestant decline prompt some to believe that members deserted the mainstream denominations for more conservative alternatives. Others argue that the concern about membership was a misplaced obsession with institutional survival or that as the church declined, those who remained were more committed. A leaner church, in other words, was a more faithful church.

Fortunately, a great deal of research has now swept away much of the polemics of this debate and clarified many of the reasons for membership growth and decline in twentieth-century mainstream Protestantism. The research has set the membership patterns of the last twenty-five years in a broader historical perspective and compared data across moderate, liberal, and conservative denominations. The research also provides new insight into some disarmingly simple but fascinating questions: Why do people join churches? Why do they join particular churches? Why do they not join churches? Are the patterns today different from those of earlier eras?

The conclusions drawn by this research can be stated fairly simply: The Presbyterian membership decline, like the decline of other mainstream Protestant churches, was not primarily a defection of members to conservative churches. Rather, it was overwhelmingly a loss of members to no church affiliation at all. The decline was dramatically affected by changing demographics, especially lower birthrates, and the behavior of the now-famous baby boomers who have defected in large numbers. In short, the membership decline has been in part the result of factors over which these churches had little or no control.[2]

That, however, is not the entire explanation. Regional and demographic differences have had an enormous impact, particularly among Presbyterians in the Southeast and in inner cities and rural America. Long-term historical perspectives suggest that some variables are significant in certain eras and in some denominations, but are not in others. Specific denominational policies and programs do affect membership growth and decline.

Furthermore, *we want to suggest throughout this book that theological factors are important, even very important, in understanding membership patterns and the mainstream Protestant malaise.* By saying this, we do not deny that church affiliation is seriously affected by sociological factors, nor do we reject Dean Kelley's equally important observation that membership loyalty is linked to how seriously a religious group practices what it preaches. But unlike some sociological research, we do not believe that membership patterns are fully explained by the cultural and demographic environment in which a church finds itself, and unlike Kelley, we believe that the theological *content* that a church propounds, rather than just discipline, is significant in attracting and sustaining membership.[3]

One important caveat about membership statistics is in order: These figures are notoriously difficult to interpret across denominational lines. Some churches maintain fairly accurate data; statisticians call these "hard" data. Other churches have extremely "soft" data. Presbyterian figures are relatively reliable, in part because of the incentive to clean rolls regularly due to the per capita assessment of each congregation. Some suggest that Presbyterian scruples exaggerate membership loss; on the other hand, the impulse to purge the rolls also provides a better measure of active participation.

Because of the confusion and acrimony surrounding membership decline, it is wise to set these issues in a broader historical and cultural framework and to distinguish between the factors that operated on Presbyterians and other mainstream Protestants and those that they did in fact control.

Historical Background

When the American Revolution ended and as Presbyterians began to form a General Assembly during the 1780s, only 5–10 percent of the American population belonged to a church. That fact always comes as a significant shock to people accustomed to thinking of their colonial and Revolutionary forbears as models of piety. In 1790, the first census revealed a population of approximately four million,

including 500,000 African American slaves. The new Presbyterian Church in the U.S.A. numbered about 20,000 in
1790. Whether members or not, the population was overwhelmingly Protestant. Roman Catholics constituted only
100,000 people; there were so few Jews that genealogists
have been able to identify virtually every one of them by
name.[4]

At the dawn of the new nation, the American people were
unchurched. All the evidence indicates that religiosity was
vibrant, but the weakness of American churches in terms of
membership is remarkable. The percentage of membership
also grew relatively slowly, reaching 26 percent by the Civil
War, 46 percent by World War I, 57 percent by World War
II, and 69 percent by the late 1980s.[5]

The denominational patterns of American Protestantism
also changed dramatically. Colonial American religious life
was dominated by Anglicans (or Episcopalians), Congregationalists, Presbyterians, and Quakers. In the early nineteenth century, Methodists and Baptists moved to center
stage of American Protestantism. As early as 1850, the Roman Catholic Church became the largest single Christian
church in the United States. It has maintained that position
into the late twentieth century.[6]

Although Presbyterians ceded numerical dominance to
Baptists and Methodists, they did share in the growth of
American Christianity. In 1690, there were approximately
1,000 Presbyterians in eighteen churches. By 1800, there
were more than 23,000 members in 449 congregations. Despite divisions, Presbyterians numbered more than
500,000 by 1860; 1.5 million by 1900; and more than 4
million by 1960.[7]

Presbyterians have always been a small minority of the
American population, but their membership growth rate
exceeded the growth rate of the American population
throughout the nineteenth century. During the 1920s Presbyterian and mainstream Protestant membership began to
decline relative to the American population as a whole.[8] In
other words, the mainstream Protestant denominations
have been in relative membership decline for more than a

half-century. The pattern since the mid-1960s is, however, dramatically different and unique, for this has been a real or actual decline in members, rather than a decline relative to the population as a whole.

Two other fascinating historical trends should be noted. First, divisions and schisms seem to have had no long-term effect on Presbyterian membership.[9] The religious ferment of American culture seemingly breeds religious fertility; the more religious options there are, the more active people become. Second, the twentieth century has witnessed growth in the average size of Presbyterian and other Protestant congregations. During the nineteenth century, an average congregation was approximately 100 members. Throughout this century the average size has increased steadily to more than 200 today. This should not be surprising, given rising costs for congregational programs and demands for specialized ministries, but it does indicate a significant change in the nature of the congregations that Presbyterians and other mainstream Protestants join.[10]

Religious Preference in Contemporary America

Gallup polls indicate that 86 percent of the American people identify themselves as either Protestant, Roman Catholic, or Jewish. The majority (56 percent) are Protestant, 28 percent Roman Catholic, and 2 percent Jewish. The remaining 14 percent declared either attachment to another faith (4 percent) or "no religious preference" at all (10 percent). While Protestants enjoy the largest representation, their share has declined 11 percent since 1952. Those with "no religious preference" have, on the other hand, grown faster than any other group—from 2 percent in 1952 to 10 percent in 1988–89.[11]

When Protestants have been asked about their specific denominational preference, Baptists constitute 20 percent, followed by Methodists with 10 percent, Lutherans with 6 percent, Presbyterians with 4 percent, Episcopalians, Disciples of Christ, and United Church of Christ members each with 2 percent. All others total 11 percent.[12]

Of course, religious preference does not mean actual membership. In one 1988–89 survey, approximately nine in ten adults (88 percent) stated some religious preference. Yet only seven out of ten (69 percent) belonged formally either to a Protestant congregation, a Catholic parish, or a Jewish synagogue.[13] A similar relationship prevails between membership and attendance. Seventy-two percent of all Americans with a Protestant preference also claim Protestant membership, but only 45 percent actually attend regularly. For certain denominations, this disparity is even wider. Eighty-three percent of those declaring themselves Presbyterian were also members in 1987. However, no more than 36 percent of these members attend church weekly.[14]

After World War II, Presbyterians and other mainstream Protestant denominations witnessed significant growth until the mid-1960s. Since then there has been steady and inexorable loss of members. As these denominations declined, many conservative churches grew, but by the late 1980s the growth rate had slowed or stopped in many cases. At the same time, the number of people unaffiliated with any church has grown dramatically.

To understand the pattern of decline, it is critical to account for the factors of growth in post–World War II Presbyterianism and mainstream Protestantism.

The Demographics of Mainstream Protestantism Since World War II

"For church membership, demographics are destiny." That statement may be hyperbole, but it contains a large element of truth. Most churches will not grow in the face of declining population. Most churches will grow in expanding suburbs or numerically prospering cities. For Presbyterians in post–World War II America, demographics explain much of membership increases and losses.

The growth was fueled primarily by the postwar baby boomers. The 1950s witnessed a religious revival that was both hailed and reviled, and it did produce more church members. The babies brought their parents to church. The classic sociological article explaining this phenomenon takes as its title the biblical text, "A little child shall lead them."[15] Total Presbyterian membership in the PCUSA, PCUS, and UPCNA in 1946 was 3,035,755; by 1956 it had grown to 3,964,778; in 1966 it peaked at 4,249,765. For twenty years a growing church school enrollment meant a growing church, a pattern that is frequently but not always the case.[16] The expansion of membership in American Presbyterianism and mainstream Protestant denominations during the 1950s is largely the story of parents seeking out religious instruction for their children and church membership for themselves. The postwar baby boom ended in 1964; membership decline quickly followed.

The baby boomers are very significant, for they help explain not only the growth of the late 1940s through the mid-1960s but also the decline of the last twenty-five years. This generation, which had such a disproportionate influence in every area of American society when compared with previous generations, also had a dramatic effect on mainstream Protestant churches. They have not affiliated with the church in the same numbers as their parents, and much of the decline is because the baby boomers have behaved differently from their parents.

As a group, they have delayed marriage. When they married, they delayed having children and divorced more often. When they had children, they had fewer than their parents. They also divorced more frequently than did their parents.

Wade Clark Roof and William McKinney provide data to support this conclusion. They divided the American population into six families of religious affiliation. Although their designation of Presbyterians as "liberal Protestants" can be disputed, their findings show several reasons why the decline has been particularly telling for the PC(USA).

Among "liberal Protestants," women over forty-five (the mothers of the baby boomers) had a birthrate of 2.27; women under forty-five had a birthrate of 1.60. As one moves across the Protestant spectrum, the more moderate and conservative churches have not only higher birthrates for the parents of baby boomers but also for the boomers themselves. But even conservative Protestant women under forty-five have a birthrate of only 2.01, and Catholic women under forty-five have a birthrate of only 1.82, a dramatic contrast with those over forty-five—2.75.[17] In short, one can conclude that demography will not solve the problem of membership decline for Presbyterians and other mainstream Protestants. American Presbyterian families are not even reproducing themselves.

Roof and McKinney also discovered that "liberal Protestant" congregations have a smaller percentage of married people than do conservative churches, and their members' average age is older than members of conservative denominations. Liberal Protestants' average age is four years older than conservative Protestants, and the age disparity is growing.[18]

Gallup polls confirm the "graying" of the Presbyterians. Fifty-one percent of Presbyterians are over the age of fifty, even though the general population contains only 35 percent in that age bracket. Similarly, those under 30 represent 27 percent of the larger population. But no more than 17 percent of the Presbyterian membership falls within that category.[19]

What happened to the baby boomers? This question has been addressed by several researchers, including Dean Hoge, Benton Johnson, and Don Luidens. They recently conducted extensive interviews with Presbyterian baby boomers whose names were drawn from confirmation lists of the 1950s and 1960s. Wherever possible, they also questioned the parents of the baby boom generation in order to learn more about their religious aspirations and beliefs.

According to these researchers, Presbyterian baby boomers left their denominational family in significant numbers. Of the 500 baby boomers questioned, 52 percent remain active in a Christian church, and only 29 percent are members of the PC(USA). The rest are now involved in fundamentalist churches (6 percent), other mainstream

Protestant denominations (10 percent), or another Christian church—for example, Roman Catholic (7 percent). What the researchers call the "unchurched" amounts to 48 percent of their sample. These may be individuals who attend church but are not members (10 percent), are members but do not attend (9 percent), are neither members nor attend but claim to be religious (21 percent), or are nonreligious (8 percent).[20]

The defection of the baby boom generation from mainstream Protestant denominations has long been recognized. What has not been clear was why they left and whether they would ever return. The Presbyterian baby boomer study indicates that the cultural upheaval of the 1960s and 1970s—debates over war, race, sexual morality, gender roles, and more—played a critical role. Life crises, especially divorce, had a significant impact on church affiliation among the baby boomers.[21]

Will the baby boomers return? Or have they been permanently lost to the church?

Some observers interpret the exodus of the baby boomers in the 1960s as a temporary phenomenon linked to adolescent rebellion. This, they assume, would subside particularly after the baby boomers had their own children. In order to provide ethical and religious instruction for their offspring, they would return to their former home churches. The Presbyterian baby boomer study suggests that the boomers do in fact want religious instruction for their offspring, and the church is one of the few places where such training can be received since it is not available in the public school system.[22]

Another study, however, concludes that the baby boomers have already begun to return. This research divided the boomers into two groups—those born from 1945 to 1954 (the "Older Baby Boomers") and those born from 1955 to 1965 (the "Younger Baby Boomers").[23]

Some Older Baby Boomers started attending worship more frequently in the 1980s. By 1984, 42.8 percent attended three times a month or more. These Older Baby Boomers had sustained at least minimal associations with congregations over the years. In contrast, the Older Baby Boomers who did not return to worship had in most cases made a clean break with the church at some point in the past. This confirms another study that found 64 percent of those who had dropped out of formal religious involvement for two or more years did not return.[24]

The attendance rate of Older Baby Boomers also did not equal that of the generation they were replacing nor did it come close to the attendance marks of those in their thirties and forties during the peak of church attendance in the 1950s.[25]

Media attention to the return of the baby boomers has often overlooked the fact that their religious participation is matched by similar modest increases in involvement by older people. So the baby boomer return to the church may be part of a very modest general increase in church participation rather than one localized in this single generation which left the church community in such large numbers during the 1960s.[26]

Two other demographic factors have decisively shaped Presbyterian and other mainstream Protestant membership patterns—race and economic status. Mainstream Protestant churches, indeed predominantly white churches generally, have a limited reach beyond the white community. In his classic study *The Social Sources of Denominationalism* (1926), H. Richard Niebuhr estimated that only 12 percent of all African American Christians affiliated outside of traditionally Black denominations. Roof and McKinney have found that in the late twentieth century that figure has only risen to approximately 15 percent. White mainstream denominations typically have 2 to 3 percent Black members, although sociologists do note that more whites have contact with Black Christians in these churches than ever before.[27]

The PC(USA) in 1990 reported that only 2.47 percent or 64,841 of its membership were African Americans, and the case of Black Presbyterians is only a microcosm of mainstream Protestantism's inability to incorporate a range of ethnic communities. In 1990, the General Assembly statistics documented 1.54 percent or 40,276 Asian American members, 0.87 percent or 22,744 Hispanic American members, and 0.73 percent or 19,108 Native American members. Other minorities amounted to 9,413 or 0.36 percent of the total.[28]

United States population projections reveal the practical significance of these numbers. By the middle of the next century, if current immigration and birthrate trends continue, the white population that has traditionally dominated Presbyterian membership rolls will no longer comprise a majority of Americans. Growth rates in the African American and Hispanic American communities already surpass white growth. Within the PC(USA), Korean American Presbyterians are the fastest growing racial ethnic constituency.

Niebuhr also found that socioeconomic status influenced how people chose their church home. Since Niebuhr's classic work on denominationalism, scholars have argued that the American Christian community resembles a ladder of church options that individuals climb as their social, financial, or educational status rises.[29]

In the past, this pattern favored Presbyterian, Episcopal, and Congregationalist (or United Church of Christ) churches because of their members' disproportionate prominence in American culture. More recently, these denominations continue to gain from "social climbing," although conservative churches have been more successful at slowing this trend by retaining their more prosperous and educated members. Indeed, since the mid-1940s the educational background of members of evangelical and fundamentalist denominations has grown faster than that of Presbyterian, Episcopalian, and UCC members. Similarly, the status of Mormons and Catholics rose dramatically after 1944, when they represented much lower segments of the socioeconomic ladder.[30]

The most surprising and noteworthy shift has occurred among those with no religious preference. Between 1945 and 1980, this group rose from the bottom of the bottom on Roof and McKinney's scale of status indicators to an upper middle position. Those with no religious affiliation exceed the national average today on every status indicator. They rank almost even with liberal Protestants in education, above moderate Protestants (such as United Methodists and northern white Baptists) on most status measures, and closely parallel to Catholics in an overall socioeconomic profile.[31]

These changes indicate that social characteristics such as education and income that have traditionally favored Presbyterian affiliation no longer serve that function. In other words, Presbyterianism is losing its social and economic distinctiveness. This loss could be a potential gain, particularly if the rising level of education in American society opens up the possibility that more racial ethnic minorities will affiliate with the PC(USA) or other mainstream Protestant denominations. Or, if the better-educated members of conservative churches become disenchanted with internal bickering and constraints, the "mainline" may be in a "windfall" position, and "upward mobility" may resume with a vengeance.

Switching Between Denominations

Another side of the growth/decline question in American Protestantism focuses on the patterns of people switching from one faith or denomination to another. If it is unlikely that mainstream Protestant denominations will grow by simply reproducing themselves, what are the prospects for attracting individuals into their communities from other Christian churches?

Obviously, the socioeconomic status of these denominations is a significant factor. So also are attitudes toward evangelism and a willingness to include people of different backgrounds and race. These questions will be addressed in later chapters.

For now, it is sufficient to note that the practice of switching faiths is rampant in contemporary America. Fewer than half of the U.S. population (43 percent) remain members of the religion or denomination into which they were born.

Yet there is wide variation among different groups. Roof and McKinney found that liberal Protestants were less likely than moderate and conservative Protestants, Roman Catholics, Black Protestants, or Jews to remain in their denominations throughout their lives. Presbyterians in particular held only 60 percent of those raised in their community and only 29 percent of the baby boomers.[32]

One influential factor in switching is ethnic identity. With a few exceptions such as Lutherans, white Protestants' ethnic background has little effect upon what denomination they will join or remain faithful to. In contrast, ethnicity produces very strong allegiance for Black northern Baptists, Hispanic Catholics, and Jews.[33]

Conservative-to-Liberal Switching

Since conservative churches grew while mainstream Protestants declined, many past observers assumed that there was a direct connection between the two. Early accounts of these trends implied that disaffected mainstream Protestants crossed the street to swell the rolls of more conservative congregations.[34]

This is largely false. Presbyterian congregations have been losing members out the back doors of their churches. Some may leave for conservative alternatives. But the overwhelming majority do not. In fact, Roof and McKinney have found that the Presbyterians and other liberal Protestants attract more members from other churches, including conservative denominations, than they lose.[35] As noted earlier, the key to understanding decline is the loss of members to no religious affiliation.

The phenomenal growth of evangelical and conservative denominations appears to be due to other factors than mainstream Protestant disaffection. These churches do have "soft" membership statistics, so comparisons with mainstream Protestant statistics are misleading. The exodus en masse of some groups from mainstream Protestant denominations to conservative alternatives also attracts attention. The PC(USA) in Mississippi, for example, is a

shadow of its former self in the 1990s because of the withdrawal of many churches to join the Presbyterian Church
in America (PCA) or the Evangelical Presbyterian Church
(EPC).[36]

But the visibility and acrimony that accompany conservative defection distort the larger patterns. Even assuming
that every member of the PCA and the EPC was a former
member of the PC(USA) in 1988, that would account for
only 220,000 of the 1.4 million-member decline. Three factors do help explain evangelical and conservative growth,
and these present a far greater challenge to mainstream
Protestantism. Conservative denominations have been
more successful at retaining their youth. They keep their
current members even when those members grow more
prosperous. Members from other denominations who join
conservative denominations are also more likely to be actively involved after they switch.[37]

The Characteristics of Switchers

The contrast between those who switch to denominations like the PC(USA) and those who move to more conservative churches is significant. Switchers to liberal
Protestant denominations appear to be older. Sixty-four
percent of those who switched to liberal Protestant
churches at some point in the past are now over forty-five,
while only 50 percent of those choosing conservative
churches are in this age group. Liberal Protestants enjoy a
net gain of 17.1 percent in older members who have
switched, but they have endured a net loss of 9.4 percent
among younger switchers.[38]

Those who move to liberal Protestant churches are also
not as active as those who choose conservative denominations. Converts from other denominational families are important because they attend church more regularly than
long-time members. Converts from other denominations to
conservative Protestant churches or the Roman Catholic
church have the highest participation rates—70 and 62

percent respectively. But only 48 percent of new liberal Protestants raised in other denominational families attend church regularly, while those lost from liberal Protestant denominations to other churches tend to participate in worship more frequently (57 percent) than those who remain in the liberal Protestant camp (34 percent).[39]

The Backdoor Exit

The fastest-growing segment of the American population consists of people who have no affiliation with a church or religious institution. Since the mid-1950s, the percentage of Americans who identify themselves as having no religious preference has risen from 2 to 10 percent. The vast majority of these individuals are disaffiliated. They were once members or at least reared in a church community, but they now reject that denominational affiliation or any religious identity whatsoever.[40]

Jews, liberal Protestants, and Roman Catholics have been particularly hard hit by this trend, losing more members to nonaffiliation than they gain from the unchurched. This suggests that the loss is not just a liberal or mainstream Protestant problem. Nevertheless, it is troublesome, particularly because the nonaffiliated were the only group in Roof and McKinney's study that showed a net gain in *younger* members. Jews, liberal Protestants, and Catholics again fared especially badly with people under forty-five years of age.[41]

The countercultural movements of the 1960s did not spark this youthful disaffiliation, but it may have accelerated the trend. According to Kirk Hadaway and the Presbyterian baby boomer study, religious activity in mainstream Protestant denominations peaked early in the 1950s. Baptisms declined before membership started its descent. The antiestablishment biases of the 1960s may have accentuated but did not produce the disaffection of young people.[42]

Hadaway also finds little solace in recent observations that disaffiliation appears to be leveling off. The disaffili-

ated are spawning even more people who have never affiliated. Americans are not becoming more religious with age,
despite predictions to the contrary. Moreover, Presbyterians, Episcopalians, and the United Church of Christ were
the hardest hit by past disaffiliation, and of the three, Presbyterians continue to have the most porous membership
boundaries.[43]

The twentieth-century battles between conservatives and
liberals in American Presbyterianism and other denominations have made both groups especially sensitive to critiques from the opposing side. The recent patterns in
nonaffiliation have blindsided mainstream Protestant communions like the PC(USA) because they ran counter to previous expectations. Indeed, the research suggests that an
increasingly secular culture can undermine theological convictions and membership allegiances as seriously as any
threat from alternative forms of Christianity. But the problem is especially acute for Presbyterians and other mainstream Protestants, for when these Christians exercise their
choice and switch, they frequently choose no church at all.
In Roof and McKinney's apt phrase, the competition for
Presbyterians and other mainstream Protestants "is not the
conservatives [they have] *spurned* but the secularists [they
have] *spawned*."[44]

That finding has far-reaching implications for the future
of American Presbyterianism and mainstream Protestant
communions.

The Disaffiliated

This group is not a homogeneous mass. Scholars have
identified several different types of disaffiliated people,
with varying characteristics and interests.

Mental Members

One group is called the "mental members," the "closet
Christians," or the "believers but not belongers." These are

people who were "once churched but are now drifting." At one time they were involved in a mainstream Protestant church and still identify themselves with their former denomination in national polls. This is why more than twice as many Presbyterians appear in national polls than are represented on the church's membership rolls. Mental members consider themselves members, but they do not participate and are not carried on the rolls of a church.[45]

The number of Americans who claim to be Presbyterian dropped from 6 percent of the population in 1967 to 4 percent in 1988. Even with this drop in mental members, Presbyterian membership in 1988 should have been 9,853,160 based on an estimated population of 246,329,000. Yet PC(USA) membership in 1988 was only 2,938,830, and when the membership of other Presbyterian bodies in this country is added, it does not come anywhere close to accounting for the remaining 6.8 million mental members.[46]

Nonmember Participants

A second level of disengagement from the church is what Jon Stone has termed the "nonmember participant." These individuals are a fascinating phenomenon. They participate regularly in worship and in some other church activities. Yet like the other nonaffiliated, they refuse to join officially the congregations in which they are involved.[47]

Stone compared the opinions of a small sampling of ministers, members, and nonmember participants in one southern California presbytery. He found surprising similarities in the views of lay members and nonmember participants. Stone's study confirms other findings that denominations no longer provide the primary identity for church people. This is true for both members and nonmember participants alike, since both express strong loyalty to their particular congregation but resist the label "Presbyterian." Similarly, both types appear to be engaged in a search for self-fulfillment and the abundant life.[48]

The main difference between members and nonmember

participants lies in the willingness of members to assume responsibility for policy making and the staffing of congregational programs. This disparity is relatively minor in comparison to the glaring dissimilarities between responses from clergy and from both types of laity. Stone found that ministers are far more likely to link membership with denominational loyalty and to expect conscientious attendance, financial support, and doctrinal agreement among the laity.[49]

No Religious Preference

Scholars have identified two more groups that are now entirely disengaged from the Christian church or any other religious community. The first includes those who were once churched but now have no religious preference. The second contains those who have never been a part of the church.

The number of "never churched" appears to have been quite small in the past, but as the "once churched but no preference" group grows, the "never churched" will, of course, increase dramatically.

Studies have shown that lack of exposure to church as a youth makes it unlikely that one will participate in a congregation later in life. As indicated earlier, there are signs that baby boomers with some church background are beginning to return to the church. What brings people back to the church are continued, even if only casual, contact with the church, the presence of children in one's family, and a conservative drift in social and political attitudes as people age.[50]

The "once churched" and the "never churched" groups share certain characteristics. Although their combined number was quite small in the 1950s (a mere 2 percent), it grew rather rapidly to 5 percent in 1972, 8 percent in 1982, and 10 percent in the Gallup polls of 1988–89. The real growth spurt for those expressing no religious preference occurred between 1960 and 1978.[51]

Catholics, Jews, and liberal Protestants, including the Presbyterians, have contributed the most to the "no preference" group. Eight percent of liberal Protestants have no religious preference, and even more troubling, 11.5 percent of people under forty-five years of age and reared in liberal Protestant homes fall into this category. Eight percent of the baby boomers who were confirmed in the Presbyterian Church consider themselves outside any religious tradition.[52]

There is a strong correlation between the development of individuals with no religious preference and the generation who, as Norval Glenn has put it, "came on line" during the counterculture of the 1960s and 1970s. A mere 2.6 percent of the adolescents of the 1950s declared no religious preference by the time they reached their twenties during the 1960s. But the number of adolescents in the 1960s who defected from all religious involvement increased to 7.1 percent, and in the 1970s the figure soared to 12.6 percent.[53] Roof and McKinney describe the nonaffiliated as a group composed of "young, predominantly male [individuals who are] well-educated, committed to the new morality, and oriented generally to an ethic of personal fulfillment."[54]

David Roozen, on the other hand, has investigated differences between the individuals with no religious preference and two other groups of "churched" and "unchurched" Protestants and Catholics. He notes that those whom he designates as the "nones" are found more frequently in urban areas and western states. They have fathers with higher occupational prestige and more education. They tend to be younger, male, single, with no children. They have had some college education and are employed as professionals. They socialize more often with friends who live outside their own neighborhoods and show a tendency to be less satisfied with their community, family life, and friendships. They have less confidence in Congress, the military, organized religion, television, and educational institutions, but more trust in the press, the Supreme Court, and the scientific community.[55]

Membership Decline and Denominationalism

Our discussion so far has identified the powerful social
and cultural factors that have contributed to the loss of
members for Presbyterians and other mainstream Protestant churches. Because these forces affected all of the mainstream churches, some have concluded that there was little
these churches did to exacerbate the trend and little they
could have done to stop it. This argument is valid—but
only to a degree. It fails to account for changes within
mainstream Protestantism and within each denomination
that unwittingly and even ironically contributed to membership decline.

Furthermore, the concern about the loss of members has
drawn attention away from some equally significant
changes sweeping across the landscape of American religion and culture, particularly mainstream Protestantism.
Briefly stated, membership loss is only one facet of a major
transformation—a re-forming of American Presbyterianism and mainstream Protestantism. Much of the Louisville
research project on American Presbyterianism has been devoted to studying these other changes that put membership
growth and decline into a broader and richer context.

One major finding of the Presbyterian study and other
research concludes that denominationalism is significantly
weaker as an influence affecting religious affiliation and religious behavior. Sociologists maintain that Presbyterians
and other mainstream Protestants have little denominational loyalty or identity, a fact readily confirmed by most
parish pastors. The blurring of denominational identity is
one aspect of the transformation of denominational life,
and it affects the patterns of membership switching and
membership decline.

As noted earlier, mainstream Protestants are no longer as
economically or socially distinctive as they were earlier.
Because of their own ecumenical commitments, they are
also less theologically distinctive. Throughout the twentieth century, American mainstream Protestants, especially
Presbyterians, provided key leadership for the ecumenical

movement. In the broad sweep of Christian history, the single most revolutionary change of the twentieth century has been the end of Protestant–Roman Catholic polemics and the religious and social peace between these two contending branches of Christianity.

In congregations, people have accepted the ecumenical movement to mean that there is nothing essentially different among the various Christian churches—in part because this is what mainstream Protestant churches have taught. American religious life today is more than ever an ecclesiastical smorgasbord or delicatessen that Americans sample broadly during the course of a lifetime. The menu includes not only the various Protestant denominations but also the Roman Catholic Church and new religious movements.[56] If denominational loyalty is one aspect of membership decline, such ties have been justifiably but ironically weakened by an ecumenical vision.

Specific denominational policies also made a difference. In the Presbyterian case study, a shift of priorities away from new church development stands out dramatically. During the 1950s the three Presbyterian denominations (PCUSA and UPCNA [later UPCUSA], PCUS) averaged nearly 135 new churches per year. As the churches responded to the social crises of the 1960s, new church development suffered, and the average dropped to 75 new congregations per year. In the 1970s the figure plummeted even further to 35 churches each year, and it rebounded only slightly during the 1980s to 58 per year. The significance of the decline in new church development is underlined by research on the dramatic growth of the Southern Baptists. Their increases are primarily attributable to aggressive programs in new church development, not to the expansion of existing churches.[57]

Presbyterians cut back on new church development at precisely the time that major demographic factors began to work against the denomination. The combination of what was happening to birthrates in American society and denominational policies in new church development proved to be devastating for Presbyterian membership.

The mainstream Protestant churches also responded to the social crises of American society in mid-century with new theological accents, including the interpretation of evangelism. In the Presbyterian denominations, this produced a contentious debate over what was called "word evangelism" and "deed evangelism." The argument affected evangelism policies by shifting priorities to "deed evangelism" and by sowing confusion about the nature and even the desirability of evangelism.[58] Interestingly, even before membership began to decline, there was a decrease in affirmations of faith, adult baptisms, and confirmations among Presbyterians. This may suggest a waning of the evangelistic impulse and a weakening of evangelism programs before the demographic trends began to affect the churches. Or it may signal that some of the religiosity of the 1950s was thin and weak, and by the end of the decade it may have already spent its strength.

In the last analysis, the research on membership patterns in mainstream Protestantism concludes that most people were lost to no religious affiliation. Yet opinion polls demonstrate that religious belief has remained virtually unchanged in the past half-century. Thus, a fascinating paradox emerges. Many Americans remain religious, but they implicitly or explicitly reject the church as a necessary part of expressing their faith.[59] This is an intriguing form of secularity that poses new challenges for understanding the nature of the church and its mission in American society.

A long-term perspective on mainstream Protestantism and its membership patterns also reveals dramatic internal changes in programs and policies. During the nineteenth and twentieth centuries, American mainstream Protestants, and American Presbyterians in particular, constructed a series of institutions, organizations, and programs that formed an ecology for nurturing Christian faith. This ecology consisted of Sunday schools, church camps and conference centers, church hospitals, theological seminaries, church-related colleges, campus ministries, youth ministries, special organizations for men and women, publishing houses, Christian education curricula, and more. This system of nurture in American Presbyterianism has been fragmented, weakened, and in some cases destroyed. Its fate is part of the explanation of membership patterns but also, and more important, a chapter in the history of the re-forming of American Presbyterianism as a denomination.

It is that rich and complex story of American Presbyterians as organized denominations in the twentieth century to which we now turn.

3

The Organizational Revolution: Denominationalism and Leadership

The Presbyterian Church (U.S.A.) is undergoing an organizational revolution. This dramatic change is affecting many other denominations, as well as most profit and nonprofit institutions. Peter Drucker, an analyst of profit and nonprofit organizations, points to the organizational revolution as one of the "new realities" of American society.[1] The breadth and depth of this transformation are still inadequately analyzed and understood. Equally important, because the revolution is not yet complete, its consequences and implications remain ambiguous.

What is now obvious is that the denomination, as Presbyterians and other mainstream Protestants have known it for most of the twentieth century, is being transformed.

Part of the explanation of the current conflict within the PC(USA) and other denominations lies in different and often incompatible expectations of what the denomination can and should do, as well as in conflicting understandings of what leadership should be. These expectations are rooted in a failure to understand the massive changes that have swept through the denomination *as an organization* and that have had dramatic effects on its leadership.

The study of American religion has long relied on the

idea of denominations as a way of organizing the religious pluralism of American culture. Despite copious research on denominations and on American religion as a whole, few people have paid much attention to churches and religious institutions as organizations. For example, there is very little literature on the financing of American religion.[2] Presbyterians gave $1.34 billion to the church in 1990; the General Assembly budget that year hovered around $110 million; the Presbyterian Foundation invested $700 million in behalf of the denomination, including congregations; and the Board of Pensions controlled assets of more than $2 billion. By any economic measure, the PC(USA) and other religious institutions—both larger and smaller— are very significant *organizations* in American society that need additional study.

American Presbyterians and the
Colonial Church

After the Roman emperor Constantine established Christianity as the religion of the empire in the fourth century, churches were recognized and established by the state. Other alternatives were sects. Church and state were fused as different ways of exercising spiritual or temporal power. The church undergirded the moral and political legitimacy of the state; the state protected the church from the divisive effects of religious dissent.

The idea of a denomination arose out of the Westminster Assembly during the 1640s. The denomination emerged from seventeenth-century England as a halfway house between the church and the sect. Theologically, the notion of a denomination recognizes that certain truths are held by all Christians; on some matters Christians can disagree yet still cooperate and respect those who differ. The issues for legitimate disagreement were called *adiaphora*, and they principally involved questions of church polity and worship.[3]

Gradually, the seeds were planted for a revolutionary idea in understanding the political order—the separation of church and state—and the most important innovation in the doctrine of the church since the fourth century—the denomination. Although the seeds of denominationalism were planted in Great Britain, the plant flourished principally in the American colonies and the new nation of the United States. The idea of the denomination has now been exported throughout the world. It is based on the importance of religious toleration and ultimately the separation of church and state.

The Westminster Assembly provided the confessional basis for many branches of the Reformed tradition, including colonial Presbyterianism. When Presbyterians settled in the American colonies, most assumed that it would be desirable and even possible to recreate a state church modeled after the Church of Scotland or other Reformed churches in Europe. However, this assumption was badly flawed because of two stark realities.

First, Presbyterians settled in colonies where a church was already established (either Congregationalist or Anglican), or where the population was so diverse that the establishment of only one church would have been unrealistic (for example, New Jersey or Pennsylvania).

Second, Presbyterians founded congregations before they developed larger governing bodies that might have been "established." They migrated as extended families who in turn formed congregations. Scots and their cousins from northern Ireland, English Puritan connectionalist, Welsh, Dutch, and German Calvinists, Huguenots—all formed congregations from families who brought the piety and practice of European traditions as part of their dowry.[4]

Therefore, in contrast to the Church of Scotland and other Reformed churches of Europe, American Presbyterianism started at the local level—in congregations. In Scotland, the Reformation had brought adjustments in the government to accommodate Presbyterian polity as it replaced Roman Catholic church order. But the hierarchical patterns remained, Presbyterianism came to power by parliamentary action, and the Church of Scotland was formed "from the top down."[5]

In colonies from New Hampshire to South Carolina, but especially in the middle colonies, extended family units of Presbyterians united to form congregations. Groups of these congregations eventually created the first presbytery in 1706 and the first synod in 1716. The Presbyterian Church in colonial America grew "from the bottom up."

The elders of the early Presbyterian sessions superintended the spiritual welfare of members of congregations, exercised discipline, admitted new members, frequently led worship themselves, and represented the congregations in presbyteries. Ministers and elders worked through presbyteries, which existed primarily to ordain ministers and to organize and order congregational life. The notion of a national denomination did not exist, and the idea of a mission for a governing body, including presbyteries and synods, was yet to come. For example, only modest efforts were made at evangelizing Native Americans or African slaves. The colonial American Presbyterian Church was actually a loose confederation of congregations.

From the beginning, Presbyterians in America actually had two churches—one that remained essentially congregational and to which most members belonged and in which they remained, and another that directed them toward the rule of church courts and governing bodies. The congregation-oriented Presbyterians benefited from the governing bodies, which ordained ministers and ordered church life, and the governing body church received leaders and resources from the congregation-oriented group. The two segments struggled, but the benefits of this organizational symbiosis outweighed the cost.[6] Presbyteries generally adjudicated tensions over priorities and differences in Presbyterian styles of government and leadership. Even when congregations and presbyteries split in 1741–1758 over issues arising out of the First Great Awakening, the differences in theology and church order were eventually and informally resolved.[7]

Thus, Presbyterianism in America began with a predisposition toward tolerating and even supporting localism. Congregationalism triumphed as the functional polity not only for Congregationalists and Baptists but also for Presbyterians, Anglicans (or Episcopalians), Methodists, and others whose polities did not formally recognize the supremacy of the congregation. To a certain extent, this was true for even the Roman Catholics. The history of American Catholicism is marked by a continuing struggle to adjust a hierarchical polity to the realities of congregational power in American religious life.

The Rise of the Denomination

In 1787, shortly after the American Revolution, Presbyterians gathered to form a General Assembly. In itself, this act did not create a Presbyterian denomination, but the Presbyterian Church in the U.S.A. represented for the first time a national church body in the new nation. Legally separated from the state, Presbyterians found themselves in a competitive situation with every other Christian church for the allegiance of the American people. At the same time, Presbyterians joined in common cause with other Protestants to evangelize the American people and tame the devastating effects of frontier life.[8]

The late eighteenth and early nineteenth centuries actually represent the formative period of American Protestantism and even American religious life. Virtually all the major characteristics of American religious institutions—both their organization and their programs—took shape during this period. Central to the emerging institutions of American Protestantism was the denomination. The difference in this new conception of the church was the idea of mission—evangelizing both the millions of voluntary immigrants who settled North America as well as African slaves and Native Americans; converting people to Christianity beyond American shores; nurturing and educating people in the Christian faith, as well as all branches of human knowledge; and pursuing an astonishing agenda of "reform" that would "Christianize" (meaning "Protestantize") American society and eventually the world.[9]

The dynamo of American evangelicalism powered Presbyterian denominationalism and most American Protestant churches. It also provided the basis for individuals and denominations to make common cause to realize their goals. Presbyterians and other evangelical Protestants thoroughly accepted the idea of the church as an agent of mission, for this commitment to witness in word and in deed represented the logical result of the evangelical conversion to Christ.

The Second Great Awakening, including the Presbyterian-led frontier revivals in Virginia and Kentucky, involved a half-century of effort to organize the religious life of the early republic. As Donald G. Mathews has written, the Awakening gave "meaning and direction to people suffering in various degrees from the social strains of a nation on the move."[10] Presbyterians and their other Protestant colleagues believed that by spreading the gospel they were uplifting society. Especially after Presbyterian evangelist Charles G. Finney launched his own version of revivalism, the missionary impulse spread among Presbyterians to bring others to Christian commitment. The related goal of preaching the gospel in every tongue, as well as attending to the educational and medical needs of people, spurred Presbyterians to organize for mission. This zealous spirit produced an extension of Presbyterian membership in the United States and a broadening of its mission beyond American shores.[11]

During the early years of the nineteenth century, Presbyterians engaged in educational and mission activities primarily by cooperative work with other evangelical Protestants. The organization they developed was the voluntary or benevolent society, an institution of like-minded people committed to a particular cause. In today's parlance they would be known as parachurch organizations. The nineteenth-century voluntary or benevolent society engaged in mission alongside of and in behalf of the denominations themselves. Presbyterians actively participated in the establishment of all the major benevolent societies— the American Board of Commissioners for Foreign Missions (1810), the American Education Society (1816), the American Bible Society (1816), the American Sunday

School Union (1824), the American Tract Society (1825), and the American Home Mission Society (1826). Likewise, they helped form hundreds of other mission societies and "unions" to ameliorate an incredible array of social ills. These included the well-known American Antislavery Society (1833) and the less commonly known New York Society for Providing Trusses to the Ruptured Poor. Representatives of these societies spoke to governing bodies of the Presbyterian Church, and offerings were collected to support their work.[12]

A Presbyterian passion for education gave a unique accent to the vision of mission for nineteenth-century Presbyterians. The Sunday school, first developed in Britain and originally organized outside the churches, gradually became an integral part of congregational life during the nineteenth century.[13] In both frontier and settled areas, Presbyterian schools sprang up to provide elementary and secondary education.

Presbyterians also led in the founding of many church-related colleges and public universities. In fact, one historian concludes that during the nineteenth century Presbyterians were associated with creating more colleges and universities than any other group in American Christianity.[14] The Presbyterian emphasis on educated ministers prompted the founding of theological seminaries in antebellum America. These were a uniquely American institution for providing leadership to a denomination. By mid-century, the basic outlines of the Presbyterian mission in education—from the Sunday school through the theological seminary—were set.

The same is true for the social agenda of American Presbyterianism. Virtually every issue that consumes the attention of late twentieth-century Presbyterians and mainstream Protestants was addressed in religious reform movements of the early nineteenth century—war, racism, economic justice, substance abuse (principally alcohol), feminism, urban blight, crime, prison reform, and others. Perhaps the only exception is environmental concerns, which developed later in the nineteenth century.[15]

At the heart of Presbyterian mission was the desire to evangelize people and to admit them to the Presbyterian church—both across the United States and beyond its shores. Home missions targeted for Native Americans, African American slaves and free people, and specific ethnic groups (such as Germans in the Middle West) became the principal emphasis of presbyteries and congregations. In foreign missions, evangelical Presbyterians were sent to Latin America, Asia, and Africa to proclaim the gospel and win converts.[16]

The organization and mission of American Presbyterians were possible because of a new method of financing the church—the development of the freewill offering. In Europe, established churches relied upon a complex system of tax revenues to support the church. Dissenting churches depended on the meager contributions of their members. In nineteenth-century America, a church depended solely on the willingness of its members to contribute money for its mission.

Initially Presbyterian congregations relied on pew rentals and sales for ministerial salaries and for the maintenance of church buildings. Capital improvements generally were underwritten by subscription of funds and occasionally by lotteries. Members of various benevolent organizations paid dues or made voluntary donations, and individuals and congregations supported education and missionary work with direct gifts.

The belief in freedom of the will or Arminianism, which pervaded nineteenth-century evangelicalism, often dismayed scholastic Calvinists, who affirmed the sovereignty of God's will in salvation. But Arminianism had an organizational and financial result—the freewill offering. Religious institutions became the most conspicuous example of the financing of charity by private philanthropy, which was and remains one of the most extraordinary characteristics of American culture.[17]

Presbyterians disagreed about how mission should be conducted and what that mission should be. The Old School/New School split in 1837 was due in part to the desire of Old School leaders to bring mission under the denominational umbrella; hence, the founding of boards and agencies. But the 1837 division was also a product of the agonizing struggle over the nineteenth century's greatest issue—slavery. In the southeast, Presbyterians hotly debated the doctrine of "the spirituality of the church."

Formulated by the southern Presbyterian theologian James Henley Thornwell, this doctrine claimed that the church's focus was exclusively spiritual. Therefore, the church should not speak out on political or social issues but rather leave such matters to the consciences of its members. When the War Between the States broke out in 1861, Old School Presbyterians formed the Presbyterian Church in the Confederate States of America, which subsequently joined with Presbyterians from border synods to form the Presbyterian Church in the U.S. The spirituality of the church was its "distinctive doctrine," and it proved to be only partially effective as a "gag rule" on discussions of social and political issues in the church.[18]

Debates over the nature of the church's mission and how it would be pursued were at one level disputes over the definition of a denomination. Whether slaveholders should receive Communion was a question about the purity of the church. Whether slaves should be evangelized was an issue defining the scope of the church's mission. Whether missionary work should be conducted by boards and agencies, by presbyteries and congregations, by women's guilds, or by benevolent societies was a debate over denominational identity and the location of power and control.

But in assessing early nineteenth-century Presbyterian mission and the organizations that made it possible, what stands out is their informal character and their relative weakness as institutions. The minutes of church courts usually provided a bare minimum of information. Despite an emphasis on educated clergy, seminaries offered no degrees, and faculty members despaired in their efforts to keep students on campus for the expected three-year program. The worship life of Presbyterian congregations was eclectic; the 1788 *Directory for Worship* provided only gen-

eral instructions for celebration of the sacraments and
praise and proclamation, and it scarcely changed for decades. Mission work was diverse and diffused, energetic
and entrepreneurial; however, it was also inefficient and
even chaotic.

The denominational glue of antebellum American Presbyterianism was the Westminster Standards and evangelical Protestantism's affirmations: the authority of scripture,
the necessity of an experience of God's grace in Jesus
Christ through conversion, and a commitment to witness
in word and deed to the world. Debates over what that
witness might involve were mitigated because of the diversity of organizations through which people might work.
Presbyterians and other evangelical Protestants essentially
understood the denomination as a "constitutional confed-
eracy" of congregations loosely connected by relatively
weak institutional structures and a broadly defined constitution.[19]

But the institutional fluidity and the missionary
consensus of evangelical Protestantism disappeared after
the War Between the States. In its place would arise the
American denomination as a corporation and a civil war
within American Presbyterianism and mainstream Protestantism.

The Age of Incorporation

During the late nineteenth and early twentieth centuries,
Americans began forming complex, hierarchical enterprises in business, government, and other areas of American life. American Presbyterians adopted the imagery,
structures, and practices of the modern business corporation and applied them to the organization of the church.
The result was the corporate denomination.

The impulse for doing so arose out of the broader
"search for order" in American social, economic, and political life that characterized the Progressive period in American history.[20] Many Presbyterians participated in the
restructuring of American economic organizations into

modern corporations, and their middle- and upper-class
economic status made them likely leaders in the reshaping
of American institutions as corporations. Consequently, it
is hardly surprising that the values and ideals of the modern corporation exerted a profound influence on the Presbyterian Church as it "incorporated."

In the twentieth century the corporate denomination became the dominant image of the church for Presbyterians.
The denomination as a corporation is a bureaucratic, hierarchical organization dependent on managers and capable
of delivering goods and services to congregations as well
as mobilizing and coordinating support of national and
international mission causes. The characteristics of incorporation permeated national structures as well as congregations. Despite differences in time and degree,
incorporation became characteristic of all three major
branches of twentieth-century Presbyterianism.

Louis Weeks has demonstrated the far-reaching changes
that resulted from adopting the model of the corporation
for organizing the church's life. Loosely knit and quasi-
independent mission groups and agencies were finally
united in one denominational structure with defined areas
of responsibility and lines of authority. The primary administrative officer of the church, the Stated Clerk, moved
from part-time volunteer to full-time employee with a
staff. "Efficiency" and "businesslike methods" were the
rallying cries of the reformers who sought to bring the corporation to the church. Experts appeared for specialized
tasks; "departments" emerged with "directors" or "managers" responsible for effective and efficient administration.[21]

The process of incorporation also affected congregations
in dramatic and subtle ways. The pastor's role as shepherd
of a flock expanded to include supervision of congregational employees—sextons, secretaries, and staff for specialized ministries. Even the terminology for physical space
changed in revealing ways. "The pastor's study," used for
the preparation of sermons, retained currency, but it also
became known as "the pastor's office," where the "busi-

ness" of the church was administered. The session increasingly assumed the functions of a board of directors. Sunday
schools became more hierarchical and bureaucratic with an
increasing use of "superintendents" to monitor and manage its educational program. The introduction of Uniform
Bible Lessons was only one example of the development of
curricula—standardized courses of instruction accompanied by manuals to aid teachers in both methods and content of teaching.[22]

Presbyterian worship, like nineteenth-century evangelical Protestant services, was eclectic and spartan. A typical
service probably consisted of two or three hymns, the reading of scripture, an unwritten pastoral prayer, and a long
sermon delivered from notes. Leaders of liturgical reform
in the age of the corporation rescued the richness of Reformed worship of the sixteenth century, and Presbyterian
worship during the twentieth century was transformed. At
the turn of the century, American Presbyterians produced
their first *Book of Common Worship* (1905). For the first
time American Presbyterians had suggestions for uniform
congregational prayers, regular use of creeds, and a form
for the Lord's Supper, baptism, and offerings.[23]

The patterns of financing Presbyterian congregational
life and mission enterprises were also reorganized, with the
weekly offering made into a liturgical rubric, a system of
annual pledges instituted wherever possible, and the provision of double envelopes so people could give separately to
benevolences and current expenses. Denomination-wide
fund drives were launched, and regional efforts were
spurred by challenge grants. Financial terminology, such as
"benevolence ratios," made their way into increasingly vo-
luminous and detailed reports. By 1902, the PCUSA required sessions of particular churches to approve all special
offerings.[24]

The PCUSA led in the move toward the corporate denomination, and the reorganization of the 1920s is a text-
book case of incorporation. A committee chaired by John
Timothy Stone, pastor of the Fourth Presbyterian Church
in Chicago and known as "a businessman in religion," met

only four times over three years and streamlined a multi-
tude of competing and overlapping boards and agencies
into a fourfold structure. The new administration of the
church consisted of a Board of National Missions, a Board
of Foreign Missions, a Board of Christian Education, and a
Board of Relief and Sustentation (pensions). Overseeing
and coordinating the work was a General Council. Actually, the plan was devised by a layman, Robert E. Speer,
secretary of the Board of Foreign Missions. The proposal
was overwhelmingly approved in 1923 by the PCUSA General Assembly.[25]

Stone's committee consisted of five elders and five ministers, most of whom came from large churches. Black Presbyterian leaders protested that mission work among Blacks
would suffer by the loss of a separate mission agency for
that purpose, and women echoed the same cry. The
women's organization of the PCUSA was finally incorporated within the structure of the denomination, but the results were ironic. Women found themselves in the peculiar
situation of making decisions on national policy for the denomination through membership on boards and agencies.
And yet, they could not serve as elders on a session. In 1930
the PCUSA approved the ordination of women as elders.
The incorporation of the church raised new and pressing
questions of power, participation, and authority in the denomination. These issues grew in intensity and complexity
during the remainder of the century.[26]

Presbyterians in the South were less enthusiastic about
creating powerful boards and agencies to coordinate the
church's mission, and during the late nineteenth and early
twentieth centuries, power was largely vested in presbyteries, which had their own boards. Part of this development
in the PCUS is attributable to the thought of James Henley
Thornwell, who argued that the mission of the church was
linked to the presbytery, not to agencies that worked in behalf of the entire denomination. Southern regionalism was
also another influence. The presbyteries of the South,
which had their own boards and employees, contrasted
sharply with PCUSA presbyteries, which were weaker and

were staffed by national administrators who coordinated national programs.[27] In the last analysis, the difference was one of degree rather than of kind, and by the 1940s and 1950s the PCUS and the PCUSA looked remarkably similar in their adaptation to the model of the twentieth-century corporate denomination.[28]

The Presbyterian acceptance of the denomination as a corporation brought unquestioned benefits. Giving increased. Mission efforts abroad and at home flourished, and congregations multiplied through the first half of the twentieth century. Sophisticated denomination-wide fund drives succeeded. The denominations produced high-quality Christian education curricula that were widely used—*Christian Faith and Life* in the PCUSA and a Covenant Life Curriculum in the PCUS. Evangelism committees taught Presbyterians how to speak of their faith to those they encountered, and the global mission efforts of the Presbyterians had much to do with the development of viable, independent-minded Christian denominations in many countries throughout the world. The corporate denomination sponsored denominational magazines, and during the 1950s *Presbyterian Life* had a larger circulation than *Newsweek*. The denominational publishing houses, Westminster Press and John Knox Press, produced books of general interest and substantive scholarship, earning a reputation for excellence in religious publishing. The corporate denomination also provided the organizational structure for sound fiscal administration and for ecumenical cooperation.[29]

At its zenith, the corporate denomination was something to behold. Cohesive and powerful, it was a very effective organization for mobilizing religious benevolence. Led by widely recognized leaders, it left a lasting mark on American Protestantism and shaped the character of world Christianity in the first part of the twentieth century. But the post–World War II period brought new strains to American Presbyterianism and mainstream Protestantism, and in its wake came the organizational revolution in American denominations.

The Organizational Revolution

The corporate denomination is remarkable for its success over a relatively long period of time. But beginning in the 1950s, it began to falter. What Presbyterians and other Protestants are witnessing today is in part the unraveling of the corporate idea of the denomination. The vitality of the corporate denomination depended on a high degree of trust between congregations and governing bodies and significant agreement about Presbyterian goals and values. Factors in both American Presbyterianism and American culture have combined to erode both the atmosphere of trust and the consensus about common values.

The organizational revolution can be seen by tracing the financial history of American Presbyterian giving and the allocation of denominational resources. These studies reveal that the corporate denomination had significant support from congregations until the 1950s. Curiously, amid the so-called revival of the 1950s and at the height of the postwar expansion of American Presbyterianism, congregations slowly but steadily began to reduce their commitment to General Assembly mission support. The erosion continued and accelerated from the 1960s through the 1980s. The new financial patterns both reflected the fragmentation of the denomination and produced the organizational revolution of the corporate denomination. In short, the capability of the PC(USA) to fulfill the role of a denomination in mission—at least through its General Assembly administrative structure—has been seriously weakened.

During the first two decades of the twentieth century, the denominations that now comprise the PC(USA) reaped benefits from the process of "incorporation." Giving to General Assembly mission causes increased in the PCUSA from $2.8 million in 1900 to $9.8 million in 1920. During the same twenty years, per-member giving to General Assembly causes soared from $2.86 to $6.16.[30] The Great Depression devastated General Assembly receipts, and in one sense General Assembly causes never quite recovered from the Depression. Giving to General Assembly causes was at its height in the 1920s and early 1930s, reaching 12–13 percent of total benevolences in the PCUS and the PCUSA. Though support for GA causes recovered somewhat in the PCUS during the 1940s, it began a steady decline during the 1940s and 1950s. By the 1980s, congregations in both denominations were allocating less than 3 percent of total benevolences to General Assembly causes.[31]

Figures from the United Presbyterian Church from 1963 to 1983 starkly illustrate the financial revolution. In 1963 United Presbyterians allocated $10.9 million for synod and presbytery causes and $29.9 million for General Assembly causes. Twenty years later, in 1983, giving to synod and presbytery mission had more than tripled to $36.5 million, while giving to General Assembly causes actually declined by more than $5 million to $24.7 million. The increase for synods and presbytery causes is illusory, for when the figures are adjusted for inflation, it becomes clear that synods and presbyteries saw virtually no increase. Inflation-adjusted General Assembly revenues, however, fell by more than 50 percent in the period from 1973 to 1988.[32]

Throughout the twentieth century, Presbyterians have increased their donations to the church—steadily and dramatically. In the early 1920s the average Presbyterian in both denominations gave approximately $56 per year. By the early 1980s, even when adjusted for inflation, the average PCUS member gave $141 per year; the average UPCUSA member contributed $121 per year.[33]

Where did the money go? The overwhelming answer is that congregations gradually and inexorably exercised more control over their own benevolences by retaining more for local mission and by designating funds for specific causes. Analysts of Presbyterian giving conclude that in the 1950s almost two-thirds of the money given to congregations went beyond the congregation; thirty years later, at least two-thirds stayed within the congregation, either for its maintenance or for its own mission efforts. By the late 1980s, congregations designated more money for Presbyterian and non-Presbyterian causes than for General Assem-

bly support.[34] Congregational autonomy has triumphed in
the financing of Presbyterian mission since the 1950s, and
this economic change has produced a dramatic shift of
power.

Both denominations encouraged the trend toward localism by administrative reorganizations in the early 1970s.
The byword of these tumultuous restructuring efforts was a
desire to carry out mission "at the lowest practical level of
the church." Large numbers of Assembly staff were termi-
nated or relocated in other governing bodies. The shift toward congregational concerns and local mission was, in
part, a result of both denominations' policies during the
1970s as well as a recognition of reality.[35]

The economic transformation of American Presbyterianism and the weakening of General Assembly mission support are clear. Explaining why these changes occurred is
quite another matter. Robin Klay argues that in the PCUS,
General Assembly support declined during the 1950s
because of strife over the allocation of money in the Assembly's budget. In her account, southern regionalism played
a powerful role in the shift of resources away from Assembly priorities. Scott Brunger's analysis of the PCUSA/
UPCUSA's financial history concludes that no one factor
can explain the decline, which began somewhat later in the
UPCUSA during the early 1960s.[36]

D. Scott Cormode tested three hypotheses to interpret
the change: controversies over social action (the Angela
Davis case in the UPCUSA), the restructuring of the denominations during the early 1970s, and increasing pastoral compensation. None of these, he concludes, in itself
explained why congregations have reduced support for
General Assembly causes. The answer, he proposes, lies in
the complexities of local ecclesiastical factors and in a
broader process of alienation from institutions that are
seen as distant and remote. As the concept of Presbyterian
mission became more variegated and unfocused, Cormode
maintains, congregations became uncertain about the direction of the denomination and less likely to support its
General Assembly causes. In contrast, the mission of the

congregation triumphed at the Assembly's expense, as did appeals for specific causes and organizations with clearly defined goals and affinities to congregations.[37]

The process of alienation from large institutions clearly represents a major feature of American culture since the 1960s. American Presbyterians and their denominational structures were swept along by the rising tide of anti-institutionalism and individualism spawned in part by the countercultural movements of the 1960s.[38] The organizational revolution in American Presbyterianism must be placed in the context of significant cultural changes that left their imprint on all denominations and virtually every area of American institutional life.

Accompanying the antiinstitutionalism of recent decades has been a sharp polarization within mainstream Protestantism and American Presbyterianism. Observers interpret these polarities in different ways. Robert Wuthnow sees conservatives and liberals pitted against one another on a wide range of theological and political issues.[39] Others see the division as a conflict between clergy and laity, with differences over social and political issues as well as priorities in church life playing important roles in defining the areas of disagreement.[40]

Peter Berger and James Davison Hunter argue that clergy are members of a "new class," composed of people whose education and skills lead them to be managers of information. As noted in chapter 1, this "new class" is different from the "old class," whose influence and power are based on the production of goods. The values of the "new class" (liberal) frequently conflict with those of the "old class" (conservative), and the result is what they describe as "culture wars" in American religion and American culture.[41]

The reality of alienation between congregations and the governing bodies of the PC(USA), however, is indisputable. A 1989 *Presbyterian Panel* poll offered the following statement for reaction from its sample population: "Most of the national level staff in the PC(USA) seem out of touch with what is happening in congregations." Forty-eight percent of the pastors agreed; 47 percent of the specialized clergy agreed; 53 percent of the elders agreed; and 41 percent of the members agreed. Perhaps equally disturbing was the high level of "don't know" answers—22 percent among elders and 36 percent among members. This poll and other findings suggest that the division between clergy and laity is less severe than the gulf between congregations and governing bodies.[42]

Exacerbating the intradenominational divisions in the PC(USA) were specific denominational policies, some of which were intended as reforms. As the reorganization of the PCUSA in the 1920s makes clear, power in the denomination was lodged in white men, particularly pastors and elders of large congregations. The corporate denomination they constructed also had roles for highly visible male leaders who were both recognized and acknowledged as individuals who could garner support for their particular agency or cause. The 1960s and the concern to recognize the roles of women and minorities in the life of the church involved a significant power struggle within American Presbyterianism. Power was redistributed, but frequently at the cost of radically reducing, if not eliminating, leadership from large churches.

In short, just as congregations were beginning to reduce their support for General Assembly mission, the church launched a necessary and needed reform of its political structures to include people who previously had little or no power. As desirable as the reform was, it undermined the corporate denomination's ties with many pastors and lay leaders of large congregations, as well as the majority of the denomination's members and their benevolences in these congregations.

The administrative reorganizations of the 1970s unwittingly contributed to the disengagement of congregations from denominational mission. In both the PCUS and the PCUSA, the reorganizations produced umbrella structures that attempted to unify the concept of mission in units named "the Program Agency" (UPCUSA) and the "General Assembly Mission Board" (PCUS). Unity, however, bred anonymity. Members, elders, and pastors frequently found it difficult to identify what office was responsible for a particular area of the church's life.

The reforms of the 1970s were also designed to curtail the strong, visible leadership of the corporate denomination, and in its place emerged administrators who saw their primary role as managers and facilitators of consultation and consensus. Richard Reifsnyder's study of the biographies of General Assembly leadership in the 1970s and 1980s concludes that these individuals entered administrative work earlier in their ministries and had less parish experience than their counterparts prior to the 1960s.[43] Thus their ties to congregations and their awareness of congregational needs were weaker.

The organizational revolution in American Presbyterianism since the 1960s has brought not only racial ethnic minorities into new positions of leadership and power but also women, and the impact of women as ministers constitutes one of the most far-reaching changes in American Presbyterianism and mainstream Protestantism in the late twentieth century. Even though the ordaining of women as ministers began in the UPCUSA in 1956 and in the PCUS in 1965, few women entered seminary and secured ordination until the 1970s. For example, in 1966 there were only 69 women ministers in the UPCUSA and 12,865 male ministers. Beginning in the 1970s and at an escalating rate during the 1980s, women increasingly sought a theological education and ordination. By the late 1980s, women constituted approximately one-third of all students enrolled in Presbyterian seminaries.[44]

The first generation of Presbyterian women ministers has encountered both significant opposition and gradual acceptance. Women ministers have been generally more successful in winning appointments to presbytery, synod, and General Assembly staff positions than calls to ministry in congregations, particularly large congregations. However, as Lois Boyd and Douglas Brackenridge found, even congregational attitudes, if not congregational behavior, show signs of changing in response to what is perhaps the most significant transformation in Protestant leadership since the Reformation.[45]

Women ministers pose at least two significant challenges for American Presbyterianism and mainstream Protestantism during the 1990s and the twenty-first century. First, if the present seminary enrollment trends continue, women may well become a majority among Presbyterian ministers during the next century. Congregations and the denomination will eventually have to accept them as ministers of the Word and Sacrament. Second, their presence has already contributed new and profound theological questions about the nature of the church, leadership, and the Christian faith, as Barbara Brown Zikmund has shown. Inclusive language for people and for God may attract the most attention, but even more important has been the questioning of Christianity itself as hierarchical and patriarchal. Proposals to recast the understanding of sin and salvation and the nature of God represent a fundamental reconception of Christianity. Women as ministers not only enrich the quality of the church's leadership but also raise new questions about the nature of Christian doctrine.[46]

Presbyterians may have proclaimed the unity of the denomination's mission in the 1970s and 1980s, but congregations were increasingly confused about what that mission was. Presbyterians may have included more people in the process of determining that mission, but managing the process seemed to overshadow the mission. Both the mission and its leadership seemed to be unclear.

In fact, as American culture lost its cohesion and fragmented during the 1960s through the 1980s, so did the sense of a unifying mission for American Presbyterians. Congregations, presbyteries, synods, and the General Assembly all attempted to deal with variously defined "crises"—race, urban and rural problems, sexual behavior and gender roles, the environment, war, armaments, poverty, and so on.

The connection between cultural cohesion and American Presbyterianism is illustrated by the fate of Presbyterian men's organizations during the twentieth century. Dale

Soden found that these groups flourished during the early years of the century and again during the 1950s. Their strength was directly related to their ability to appeal to the spirit of the age—moderate political reform in the first decades of the century and anticommunism during the 1950s. When these ties to American civil religion were loosened, Presbyterian men's organizations languished.[47] The disintegrating forces of American society have been met by committed and courageous attempts by Presbyterians to deal with epochal changes, but in the process the clarity of mission has suffered.

The debate over denominational mission and the fragmentation of denominational goals help explain the extraordinary proliferation of special-interest groups in American Presbyterianism since the 1960s. Most of these groups are designed to advocate specific causes, ranging from social and political agendas to the nurturing of Christian disciplines. The scope of mission expanded so broadly that these Presbyterian groups provided a sense of identity and purpose for members in a pluralistic denomination. At the same time, these groups often sapped energy from the denomination as the governing bodies sought to deal with the special interest groups' intensely competitive claims for priority.[48] Since the 1960s, the phenomenon of "single-issue politics" has characterized American politics, American Presbyterianism, and mainstream Protestantism.

The fractious debates over mission are related to the theological changes in American Presbyterianism and mainstream Protestantism during the twentieth century. As compelling challenges to denominational mission arose in post–World War II America, major reformulations of Christian theology were advanced within American Presbyterianism and recognized from other Christian traditions. For a denomination committed to ecumenism and a recognition of the diversity of Christian belief and discipleship, the theological ferment of the last thirty years has been both bane and blessing. On the one hand, it has enriched the church's vision of the Christian faith; on the other, it has so expanded the ways of understanding Christianity that both pastors and lay people are left confused as to what is the distinctive theological stance of Presbyterians.[49]

The New Denomination

The organizational revolution has transformed the corporate denomination. The changes can be traced in financial patterns, leadership, administrative structures, the nature of denominational mission, and theological developments. The congregation is now the locus of power and mission in American Presbyterianism. But congregations are also characterized by tremendous diversity and frequently by confusion about their own identities.[50] What then will happen to the denomination? The organizational revolution is not over, and the next stage of denominationalism is not yet clear.

Obviously, the corporate denomination that relied on close ties with congregations and common agreement about goals in mission has been transformed. In financial terms, the contemporary denomination simply cannot meet the expectations of individual church members or congregations because of the lack of money and personnel. The fragmentation of mission and the escalating proliferation of mission causes also pose serious obstacles to reviving the corporate denomination. Indeed, after studying the history of presbyteries, Lewis Wilkins concludes, "The era of the American evangelical denomination as a connected, coherent, and potent mission enterprise is over."[51]

Such a bleak assessment may be premature, for the history of denominations demonstrates their enormous flexibility in responding to religious and cultural change. A number of intriguing hypotheses have been advanced to describe the current state of the organization of American denominations and American Presbyterianism.

Louis Weeks and Bill Fogleman have proposed the "two-church hypothesis" to explain the divisions in the PC(USA). They suggest that American Presbyterians have always functioned within two churches—one dominated by people oriented to the needs of individuals and congregations and another focused on the interests of governing bodies. Each has its agenda and networks of support, but the agendas are different and produce internal conflict within the denomination.[52] Wuthnow's description of the polarization of mainstream Protestantism, together with other studies, confirms this interpretation.[53]

A similar interpretation portrays mainstream Protestant denominations as "holding companies," organizations that provide a canopy for a wide diversity of people with varying visions of the Christian faith and the church's mission. This image suggests that the denomination's role is not to provide either a common witness or a coordinated mission; rather, the denomination attempts to strengthen the diverse groups and congregations moving in disparate directions, and to manage and minimize their conflicting goals and strategies. Because of internal conflict, the "holding company" denomination is inherently unstable and faces a monumental challenge in retaining the allegiance of diverse groups and/or in monitoring the manifold forms of mission.[54]

The task of managing pluralism has prompted Craig Dykstra and James Hudnut-Beumler to propose the image of the "regulatory agency" for the modern mainstream Protestant denomination. According to them, as funds for national denominational structures declined and as the idea of mission fragmented, denominations increasingly rely on their ability to legislate the terms under which congregations can and should conduct their mission work. Unable to provide goods and services or to conduct mission as the corporate denomination did, denominations now rely on monitoring and regulating mission. This regulatory function is seen by many as coercive or oppressive in a voluntary organization like the church. Therefore, the organization is often itself the source of conflict and is frequently "dysfunctional."[55]

David McCarthy and James Moorhead argue that the unifying force in the PC(USA) may no longer be theology but polity. Because of the diversity of theological convictions and views of the church's mission, Presbyterians are united by a common process, rather than one vision.[56]

None of these interpretations offers prescriptions about what denominations might do to recover a greater degree of organizational vitality and direction. They do, however, clarify what is happening to the PC(USA) and mainstream Protestant denominations. The new organizational life of the denomination may be the beginning for understanding its present predicaments and its future.

Does the denominational revolution and the triumph of the congregation represent a qualitative decline in the witness of American Presbyterians and other mainstream Protestants? The answer is unclear. Amid the organizational problems of American Presbyterianism are reservoirs of vitality and strength in congregations, governing bodies, and denominational institutions. But for Presbyterians with a conviction of the connectedness of the body of Christ and a vision of the ecumenical character of Christian witness, the denominational revolution—with its accompanying alienation from the General Assembly on the part of many and the preoccupation with congregational concerns—presents a sobering challenge.

Furthermore, the transformation of the denomination as an organization may compel Presbyterians, who stand in a confessional tradition, to ask deeper questions about the theological basis of their common life and to acknowledge the new challenges to the Christian faith as a new century approaches.

4

The Predicament of Pluralism: Theology and Confessions

"The Bible is to the theologian what nature is to the man of science," declared Charles Hodge, the preeminent Presbyterian theologian of the nineteenth century, adding:

> It is his store-house of facts; and his method of ascertaining what the Bible teaches, is the same as that which the natural philosopher adopts to ascertain what nature teaches. . . . The duty of the Christian theologian is to ascertain, collect, and combine all the facts which God has revealed concerning himself and our relation to him. These facts are all in the Bible. . . . The theologian must be guided by the same rules in the collection of facts, as govern the man of science. . . . In theology as in natural science, principles are derived from facts, and not impressed upon them.[1]

Hodge's serene confidence in the Bible as the repository of truth and in the theologian's capacity to mine successfully the biblical record for that truth was shared by the vast majority of Presbyterians and mainstream Protestants in the 1870s. However, significant voices within his own communion were already questioning whether the theologian's yield was the pure ore of divine revelation or, more likely, a cruder mixture of revelation and erroneous human interpretation.

Employing imagery reminiscent of Hodge, the New School Presbyterian Albert Barnes observed in 1867 that "the work of the Christian theologian is to sit down to the New Testament simply as an interpreter of language, as the learner of science sits down to the study of the works of nature, to learn what nature *is,* not to determine what it *should be.*" Barnes insisted that the "authority to modify" the system of Christianity found in scripture was not "entrusted to mortals." That system would not be "made different at one time from what it is at another." But Barnes went on to note an important qualification: "It is not to be assumed . . . , by the Christian or the infidel, that we have in fact, in our creeds and in our interpretation of the Bible, *precisely* the system which is revealed. That we have the true *record* in the Bible [—that] we are to believe; and the infidel may hold us to that; but that we have the proper *interpretation* of that record is not to be assumed as certain."[2]

During the twentieth century, this important question of interpretation would raise even deeper challenges to Presbyterian theology and its tradition as a confessional church. The responses to these challenges have been mixed, and they pose a genuine predicament to a denomination that has traditionally emphasized the Bible as its theological and confessional base.

Presbyterians, along with other mainstream Protestants, have awakened in the late twentieth century to the diversity of cultures and the pluralism of theological outlooks present in the world Christian community. This has enriched and expanded the Presbyterian perspective on scripture, theology, and discipleship. But it has also fragmented the church and blurred its own identity as Presbyterians have struggled to discover a commonly acceptable locus of authority for interpreting scripture, defining Presbyterian theology, and determining Presbyterian practice.

The story of the theological changes in American Presbyterianism constitutes one of the most important chapters in the re-forming and reshaping of American Presbyterianism, mainstream Protestantism, and American culture. Indeed, because theological pluralism includes perspectives from other areas of the world, the study of theology in twentieth-century American Presbyterianism illumines part of the transformation of world Christianity.

The Critical Period and Protestantism's Civil War

Charles Hodge and Albert Barnes wrote at the beginning of what Arthur M. Schlesinger, Sr., labeled "a critical period" in American religion; Sydney E. Ahlstrom emphasized the point by changing "a" to "the"; Paul Carter described it as "the spiritual crisis of the Gilded Age." The crisis began in the 1870s and extended into the early twentieth century, and it involved two different challenges to American evangelical Protestantism—one to its system of thought and another to its program of "Christianizing" America. The intellectual challenge came from new forms of biblical criticism, Darwinian science, and the study of world religions. Later, the emergent social sciences, particularly sociology and psychology, raised new and troubling issues. The social challenge arose out of far-reaching changes in American culture prompted by urbanization, the "new" immigration from eastern and southern Europe and Asia, and industrialization. The strains of the late nineteenth and early twentieth centuries launched American Protestants on a quest to redefine their faith amid the perilous seas of modernity.[3]

One clear result has been the end of an evangelical Protestant consensus, which itself was short-lived because it was forged amid deep divisions. The twentieth century marked the beginning of a civil war within American Protestantism. The divisions can be variously labeled—liberals vs. conservatives, modernists vs. fundamentalists, and so on. It is also true that the two contending factions have been divided among themselves. Evangelicals, fundamentalists, charismatics, and Pentecostals are not of uniform mind; similarly, twentieth-century liberalism has many schools and considerable diversity.[4]

Late nineteenth-century Presbyterians were divided by
the other Civil War, the War Between the States. The Old
and New Schools had consolidated into regional divisions
by forming the PCUS in the South and the PCUSA in the
North. The Old School had always been the larger faction
in both traditions, and it exerted overwhelming influence
in the PCUS.

Dominating Old School Presbyterianism was a rigorous
school of thought given various names but widely known as
"the Princeton theology." In one sense, the identification
with Princeton Seminary is inaccurate, for it had many formulators outside of Princeton. For example, James Henley
Thornwell and Robert Lewis Dabney made significant contributions from the South. But in its heyday and thereafter,
the Princeton theology has been rightly identified as the
dominant theological movement of nineteenth-century
Presbyterianism. Hodge was its foremost proponent. Because he taught so long (1820–1878) and had so many students from other denominations, his influence spilled far
beyond American Presbyterianism into other traditions,
affecting Methodists, Episcopalians, and Southern Baptists.[5] His three-volume *Systematic Theology* (1872–73)
was not published until near the end of his life out of concern that publication might produce an enrollment decline
at Princeton, but the work spread his influence and continues in print even today.

Hodge's thought and the Princeton theology drew on a
variety of traditions—the Westminster Standards (the
Confession of Faith and the Larger and Shorter Cate-
chisms), seventeenth- and eighteenth-century scholastic
Calvinism (especially the thought of the Swiss theologian
Francis Turretin), Scottish common sense realism, and Ba-
conian science. Its popularity rested in part on the widespread acceptance of the philosophy of common sense
realism in nineteenth-century America. It attempted to
combat what it viewed as the equally pernicious forces of
the Enlightenment, with its faith in reason, and romanti-
cism, with its confidence in subjective feeling. Hodge is
known for his widely quoted aphorism that "a new idea

never originated" at Princeton Seminary while he was there. Hodge's remark emphasized his conviction that all Presbyterian theology must remain faithful to the Bible as interpreted in the Westminster Standards. In fact, for all of its rigor as an intellectual system and its rational apologetics, the Princeton theology also contained a vibrant form of evangelical piety, whose influence vastly exceeded its intellectual endeavors.[6]

They were an odd couple: the Westminster Standards, with their stress on the sovereignty of God, the eternal decrees of God, predestination, election, and reprobation, on the one hand, and the Arminianism of evangelicalism, with its emphasis on an individual's decision for Christ, on the other. No group of Presbyterians recognized this more than Hodge's theological opponents, the New School Presbyterians. Informed and invigorated by the revivals of the Second Great Awakening as well as the evangelistic opportunities in the Old Northwest, the New School pressed for an even more vital and socially aggressive piety than that of the Old School. They also openly questioned the Westminster Standards wherever its predestinarian elements discouraged individual initiative in conversion.

American Presbyterians struggled mightily with the legacy of Westminster and how strictly it was to be enforced throughout the eighteenth and early nineteenth centuries. Westminster itself had introduced the distinction between core doctrines of the Christian faith, to which all Christians must subscribe, and the *adiaphora,* issues where Christians could agree to disagree. In 1729, colonial Presbyterians adopted the Subscription Act, which declared that candidates for ordination could disagree with anything but the "necessary and essential articles of faith" and then conveniently left those unspecified. After the American Revolution, Presbyterians amended Westminster to take out the embarrassing section on loyalty to the king, but controversy over how far one must go in endorsing Westminster erupted again in the early nineteenth century.[7] This time the debate involved Old School–New School arguments and eventual schism over the Old School asserting a sover-

eign God electing unilaterally a predestined elect and the
New School Presbyterians contending that the individual
can and must reach out to receive saving grace.

The reunion of the PCUSA (New School) and the
PCUSA (Old School) in 1869 signaled the latter's declining interest in a rigorous interpretation of predestination
and both parties' concern to stress God's love for humanity. This shift increased the pressure for further revisions
of the Westminster Standards in the 1880s. In 1889, fifteen
presbyteries overtured the PCUSA General Assembly, ask-
ing for revisions. In the ensuing debate, some argued that
changing Westminster would damage its integrity and that
a new confession was needed. The PCUSA decided in favor of revisions, but in 1892 all of the proposed changes
received the endorsement of a majority, but not the necessary two-thirds, of the presbyteries. A decade later, in
1903, some amendments were approved that softened
some of Westminster's hard edges. Two new chapters on
the Holy Spirit and the love of God and missions were
added, as well as a "Declaratory Statement," which affirmed God's love for all humanity and the salvation of
those dying in infancy. But revisions alone were insuffi-
cient; presbyteries steadily interpreted Westminster more
expansively.[8]

Adding fuel to the increasing attack on Westminster was
what William M. Hutchison calls "the modernist impulse"
in American Protestant theology. Modernism had relatively few prominent proponents in American Presbyterianism, although it did raise its head in the celebrated trials
of David Swing of Chicago in 1874 and Charles A. Briggs
of Union Theological Seminary in New York in 1893, the
latter for his position on biblical criticism.

Although modernism had diverse and eclectic elements,
it accented three primary themes. First, the Bible should be
interpreted with the use of higher criticism, including historical analysis of the origin and development of the text.
Second, Christian doctrines needed to be modernized—reinterpreted to fit contemporary forms of thought, including
Darwinian science. Third, history was the gradual, evolu-

tionary unfolding of God's benevolent will for human life. History was the story of progress, guided by God but decisively shaped by human endeavor. At the time, modernism seemed to attack biblical authority and scholastic Calvinism, and the conservatives—Charles Hodge and especially his successors, son A. A. Hodge, Benjamin Warfield, and J. Gresham Machen, as well as others—reacted angrily and vehemently.[9]

Beginning in 1892, successive attempts were launched in the PCUSA General Assembly to confront what some saw as the modernist beast at the gates and to deal with presbytery laxity in strictly enforcing the Westminster Standards. In 1910, 1916, and 1923, the General Assembly passed resolutions to define "the essential and necessary articles" of faith for ordination. The number varied, but the five "fundamentals," as they would eventually be called, narrowed the heart of the Christian faith to these beliefs: the inerrancy of scripture, the virgin birth of Jesus Christ, the historical accuracy of the miracles of Jesus, the bodily resurrection of Jesus, and his substitutionary atonement. Lingering beneath the surface but very powerful in fundamentalist circles outside of American Presbyterianism was the belief in premillennialism—the triumphant return of Christ in human history prior to the inauguration of Christ's thousand-year reign.[10]

Two basic issues lay at the heart of the fundamentalist controversy in the PCUSA—what was the confessional basis for the denomination and who should determine it. Differently stated, the challenge was the nature of authority and where it was lodged—agonizing questions posed by modernity that have convulsed both Protestants and Catholics since the nineteenth century. In the late nineteenth century Presbyterians reemphasized the infallibility of the scriptures, and in the early twentieth century they reinterpreted the doctrine as the inerrancy of the original manuscripts. Coincidentally, the First Vatican Council in the 1870s issued its formal decree on papal infallibility. The Protestant and Catholic responses to modernity, which seemed to undermine the idea of transcendent truth, represented a desire to define precisely the mystery of faith and the location of authority.

At a more mundane level, the fundamentalist controversy in the PCUSA was a dispute over the standards of ordination. It was no accident then that a Presbyterian seminary—Princeton Theological Seminary—became the site of a titanic struggle for control in the PCUSA. Princeton was, after all, the birthplace of the Princeton theology, a key element in the fundamentalists' rationale for biblical inerrancy. It also included on its faculty J. Gresham Machen, the theological leader of the conservatives. But no less important in its selection as a battleground was the fact that by 1912 Princeton had enrolled over 1,000 more students than any other U.S. seminary.[11]

In retrospect, the fight in the PCUSA involved people with remarkably similar backgrounds and intellectual worlds. During the 1920s the sociologist E. A. Ross observed the verbal violence in American religion and society and astutely commented, "Conflict is sharpest and most passionate when it comes between those who have been united."[12]

That is how it appeared to Machen. "The greatest menace to the Christian Church to-day comes not from the enemies outside, but from the enemies within," Machen declared. "It comes from the presence within the Church of a type of faith and practice that is anti-Christian to the core." Machen was unwilling to conclude that liberals were not Christian, but he believed that "it is at any rate perfectly clear that liberalism is not Christianity." His verdict: "A separation between the two parties in the Church is the crying need of the hour."[13]

Machen and his allies were defeated at the 1926 and 1927 meetings of the PCUSA General Assembly. He subsequently left Princeton Seminary to establish Westminster Seminary and the Orthodox Presbyterian Church. The resolution proved to be a major turning point in twentieth-century American Presbyterian history. The PCUSA decided it would not require affirmation of any set of "essential and necessary articles" of faith, precisely and clearly defined, for ordination. The responsibility for examining candidates' orthodoxy and for ordaining them was lodged in the presbyteries, as it had been at the conclusion of the eighteenth-century subscription controversy. The denomination was launched into the future as "the broadening church."[14]

Ironically, at the very moment that American Presbyterianism reaffirmed this theological decentralization, it was also adopting the model of the corporate denomination. The streamlining of denominational administration presupposed a broad consensus about theology and mission, but the fundamentalist controversy prompted the PCUSA to strip the denomination of its ability to define its faith, by lodging theological authority in presbyteries.[15] This meant that as the denomination organized for pursuing a coordinated mission, it lacked a national institutional mechanism for defining and sustaining a common theology to direct that mission.

The implications of these movements in two different directions were scarcely evident at the time. But as early as 1954, Loetscher, who was certainly no fundamentalist, offered a perceptive and prophetic conclusion. "In sweeping away by a stroke of interpretation much of the previously exercised power of the General Assembly to define and thus to preserve the Church's doctrine, the commission established a principle which has much broader implications than the Church has yet had occasion to draw from it," he wrote. "If the Church now has no means of authoritatively defining its faith short of the amending process—which could hardly function in the midst of sharp controversy—ecclesiastical power is seriously hindered for the future from preventing more radical theological innovations than those discussed in the 'five points.' " Noting the "increasing odium against heresy prosecution," Loetscher believed that the PCUSA now depended upon "its group mind" or its consensus of opinion rather than any form of authoritative doctrine or ecclesiology.[16]

It was precisely this "group mind" of American Presbyterianism which fragmented after the 1920s. The result is a denomination that sees authority, confessions, and Christian doctrine itself in diverse ways.

After the Battle: A Neo-Orthodox Consensus

The Princeton theology and conservative voices did not disappear from PCUSA and American Presbyterianism. The fundamentalist controversy also touched the UPCNA and the PCUS, but with less acrimony. In 1925, the UPCNA adopted a new confession, which described the scriptures as "inspired throughout in language as well as thought." It added that the biblical "writers, though moved by the Holy Spirit, wrought in accordance with the laws of the human mind." Inerrantists and noninerrantists alike found this acceptable. In the PCUS, the issue was never joined—directly. Occasional skirmishes arose over people like Kenneth J. Foreman, later of Louisville Presbyterian Seminary, who attacked the plenary inspiration of scripture in 1930, and Ernest Trice Thompson of Union Seminary in Richmond, who advocated higher criticism of the Bible. Amid the "noise of conflict" in the 1920s and 1930s, the PCUS and the UPCNA remained intact.[17]

But the door had been opened to a greater degree of doctrinal pluralism. Into the breach came Karl Barth, whose commentary on Romans had already exploded like "a bombshell on the playground of the theologians."[18] What came to be known as the neo-orthodox movement in Protestant theology represented a clear break with scholastic Calvinism and the Princeton theology as well as an attack on various forms of modernism and liberalism. Its influence grew in American Presbyterianism throughout the 1930s and 1940s, particularly through a new generation of faculty appointments at Presbyterian seminaries.[19]

Neo-orthodoxy was a movement, rather than a unified school of thought. It had various names besides neo-orthodoxy—such as theology of crisis, Christian realism, dialectical theology, neo-Reformation theology, and others. Its proponents were an eclectic group, disagreeing with one another in significant ways. In Europe the movement was associated with Barth, Emil Brunner, Friedrich Gogarten, and Eduard Thurneysen; in the United States its most prominent figures included Reinhold Niebuhr, H. Richard Niebuhr, and perhaps Paul Tillich. From the 1930s through the 1960s, its banner was carried by a host of Presbyterian-seminary based professors, including Arthur C. Cochrane, Edward A. Dowey, Kenneth J. Foreman, Shirley C. Guthrie, Jr., Joseph Haroutunian, Elmer Homrighausen, Hugh T. Kerr, John H. Leith, John A. Mackay, James I. McCord, and others.[20] Its primary ally was the biblical theology movement, and the two streams found forums for expression as well as institutional homes in two journals founded at Presbyterian seminaries—*Theology Today,* established in 1944 at Princeton and *Interpretation: A Journal of Bible and Theology,* created in 1947 at Union in Richmond.[21]

Neo-orthodoxy resisted liberalism by asserting the centrality of scripture, and it opposed fundamentalism by arguing for the validity of biblical criticism. It sought to recapture the radical character of human sinfulness, both in individuals and in the structures of human society. Reinhold Niebuhr once declared that his early pathbreaking work *Moral Man and Immoral Society* should have been called "Immoral Man and More Immoral Society." Neo-orthodoxy also broke with nineteenth- and early twentieth-century liberalism by emphasizing the transcendence of God. H. Richard Niebuhr's sarcastic and oft-quoted indictment of liberalism sums up this spirit: "A God without wrath brought men without sin into a kingdom without judgment through the ministrations of Christ without a cross." Neo-orthodoxy, however, did concede one point in the liberal platform; theology was a human and historical construct, changing over time. The Christian faith must be interpreted and reinterpreted in each age. Therefore, all confessions are historically conditioned. The neo-orthodoxy represented by Reinhold Niebuhr was also determined to address the social and political crises of American culture and the world. Its clear commitment to a social ethic put it at arm's length from the Princeton theology and its fundamentalist and evangelical heirs in mid-twentieth-century America.[22]

The emphasis on social ethics was particularly influential and especially inflammatory in the PCUS with its distinctive doctrine of the "spirituality of the church." For Presbyterians in the South, the emergence of neo-orthodoxy actually constituted an attempt to overthrow the spirituality of the church and consign it, in Kenneth Foreman's words, "into everlasting discard." The doctrine had always been applied imperfectly, but it had served as an effective barrier to the social witness of the PCUS and forestalled the denomination's agonizing confrontation with race. Neo-orthodoxy in the South was not only an attempt to reformulate Christian doctrine but also a debate over the nature of the church and a political struggle over the soul of southern Presbyterianism.[23]

The triumph of neo-orthodoxy in American Presbyterian theology—and indeed in mainstream Protestantism—was complete by the 1950s and 1960s. Its impact was everywhere. Neo-orthodox books poured from Westminster and John Knox presses. New curricula, *Christian Faith and Life* (PCUSA) and the Covenant Life Curriculum (PCUS), were launched, emphasizing full-length books written by seminary professors. Long after the curricula themselves have died, some of these books remain as stalwarts for congregational and seminary use in the 1990s, including Robert McAfee Brown's *The Bible Speaks to You* (1955), Shirley C. Guthrie's *Christian Doctrine* (1968), and A. B. Rhodes's *The Mighty Acts of God* (1964). *Presbyterian Life* and *Presbyterian Survey*, the denominational magazines, featured articles on neo-orthodox thinkers. Reinhold Niebuhr appeared on the cover of *Time*, advised politicians, and crisscrossed the country speaking on college campuses. Preaching and worship resources accented neo-orthodoxy's emphasis on the Word as preached and celebrated in the sacraments.[24]

Neo-orthodoxy left two other profound and pervasive imprints on American Presbyterianism in mid-century. First, although it was not the prevailing theology of the ecumenical movement, it made significant contributions to both the "Life and Work" and "Faith and Order" discussions. Its simultaneous concern to reformulate Christian doctrine and to address the world's social and political problems made neo-orthodoxy a welcome resource for ecumenical understanding and ethical reflection. Second, through the influence of the Niebuhrs a concern for social ethics both prepared and prompted Presbyterians to look far more critically at the social and economic structures of American society. One clear result was the addition of faculty positions in social ethics at Presbyterian seminaries and the explosion of seminary courses addressed to specific, contemporary social problems.[25]

Neo-orthodoxy rode the boom of religiosity in the 1950s, although its leaders were skeptical and even cynical about the depth and breadth of the postwar revival. In *The Surge of Piety in America* (1958), A. Roy Eckardt declared, "It is rather hard to see how we can stand very long the terrific pace our surging piety has set for itself. There will probably be a reaction." Then, in prescient words he added, "If the new piety does expire, as it may already have begun to do, the few younger souls who tomorrow or the next day chance to pick up this particular volume will be extremely puzzled over what all the fuss was about."[26] Other popular critiques of the religiosity of the postwar period include Will Herberg's *Protestant-Catholic-Jew* (1955), Peter Berger's *The Noise of Solemn Assemblies* (1961), Gibson Winter's *The Suburban Captivity of the Churches* (1961), and Martin Marty's *The New Shape of American Religion* (1959).[27]

Despite its vitality and strength, neo-orthodoxy as a movement left an ambiguous legacy on American Presbyterianism and mainstream Protestantism. Its chief contribution was its role as critic—of popular piety, denominational life, denominationalism, political passivity, fundamentalist precisionism, liberal idealism. Its strength was its defining what people should eschew. Its appeal was based in part on the relative consensus about social values that still prevailed in American society. Its attack on institutions seemed plausible, even during the 1950s, which witnessed the signs of the erosion of the corporate denomination in American Presbyterianism.

But neo-orthodoxy's critique of church and society emerged from denominations and thinkers who still operated with a sense of theological confidence and cultural recognition.[28] As critics, Sydney Ahlstrom charged, neo-orthodox theologians put down "a very thin sheet of dogmatic asphalt over the problems created by modern critical thought." James Moorhead further maintains that neo-orthodoxy's dynamic conception of Christian doctrine also created "a principle of self-criticism and volatility conducive to further change."[29]

In retrospect, neo-orthodoxy helped pave the way for the theological, ecclesiastical, and cultural traumas of American Presbyterianism and mainstream Protestantism since the 1960s. Its confidence about vanquishing liberalism proved to be unwarranted as new forms of theological liberalism assumed compelling force in the 1960s and subsequent decades.

Its assumption that fundamentalism was dead was equally false. During the 1940s, fundamentalism and evangelicalism regrouped with new initiatives and even new accents. In 1943 conservatives founded their own ecumenical organization, the National Association of Evangelicals, and in 1947 they established Fuller Theological Seminary as the self-conscious perpetuator of the old Princeton theology. In 1956, largely through the efforts of Billy Graham, *Christianity Today* was launched as the principal journalistic forum for fundamentalism-evangelicalism.

Scarred as they were by the bitterness of the fundamentalist controversy and by continuing harsh attacks, American mainstream Protestants, and especially American Presbyterians, treated conservative Protestantism as a fundamentalist monolith. They were blinded to the mutations, fragmentation, and creative developments in conservative circles. By the 1960s conservative American Protestantism had changed, and it was poised for a renaissance. But the categories of division—forged by the controversies of the past—remained in place.[30] The civil war in American Protestantism tragically continued, with the contenders sometimes more entrenched and more vehement than ever before.

The Rise of Theological Pluralism

For historian Ahlstrom, the 1960s were the era of "the radical turn in theology and ethics." It represented the end of "a Great Puritan Epoch" in Anglo-American history, spanning more than four centuries. Writing at the end of the '60s, Ahlstrom argued that the decade "was a time . . . when the old grounds of national confidence, patriotic idealism, moral traditionalism, and even of historic Judeo-Christian theism, were awash. Presuppositions that had held firm for centuries—even millennia—were being widely questioned. . . . The nation was confronting revolutionary circumstances whose effects were . . . irreversible."[31]

The decade began in the wake of the union between the UPCNA and the PCUSA to form the UPCUSA in 1958. The UPCNA agreed to accept the Westminster Standards as the confessional basis for the merged church, even though its 1925 Confession and a subsequent revision in 1945 superseded Westminster. Acceptance of Westminster was considered a temporary arrangement since the first General Assembly of the UPCUSA appointed a special committee to develop a "brief" statement of faith. The committee, led by Edward A. Dowey, won a broader mandate to formulate a more complete statement of the Christian faith, as well as the preparation of a *Book of Confessions*. The new statement would be one among several confessions of the church catholic and the Reformed tradition. Nine years later, the "Confession of 1967" and the *Book of Confessions* were approved.[32]

"C-67," as it became popularly known, represented the triumph of neo-orthodoxy in American Presbyterianism. Its theme was reconciliation, and it focused on Jesus Christ: "In Jesus Christ God was reconciling the world to himself." C-67 decisively broke with the understanding of scripture in Westminster, declaring, "The one sufficient revelation of God is Jesus Christ, the Word of God incarnate, to whom the Holy Spirit bears unique and authoritative witness through the Holy Scriptures, which are received and obeyed as the word of God written." The introduction to C-67 made it clear that this confession was designed to supplant Westminster, particularly on the doctrine of scripture. "This section is an intended revision of the Westminster doctrine, which rested primarily on a view of inspiration and equated the biblical canon directly with the Word of God," it stated. "By contrast, the preeminent and primary meaning of the Word of God in the Confession of 1967 is the Word of God incarnate." Furthermore, as Moorhead has noted, "for the first time in a creedal statement, American Presbyterians endorsed modern biblical scholarship" through C-67.[33]

In two areas, C-67 both captured the spirit of twentieth-century American Presbyterianism and planted the seeds for future theological difficulty. First, the theme of reconciliation was used as the basis for developing the social witness and ministry of the church. It cited four areas of urgent concern: racial and ethnic discrimination; the dangers of nationalism in achieving peace, justice, and freedom; the prevalence of "enslaving poverty" throughout the world; and "anarchy in sexual relationships." Coming as it did at the height of the civil rights movement and the beginning of significant protest against the Vietnam war, these accents are not surprising. Arnold B. Come concluded, "The most original and distinctive contribution of C-67 [is that] it brings a social ethic within the scope of God's reconciling work in Christ."[34]

Second, Moorhead has pointed out that both C-67 and the *Book of Confessions* suggested a looser understanding of confessional authority. The framers of the document emphasized that all creeds were human documents and therefore conditioned by the historical circumstances under which they were written. Furthermore, the very specificity of the ethical concerns identified in C-67 made it clear that the church was trying to identify the major challenges to Christian witness in the 1960s. Thus, Moorhead notes, "despite the intention of its authors, C-67 gave a potential charter to redefine Presbyterian theological identity by retail—that is, on a case by case basis in response to 'particular problems and crises.' "[35] After nearly a century of trying to emancipate itself from Westminster, one branch of American Presbyterianism, the United Presbyterian Church in the U.S.A., had a new confession, only to discover that it would not serve as a unifying basis for its theological identity.

The confessional history of the PCUS traveled a similar but slightly different path. Even in the early part of the twentieth century, the PCUS never witnessed the same movement to dethrone Westminster as the confessional basis of the church. For example, the catalog of Union Seminary in Virginia declared in 1926, "The interpretation of Scripture teachings promulgated by the Westminster divines is believed to be the most perfect creedal statement drawn from the Scriptures to date."[36]

Within the context of Westminster, reformers and neo-orthodox theologians did attempt to dislodge the PCUS from its position on "the spirituality of the church" and *jure divino* or "divine law" Presbyterianism, which held that church order was and must be grounded in scripture. But the same forces that brought confessional revision in the UPCNA/PCUSA tradition also worked on the PCUS—the need to redefine biblical authority, the compelling urgency of the church's social witness, and the desire to have a confession stated in modern terminology and forms of thought.

In 1962 the PCUS General Assembly adopted "A Brief Statement of Belief" as an educational document to help interpret Westminster. It was never submitted to the presbyteries for approval and thus had no confessional status. During the 1960s and 1970s, a committee led by Albert C. Winn produced "A Declaration of Faith," a poetic statement that captured neo-orthodox emphases. "A Declaration" was less stridently and obviously intended to be a replacement for the Westminster standards, but like C-67 it was accompanied by a proposed Book of Confessions. The 1976 PCUS General Assembly approved both "A Declaration" and a Book of Confessions, but the documents failed to win the approval of two-thirds of the presbyteries. In this case, failure bred victory, for "A Declaration" proved to be highly adaptable for liturgical use. Even though it was never approved by the PCUS, "A Declaration" undoubtedly gained wider currency in both the UPCUSA and the PCUS than the Confession of 1967.[37]

The theological debate over confessions in the PCUS did take its toll. In 1973, exactly 112 years after the formation of the Presbyterian Church in the Confederate States of America, some conservative Presbyterian leaders withdrew from the PCUS and established the Presbyterian Church in America. Their concerns were several, including the denomination's stand on civil rights and other political issues, and the ordination of women as elders and ministers. But, as Rick Nutt has shown, the driving force behind the PCA was also adherence to the Princeton theology and the Westminster Confession. What the PCA did not embrace was "the spirituality of the church," for it simply saw the Bible applied differently to the same divisive political issues—abortion, war, race, gender roles. Nutt concludes that even though the PCA accused the PCUS of taking on a secular agenda, "unconsciously it has done the same. Perhaps it is this paradoxical tie that even now binds these 'cousins' together."[38]

Even as neo-orthodoxy triumphed, formally or informally, as the confessional basis and theological identity of American Presbyterianism, the consensus it forged began to crumble. The transformation of theology since the 1960s arose in part out of the awareness of a moral crisis in American society and the world—racism and civil rights, Vietnam, the environment, sexuality, and gender roles. However, it was also fed by a growing sense that the nature and task of theology itself had changed.

One revolutionary development, measured against the larger framework of the history of Western Christianity, was the collapse of Protestant–Roman Catholic polemics and the emergence of Roman Catholic theology. During the nineteenth and early twentieth centuries, anti-Catholicism was a dominant theme in American Protestantism; Catholics often responded in kind. The first sign of change came after Pius XII's landmark encyclical in 1943, *Divino Afflante Spiritu*, which sanctioned the use of modern biblical criticism. Catholic biblical scholars began to participate in scholarly organizations once dominated by Protestants, and Catholic commentaries became widely used in Protestant circles. The work of Raymond Brown and Roland Murphy, as well as the publication of the *Jerome Biblical Commentary*, were harbingers of this new era in biblical scholarship. Pope John XXIII's call for *aggiornamento* and the Second Vatican Council, with its Protestant observers, further opened the doors for Protestant-Catholic dialogue. By the mid-1960s, the work of Karl Rahner, Hans Küng, Gregory Baum, and Pierre Teilhard de Chardin were widely read and discussed by Protestants. The shift, which was remarkably sudden and extraordinarily irenic, symbolized the predicament of pluralism that would escalate in the 1960s.[39]

Hugh T. Kerr's *Theology Today* editorial of 1964, "Time for a Critical Theology," was an early and insightful analysis of the new theological climate brought about by religious and social upheaval. Marking the twentieth anniversary of the journal, Kerr declared that "if anything can teach the Christian church in these days what it means to think and act self-critically, it will be the racial revolution." Furthermore, Kerr declared, "one of the massive ironies of religious history is being dramatized before our eyes: the Roman Catholic Church is rapidly emerging in the eyes of the world as the symbol of progressive ecclesiastical *reform*!" The response, Kerr suggested, should be twofold: "First, the times call for an interpretation of the *function* of theology as a critical discipline; and second, the *perspective* of theology must be open enough to take in a multiplicity or pluralism of possibilities." Theology would be "not so much a structure or content as . . . a way of thinking,

[and] since we have begun to accept the pluralism of denominations, even of faiths, and perhaps someday of religions," Kerr said, "why should it be so difficult to accept the
plurality of theological expression at many levels?"[40]

Kerr's inquiry was answered affirmatively, since what
appeared in the 1960s was precisely the "plurality of theological expression at many levels." Presbyterians and mainstream Protestants perceived a religious and cultural crisis
in Western society that required the church to reorient its
thought and its mission. Rather than the church setting the
agenda for the world, theologians argued that the world and
its desperate needs provided the priorities for theological
reflection and the church's mission. Many theologians
urged the church to recognize the value and promise of secularization.

No other work so thoroughly captured the spirit of the
'60s as Harvey Cox's *The Secular City* (1965), a book that
heralded the promise of secularity and technology. Cox and
others argued that secularity would liberate people from
false securities and provide the freedom for what Dietrich
Bonhoeffer had elliptically described as "the non-religious
interpretation of biblical concepts." Works sounding similar themes such as John A. T. Robinson's *Honest to God*
(1963), Joseph F. Fletcher's *Situation Ethics* (1966) and
Thomas J. J. Altizer's *The Gospel of Christian Atheism*
(1966) were published by the Presbyterian publishing
house, Westminster Press.[41]

Secularity was hailed for its promise; ethics became the
road to deliverance. Building on neo-orthodoxy's strong social concern and in responding to the crises of American
society, Presbyterian and mainstream Protestant theologians focused on ethics to an extraordinary degree. The
civil rights movement brought with it theological voices
that attracted the attention of mainstream Protestants.
Most notable were Martin Luther King, Jr., James H.
Cone, and J. Deotis Roberts. Their critique of the racism of
American society was sharp and pointed, and some
mounted an even more radical attack on Christianity as
racist itself.[42]

The rise of Black theology marked the first of several movements that highlighted justice as the primary agenda for theology and the church. Loosely grouped as liberation theologians, these thinkers were both Protestant and Catholic, and many came from the Third World—Latin America, Africa, and Asia. Driving their theologies were several critical concerns—the dramatic disparity between white, Western wealth and the poverty of the rest of the world; God's "preferential option" for the poor; the critique of the West for its economic and political oppression of the Third World; and the mandate to the church to identify with forces of resistance and even revolution that sought justice for the poor and the oppressed.[43] Even when the call for justice was less strident, many theologians outside the West were also attempting a basic reformulation of Christianity. Instead of using traditional Western philosophical categories, they plumbed the resources of their own cultures to propose new constructions of Christian doctrine.

By the 1980s feminist theologians became perhaps the most prominent new theological voices espousing the call to justice in American mainstream Protestantism. Their influence is due in large measure to two factors. First, they speak self-consciously to women, a neglected constituency, whose numbers and labors in the church have been far greater than the voice or vote traditionally permitted them. Second, particularly in Reformed circles, they have lifted anew the iconoclastic challenge by questioning the limited anthropomorphic image of God as male.

Women have been the majority in mainstream Protestant denominations at least since the early eighteenth century, the earliest point for which accurate data exist. The early nineteenth century brought forth the first stirrings of feminism, partly a spillover from the abolitionist movement and its concern for racial freedom and partly a product of evangelicalism and its proclamation of spiritual freedom. During the late nineteenth and early twentieth centuries, feminism focused on woman suffrage and prohibition, which it won simultaneously in 1920.[44]

Because women had no access to ordination as either
minister or elder in nineteenth-century Presbyterianism,
women constructed their own organizations, both inside
and outside the church. These structures had two forms of
power and influence. First, they amassed significant
amounts of money for religious and other charitable purposes, especially for foreign missions. Second, they provided women with leadership roles, mutual support, and a
common community that was denied them within most of
the structures of American Protestantism, including American Presbyterianism.[45]

As we have seen, the adoption of the model of the corporate denomination brought women within the structure of
the denomination; and if they were to have voice and vote,
ordination as elders and ministers became critically important to women. The PCUSA adopted a provision for
women to be ordained as elders in 1930; the constitution
was changed in 1956 to permit ordination of women as
ministers; the PCUS made both changes in 1964. Women,
however, did not seek ordination to ministry in large numbers until the 1970s. By 1975, 313 were enrolled in Presbyterian seminaries. By 1980, the number had grown to 419
and by 1985 to 600; by 1990 it had soared to 1,240, 31
percent of the entire enrollment of the Presbyterian seminaries. Similarly, the number of women ministers multiplied dramatically. Statistics for women pastors in the
PCUS during the 1970s do not exist. But the UPCUSA had
131 women as ministers in 1972 and twenty of these served
either as pastor or co-pastor, while thirty-six more were associate or assistant pastors. By 1990, the combined
PC(USA) was served by 2,257 women ministers, 1,052 of
whom labored as parish pastors.[46]

The feminist influence in American Presbyterianism has
grown steadily since the 1970s. Initially, it emphasized the
neglected roles of women in the Bible and the history of the
church, inclusive language about people, and the equality
of both genders. Its concerns grew broader as it launched a
more thorough and fundamental critique of Christianity as
a patriarchal religion.

By the end of the 1980s, feminist theologians were divided into at least three groups. One proposed a reconstruction of Christian doctrine freed from patriarchal and hierarchical assumptions and structures. Another professed allegiance to the Christian faith but rejected traditional organizations of the church for new experimental churches. A third group abandoned Christianity altogether as irretrievably patriarchal, masculine, and sexist and endorsed instead naturalist or spiritualist alternatives.[47] In short, in two decades feminist theology had moved from a form of liberation theology with ethics and justice as its primary theme to a searching critique of Christian doctrine and a fundamental attempt to reconceive the Christian faith.

Another movement in mainstream Protestant theology brought new diversity by relying on the insights of other disciplines and by focusing on theological method. The disciplines employed were varied—sociology, phenomenology, literary criticism, psychology, process philosophy, communication theory, and more. The preoccupation with method and interdisciplinary inquiry produced genuine intellectual excitement and ferment, but the enthusiasm was largely restricted to the academy, particularly departments of religion in colleges and universities. The new theological climate made theology seem increasingly the province of the professional and alien to both the church and its members.[48]

One clear result of theological pluralism and the emphasis on social ethics since the 1960s is what Benton Johnson calls the shift from old to new agendas in American Presbyterianism. The old agenda, according to Johnson, focused on moral and ethical issues related to individuals and the family. The new agenda shifted attention to social problems that involve institutions and structures of society. Furthermore, the scope of American Presbyterian ethical concern has expanded dramatically since the 1960s and has developed a discernible, if not predictable, liberal stance.[49] The shift confirms Wuthnow's contention that American Presbyterianism and mainstream Protestantism have become steadily more politicized and polemical since the 1960s.[50]

It should be noted that American Presbyterians formally endorsed racial ethnic and gender diversity as well as theological pluralism, albeit grudgingly at times, and have now institutionalized them in various ways. It would have been impossible to resist and combat the cries for justice and participation without succumbing to the injustice wrought by divisions of race, nation, class, and sex in American society and mainstream Protestantism. Diversity, understood as equal participation, became a key way of understanding the nature of the church itself for American Presbyterians and mainstream Protestants. Theological pluralism, understood as the equal validity of different visions of the Christian tradition, emerged as a basic theological principle.

Diversity and theological pluralism have brought unquestioned benefits to American Presbyterianism and mainstream Protestantism. They have made these churches far more sensitive to the world Christian community and its ecumenical variety; they have heightened churches' ethical awareness of the injustice suffered by women and racial ethnic minorities in its own membership and American society; they have encouraged experimentation with new philosophical and cultural understandings of Christianity itself.

However, the scope of acceptable diversity and pluralism for many Presbyterians is still partial and distorted. The bitter legacy of the fundamentalist fissures in American Presbyterianism has often made Presbyterian leaders instinctively defensive and hostile to conservative and evangelical movements and blind to the variety and change in evangelicalism itself. Nowhere is this more clear than in Presbyterian reaction to the founding and development of Fuller Theological Seminary.[51]

Furthermore, Presbyterians remain deeply suspicious and distrustful of the "third force" in Christianity—the Pentecostal and charismatic movements that have demonstrated considerable power in American culture and are transforming Christianity in other parts of the world.[52]

Ironically, Presbyterians also exhibit ambivalence within their own community when, for instance, Korean American Presbyterians are welcomed because they bring diversity of participation but are criticized for their refusal to ordain women, a position grounded in a conception of biblical authority forged by earlier strands in Presbyterian theology.[53] The Presbyterian preference for diversity and pluralism has become a bias for the options of the left, more than those of the right.

Theological pluralism is also inherently unstable as a foundation for Christian identity and denominational mission. The rise of pluralism in mainstream Protestantism and the politicization of theology have created a chasm between denominational structures and congregations. Many PC(USA) congregations are not only alienated but finally confused and ignorant about what their denomination is or does. This internal division exacerbated the loss of these denominations' mediating function in American religion and American society.

But even more importantly, theological pluralism raises deep and troubling questions about Christian identity—what it is and what it means. The PC(USA)'s adoption of "A Brief Statement of Faith" in 1991, plus a *Book of Confessions*, may mean that the church has not rejected its confessional character or its Reformed legacy. The document itself is tribute to the triumph of, at least, persistence in the face of cultural diversity and theological pluralism. The committee responsible for drafting it contained people with widely different and sharply antagonistic points of view. The text also reflects the prevailing concerns of late twentieth-century Presbyterians and their commitment to inclusiveness: strong social and ethical emphases, explicit recognition of the call of both women and men to service, inclusive language for people and God.

Others believe that theology and confessions can no longer bind a denomination like the PC(USA) together. The growing cultural diversity and ideological pluralism of American society, the steady erosion of institutional vitality in all areas of American life, and the pervasive power of individualism make theological and doctrinal ties both weaker and less relevant. Instead, argue Moorhead and McCarthy, polity prevails over theology.[54]

Presbyterian polity certainly has theological content. But polity alone offers only the mechanism for decision making, not the cement of common purpose that bonds minds, hearts, and bodies in a shared understanding of mission. Throughout the twentieth century, American Presbyterians have led and been engulfed in the internecine civil war of American Protestantism. This Protestant fight focused on the nature of Christian theology and doctrine and the church's mission in the world.

Tragically, the debate has been waged between a variety of conservative and liberal options, blurring the identity of these denominations as bearers of distinctive Christian emphases. To embrace the contending parties, "pluralism"—used as a code word both for theological pluralism and for cultural, racial, and gender diversity—became a political strategy and a theological principle. Few Presbyterians would argue for a return to the Westminster Standards and the world of the Princeton theology. In this regard, Edward Farley is right in celebrating the "critical modernism" of contemporary Presbyterianism.[55]

But pluralism as a political platform and theological principle represents a genuine predicament for the church's mission. The diversity of voices and values inevitably raise agonizing questions about what American Presbyterians should or could say together and what they would do cooperatively as witnesses to Jesus Christ.

There is no quick or easy solution to this predicament. But its resolution certainly depends on two factors. First, Presbyterians must resist the divisive temptation of relieving the tensions of living in a theologically pluralistic community either by retreating into insulated special-interest enclaves of like-minded Presbyterians or by ignoring the disaffiliation of Presbyterians with different viewpoints.

Second, Presbyterians must begin to address the problem of theological pluralism by making theology the central focus of conversation whenever and wherever Presbyterians gather in congregations and governing bodies so that sincere differences in perspective can be recognized and evaluated openly in a spirit of shared searching for God's word today.

Such a strategy will not ensure theological consensus. But it is a necessary first step to such a consensus, and at the very least it will place the difficult questions of Christian discipleship at the center of Presbyterians' common life, thereby fulfilling the church's most important function.[56]

5

The Varieties of Witness: The Debate Over Evangelism

In 1803 the Presbyterian Church commissioned Gideon Blackburn as its first missionary to the Cherokees with these words:

> The Standing Committee on Missions acting under the authority, & by order of, the General Assembly of the Presbyterian Church in the United States of America, confiding very much in your piety, prudence, & diligence, & zeal, have appointed, and by these presents do appoint you the Revd. Gideon Blackburn their missionary to the Cherokee nation of Indians, for the purpose of carrying the gospel, & the arts of civilized life to them. . . . [1]

The church's charge captured the heart of the nineteenth-century Presbyterian understanding of evangelism—"carrying the gospel, & the arts of civilized life." Throughout the century Presbyterians attempted to evangelize people in the United States and throughout the world by founding churches, schools, hospitals, and other institutions that would fulfill this twofold emphasis.

But the twentieth century introduced new emphases that have frequently fragmented the assumption that evangelism carried both the gospel and the "arts of civilized life." Presbyterians have tended to divide into two camps, arguing intensely about which emphasis had priority—witnessing to the gospel by seeking salvation for individuals, or transforming the social order by seeking justice. Furthermore, as Presbyterians became increasingly conscious of other denominations, other faiths, and the pluralism of cultures, they began to doubt what their forebears took for granted—the necessity and the need to evangelize. Both the self-evident truth of Christianity and the unquestioned benefits of civilization were far less obvious to American Presbyterians who had been buffeted by the cross-currents of the twentieth century.

Evangelism

John Calvin chose to subsume the evangelistic task under a wide range of pastoral duties, but his theology seeded the Reformed tradition with the dual concerns for individual salvation and the transformation of culture. Calvin's disciples regarded their own efforts to reform the church and society as part of Christianity's fundamental evangelistic task. English Puritans focused on the need for conversion, as the basic component of Christian life, and the purification of the church and society.[2]

In North America, Presbyterians and other Protestants led an evangelical movement that eventually dominated American Protestantism during the nineteenth century and gave it cohesion. Presbyterians played prominent roles in the revivals of the First and Second Great Awakenings, and after 1810 they were also deeply involved in the formation of the complex network of benevolent societies.[3] These organizations were voluntary and interdenominational, yet an examination of their membership rolls indicates an inordinate number of Presbyterian and Reformed leaders orchestrating their programs. These Christians believed that such agencies served the double purpose of spreading civilization and the gospel by providing missionaries, Bibles, theological literature, and Christian education materials to the American frontier and foreign lands. Other associations such as the American Temperance Society, the American

Peace Society, and the American Anti-Slavery Society gave expression as well to Presbyterians' desire to reform their culture with Christian ideals.[4]

Structures for Revival

The Presbyterian Church in the U.S.A. greeted the twentieth century by establishing the first official evangelism committee in the bureaucracies of mainstream Protestantism. In itself, that action demonstrates the lure of the corporate understanding of the denomination and the impulse to organize what had previously been left to a variety of local or congregational initiatives. Although it was nowhere explicitly stated, the committee focused primarily on white Americans of northern European descent; other agencies were given administrative responsibility for outreach to other races or new immigrant groups. This, of course, set the denomination on a course that contributed to suspicions among people of color and other ethnic groups concerning the authenticity of Presbyterian invitations to share in its denominational life.[5]

PCUSA evangelism in the early decades of the twentieth century centered on the use of revivals. Under the leadership of J. Wilbur Chapman, the church developed the "Simultaneous Movement," as a new form of urban revivalism. Simultaneous revivals were evangelistic campaigns centered in major metropolitan areas. Unlike the late nineteenth-century city revivals organized by Dwight L. Moody and those of the early twentieth century run by Presbyterian Billy Sunday, the simultaneous campaigns were not restricted to a large, central meeting place. Instead, they maintained close ties with congregations by simultaneously holding evangelistic services in many local churches.[6]

The Simultaneous Movement's evangelistic teams embodied the technique of specialization, one of the characteristics of corporations. Specific evangelists in the campaign were practiced technicians at leading services devoted specifically to converting men, women, youth, the laboring class, or the "less than reputable."[7]

The Simultaneous Movement was also an ecumenical effort. Churches from other denominations participated in these citywide revivals, and the congregational activities of other churches were listed in the promotional literature distributed by Presbyterians. Indeed, the PCUSA was instrumental in creating an Evangelism Commission in the Federal Council of Churches shortly after its formation in 1908. Since that time, the evangelism programs of American Presbyterianism's major branches have emphasized ecumenical cooperation.[8] Almost all Presbyterian evangelistic activities have centered on bringing people to faith in Jesus Christ. Seldom have these efforts been reduced to mere solicitation of members for the Presbyterian denominations.

The Presbyterian Church in the U.S. developed a separate committee with staff for evangelistic work in 1908. The following year, this Permanent Committee on Evangelistic Work hired its first general secretary, the Rev. J. Ernest Thacker. However, the organization of PCUS evangelism did not approach the complexity or sophistication of the PCUSA until the late 1940s for one reason: lack of centralized funds.[9]

The practice of simultaneous campaigns continued in the South and in the United Presbyterian Church of North America (UPCNA) long after the PCUSA had abandoned the technique.[10]

During the 1920s and 1930s, the fundamentalist controversy racked American Presbyterianism and finally split the PCUSA. Heresy trials and fierce battles in the General Assembly of the PCUSA erupted. The PCUSA eventually rejected the doctrinal precisionism and biblical inerrancy of the fundamentalists. But it paid a price with schism and the formation of the Orthodox Presbyterian Church in the 1930s under the leadership of J. Gresham Machen.[11]

The fundamentalist controversy also affected attitudes toward evangelism. American Presbyterians gradually identified revivalism and eventually evangelism itself with fundamentalist theology and practice. Formal revivals declined as an evangelistic technique among Presbyterians in the 1930s and 1940s. As an alternative, the PCUSA in particular moved in the direction of person-to-person evangelism.

The New Life Movement and Person-to-Person Evangelism

Evangelism efforts at the denominational level during the 1930s and 1940s were limited largely to circulation of information about proven methods of local outreach, rather than the initiation of new national programs. But in the late 1940s, the PCUSA began a major push to foster person-to-person evangelism throughout its congregations.[12]

Known as the "New Life Movement," this effort aimed high both in its scope and its organization. Its motto was "If any man be in Christ, he is a new creature," and it predicted that by January 1, 1950, the church would be revived and re-equipped for the next half century. New Life's influence was not expected to end there; indeed, the campaign was not intended to be "promoted for a period and finished forever." Rather, it was hoped that "three years of concentrated attention" to evangelism would start a spiritual ferment that would "remain for the permanent endowment of the Church."[13]

Every board and agency of the PCUSA focused its resources on outreach during the New Life campaign, but the program's primary tool emphasized person-to-person contacts. Each year of the New Life three-year cycle was aimed at a different audience. The first year the congregation itself received attention as New Life attempted to reinvigorate the church's spiritual energies from within. The second year PCUSA members engaged individuals with some prior connections with the denomination, and finally during the last year, the membership extended an inviting hand to any who had never experienced the community of the church.[14]

New Life organizers forecasted that by 1950 there would be 1,000,000 more Presbyterians on the rolls, 300 new churches or Sunday schools, and 100,000 lay people trained in personal evangelism. The first of these impressive goals was never reached, although almost 700,000 new people did enter the communion either by profession or reaffirmation of faith, and 100,000 lay people were trained in evangelism.[15]

The timing of the New Life movement was fortuitous. New Life encouraged the development of similar programs in both the UPCNA and the PCUS, as well as in the Federal Council of Churches. Together these efforts to renew the evangelistic ethos of mainstream American Protestantism poised its denominations to ride the crest of a significant cultural wave.[16] The 1950s marked the decade of the postwar "revival" of American religion, fed in part by the ethos of "faith in faith" and the baby boom generation. Some scholars have claimed that church growth and increased synagogue participation were inevitable. While this may be so, it remains true that Presbyterians and other mainstream Protestant denominations were prepared for this surge in religious interest because they had already adopted focused programs of outreach for new members.[17]

New Questions for Evangelism Programs

Throughout the 1950s, new alternatives to the New Life pattern did not emerge. By the latter years of the decade, dramatic social turmoil combined with new theological ferment to dim the sparkle of the postwar religious boom. Four questions in particular posed difficult issues.

First, a study of new members in the late 1950s found that four out of six individuals brought into the United Presbyterian Church in the U.S.A. were inactive only three to four years after joining. Therefore, it appeared that recent evangelistic efforts had failed to assimilate new Christians and to inculcate a lasting faith.[18]

Second, a shift in American ecumenical thinking changed the paradigm for Christian unity so that denominationalism seemed a defect rather than a mainstay of Christian discipleship. The dominant neo-orthodox theologians of the 1950s had already charged that denominations were an ugly scar on the body of Christ. In 1960, the stated clerk of the UPCUSA, Eugene Carson Blake, joined with Bishop James Pike of the Protestant Episcopal Church in calling for a Consultation on Church Union that would heal the denominational divisions of Christ's church. In this ecumenical environment, the claims for denominational distinctiveness appeared to be in actual conflict with the gospel, and efforts to bring individuals into a particular denomination's understanding of Christianity were considered outdated and parochial.[19]

Third, the reaction of mainstream Protestant leaders to the postwar revival was self-critical, skeptical, and cautious. As early as 1950, Reinhold Niebuhr declared: "The evidences of a contemporary revival of religion are not conclusive. There are certain marked tendencies in both the cultural and popular interests of our day which would seem to prove the reality of such a revival. But it is not possible for a contemporary observer of any 'tendency,' whether in politics or religion, to offer conclusive proof of the reality of any 'movement.'" In 1958, the *Christian Century* greeted the latest report on increased membership acerbically: "Up and up and up we go. Church membership zoomed with 964,724 new souls put on the old lists (or old souls on new lists!) in 1957." Even the evangelical magazine *Christianity Today* was leery of the postwar prosperity of the American churches. "It would be too much to say," an editorial declared, "that the soul of the nation has undergone repentance and revival. The minister who said that 'the world at its worst needs the Church at its best' did not understate the demands posed by our decade."[20]

Fourth, the challenges to evangelism and the skepticism about the postwar revival coincided with the civil rights and anti–Vietnam war protests of the 1960s. These dramatic events raised agonizing questions about the character of America as a Christian nation and whether the church had practiced enough of what it had preached. In focusing so much on verbal evangelism, the critics charged, the church had contributed to perpetuating major social evils whose remedy required fewer words and more physical witness in solidarity with the oppressed.[21]

Theological Reformulations of Evangelism

Presbyterian evangelism literature, particularly in the UPCUSA, responded to these challenges in two ways. First, it gave tacit permission for Presbyterians to remain silent about their motivations when they were engaged in social action. Second, it insisted that the church's first duty was self-sacrificial service, not institutional maintenance.[22]

The UPCUSA Division of Evangelism drastically redefined evangelism in 1967. In a policy statement entitled "Mission and Evangelism," the division demoted evangelism from its place as the essence of mission to one of the many subsidiary enterprises of mission. At the same time, it granted permission for a muted witness in service to social advocacy. The statement insisted that "all evangelism is mission, but all mission is not necessarily evangelism. Christians are often engaged in the mission of the Church without any explicit or self-conscious verbal reference to their being Christian or to the teachings of Christ. They simply allow their Christ-formed consciences and concerns to cooperate with, and to take part with, other men [and women], whether Christians, Jews, humanists, or atheists, in working for the welfare of other men [and women]."[23]

The rhetoric of the Division of Evangelism paired this subtle muting of the Presbyterian witness with allusions to Christ's admonition that those who would lose their lives for his sake would preserve them. The adoption of this gospel passage as the standard for the church's witness was accompanied by one unintended, destructive development. In 1966 the UPCUSA membership began to hemorrhage, with an average net loss of 54,294 members per year over the next decade. As the magnitude of the losses became evident, cries for a reexamination of the evangelism program multiplied. But the logic of self-sacrifice proved impenetrable to the challenges posed by the losses of members. "The Church has no warrant for substituting a statistical graph for a cross," reported the UPCUSA Board of National Missions in 1968. It further suggested that the "winnowing" of the membership might ultimately prove the cure for the church's flagging health.[24]

The pitting of institutional maintenance against ministries of social transformation coincided with a steady decline in mainstream Protestantism's public ministries in American society. These denominations had created a host of social institutions to serve as avenues for Protestant charity and reform. By 1900, a range of identifiable mainstream Protestant colleges, hospitals, and social agencies had been established for this purpose across the nation. But throughout the twentieth century, as the states and the federal government assumed more responsibility for social services and exercised more control over these institutions, their identifiable denominational, and even their Christian, ties loosened. Denominational leaders relinquished their influence over these institutions, believing that the Christian purposes of the founders would be perpetuated.

As colleges, hospitals, and community social services blurred their Christian identity, Presbyterians and their mainstream counterparts continued to "live out their faith" through service in these structures. But the agencies themselves struggled to find ways of making their organizations acceptable to government regulation and worthy of support from a range of sponsoring community groups, religious and otherwise. These now independent structures frequently changed their names to blot out prior ecclesiastical associations and/or introduced regulations against their volunteers and staff openly declaring their religious motivations for service in the organization. While the Christian motivation of volunteers and staff remained powerful, their motives were largely eclipsed from public view.[25]

In other words, just as Presbyterians were muffling their verbal witness in the 1960s, their physical witness, emphasized by denominational pronouncements, was inadvertently masked.

The Presbyterian attempt to respond to the social turmoil of the 1960s prompted a rethinking of evangelism.
The effort to redefine the church's mission is also reflected
in significant changes in programs for new church development, campus ministries, and the denomination's use of
media.

New Church Development

During the late nineteenth century, new church development efforts concentrated almost exclusively on the needs
of the immigrants and the frontier. But between 1900 and
1940, this emphasis gave way to concern for the creation of
urban and suburban congregations, and from 1940 to 1960
the Presbyterian denominations focused on the burgeoning
suburbs of post–World War II America.[26]

As Robert Bullock has noted, the statistics for new
church development changed dramatically. The PCUSA/
UPCNA/UPCUSA and the PCUS together averaged almost 72 new churches per year in the 1940s and nearly 135
per year in the 1950s. But in the 1960s the average fell to 75
and declined even further to 35 per year in the 1970s. In
the 1980s it recovered slightly to an average of 58 per
year.[27] This slump in new church development is especially
significant in light of recent studies that indicate a strong
correlation between new church starts and the membership
growth of denominations like the Southern Baptist Convention and the Assemblies of God.[28]

The American surge of participation in religious institutions during the 1950s fueled much of the boom in new
church development. The scarcity of building supplies during World War II contributed as well. The war halted much
new construction in all sectors of society. But postwar prosperity satisfied this pent-up demand with phenomenal
growth in the suburbs and a concomitant increase in new
churches. Because of these unusual circumstances, the
1950s may be an inappropriate standard by which to measure subsequent new church development programs.[29]

Yet it is also true that, like evangelism programs in the

late '40s and early '50s, new church development received
significant attention by the Presbyterian denominations, at
both the local and national levels. The PCUS case proves
this point. The old Board of Home Missions was renamed
the Board of Church Extension in 1949. Church Extension
developed separate support agencies, such as a Survey and
Church Location division and Church Architecture and
Urban Church divisions, to provide information to local
new church development projects. Major funds were either
donated outright or facilitated by the denomination guaranteeing loans for new congregations. This money was
largely targeted at selected suburban sites where quick development of a self-sustaining congregational unit could be
expected.

For example, Mecklenburg Presbytery, covering the
Charlotte, North Carolina, area, founded a new church every year from 1946 to 1966. From 1967 to 1980 it started
none. During the same period, Charlotte's population increased by approximately one-third. The Presbyterian
presence in Charlotte declined from 13 percent of the population in 1920 to 7.6 percent in 1980.[30]

Like evangelism programs, new church development began to wane in the late 1950s. The cost of most new church
starts rose. But even where support remained, the denomination at both the local and national levels redirected its
focus toward urban churches in changing neighborhoods
and to developing inner-city ministries in shopping centers, high-rise apartments, and house churches, and in vo-
cational, special purpose, or age-group communities.[31]

Although these efforts reflected an urgent concern to address the massive social dislocations of urban America, the
resulting new congregations struggled for survival. Between
1967 and 1971, when the UPCUSA shifted its emphasis to
new "experimental" and "noninstitutional" ministries,
only twenty-five new churches or ministries a year were
started, with only a few ever reaching a membership of
more than forty adults.[32]

This redirection of resources to new ministries was
launched by its advocates in the UPCUSA as a faithful re-

sponse to the theme of reconciliation centered in the newly adopted Confession of 1967. PCUS proponents viewed this program as a response to God's leadings in the world. The PCUS moderator remarked in 1961, "Our great concern . . . should not be the rising or falling of statistics but whether or not we are an instrument of God's purpose for these times."[33]

Ministries on College Campuses

The Reformed tradition and mainstream Protestantism shared a concern for education that produced an extensive network of colleges and universities prior to the Civil War. By 1860, 175 of the 182 colleges had been founded by churches or through denominational initiatives, and Presbyterians led the way with 49. During the nineteenth century, pastoral work among students was handled informally by the president, who was often a minister; by a faculty member or groups of faculty; by an area pastor; or by students themselves. After the Civil War, organizations such as the YMCA, the YWCA, the Student Volunteer Movement, and the Student Christian Movement became especially important arenas of ministry on college campuses. But the late nineteenth and early twentieth centuries brought epochal changes in the scope and character of higher education. Presbyterians recognized the change by designating the college campus as a field of evangelism and responded by creating a specialized ministry—the campus chaplain.[34]

Early in the century, the evangelism division of the PCUSA organized regular visitations to Presbyterian-related colleges. Official visitors led services, evangelism weeks, and personal interviews on campus to encourage the spiritual development of Presbyterian students.[35] In 1905 the PCUSA General Assembly affirmed a plan to appoint "special ministers" to serve college campuses, much like Army or Navy chaplains. The PCUS lagged behind in commissioning campus ministers and appointed them largely through congregations, presbyteries, or synods. But Ronald

White has noted that by the 1920s, both the PCUSA and PCUS had "embraced campus ministry with enthusiasm."[36]

By the 1930s, three models for Presbyterian ministry prevailed on college campuses. First, some congregations continued to relate directly to a nearby college or university, and its pastors and members actively ministered to the campus community. Second, Presbyterian-related institutions had their own chaplains, most of whom had faculty status and teaching responsibilities. Third, Presbyterian chaplains also served large public universities.[37]

As early as the 1930s, however, major tensions were building in campus ministries. Leaders posed the question about whether these ministries should be focused on students and their needs, or serve the denominations and congregations that supported the ministry. Behind this dilemma was the growing tension between the ideals of the secular university and the values and commitments of the church.[38]

The post–World War II era brought an even greater transformation to higher education and posed increasingly severe challenges to campus ministry. The scope of higher education exploded, primarily through government initiatives, and public tax revenues became the major source of funding for what had become a vast enterprise in higher education. In one sense, higher education is the most visible area of American society in which mainstream Protestantism has seen itself disestablished. If the history of higher education in the nineteenth century is the story of American Protestants, in the twentieth century it is the chronicle of the secularization of higher education through state funding.[39]

Presbyterians and other mainstream Protestants could not and did not keep pace with the financial needs of their own church-related institutions. They also saw the role of these denominational colleges usurped by public institutions. This included the teaching of religion itself. After World War II, both private and public institutions added departments of religion, and the curriculum was shaped not by the needs of the church but by the standards of the academy. Seeking to maintain and improve their academic standing, the church-related institutions frequently minimized church affiliation or Christian commitment in favor of academic excellence as they hired faculty to teach religion and other disciplines as well. Thus, even at church colleges, campus ministers increasingly found themselves operating at the margins of institutional life.[40]

Presbyterians did not willingly or easily surrender the field of higher education. In fact, the 1950s saw an expansion of Presbyterian activity in campus ministry. In 1950 the PCUS, for example, had only 50 campus ministers, but by 1962 it had Presbyterian chaplains located at 100 of the 300 campuses in the Southeast.[41] The '50s also witnessed the gradual development of ecumenical campus ministries on a broad scale. The ecumenical model had minimal impact in the first half of the twentieth century, but in the 1960s Presbyterians united with other mainstream Protestants to make ecumenical campus ministry the new vision for the future.

In doing so, Presbyterians responded to the growing ecumenical involvement of their denominations, the climate of ecumenism in theology, the practical appeal of economies in staff, funds, and program, and the growing concern to inspire students to be agents of change in American society. And yet the ecumenical campus ministers were confronted by escalating and conflicting demands. They were representatives of the church, but their immediate community was usually the secular college or university. They vigorously upheld an ecumenical understanding of the Christian faith, yet they also labored in a society of discernible congregations and denominations, which funded their ministries. As a 1966 study of campus ministers discovered, the chaplains and their students found themselves increasingly at odds, both theologically and politically, with pastors of congregations and lay parishioners.[42]

The identification with and support of ecumenical campus ministries became a serious problem. The campus clergy's relationships to congregations, presbyteries, or synods remained unclear, and the gap between the increasingly secular atmosphere of colleges and universities and the faith commitments of the church stretched both parties' loyalties to these chaplains and their ministries.

In 1950 Presbyterians supported more than 500 campus ministries; by 1989 the number had dwindled to 253. One long-time Presbyterian campus minister looked back from the 1980s on the swirling changes of the last three decades and sighed, "We ministered to the students, to the graduate students, to the faculty and staff, widening the circle and losing people all along the way. Thus we ministered to the 'structures of the university,' whatever that means, and we were lost."[43] An even bleaker assessment came from San Diego Presbytery executive Neil W. Brown: "Campus ministry, as we have known it for forty years, and its ecumenical version over the last twenty years, is over and done with."[44]

The disarray of campus ministry proved to be particularly damaging because it had traditionally been for Presbyterians and mainstream Protestants an important means of evangelism to young adults. Campus ministers often comprised a significant network of people who influenced students to enter the ministry or who encouraged the development of lay leaders. College students who confronted challenges to their childhood faith found in Presbyterian and other mainstream Protestant campus pastors a recognition that the intellect is God's creation and received assistance in deepening their quest for knowledge of God and themselves.

But in the latter half of this century, campus ministries stood in disarray—battered by the secularization of higher education, emaciated by the denominations which no longer adequately funded them, and weakened by their withdrawal from evangelism in the name of ecumenical cooperation and ministries of social justice. Campus ministry as evangelism, however, did not disappear, and groups such as Intervarsity and Campus Crusade stepped into the breach and often into the budgets of Presbyterian congregations.

The PC(USA) has experienced its greatest membership losses among the young. Sociologists claim that most people's religious affiliation or lack thereof is set in their late teens and early twenties. Religious affiliation—especially among young people in the 1980s and 1990s—is increasingly tenuous and flexible. If this is so, the disarray of Presbyterian campus ministries is one factor in explaining the defection of college students during the 1970s and 1980s. To reconstruct and reemphasize campus ministries represents a new challenge and opportunity for Presbyterian evangelism in the future.[45]

Media Ministries

In the 1950s mainstream Protestants had significant, if not overwhelming, influence in the religious use of mass media. By the 1980s evangelicals—especially the televangelists—had triumphed.

This dramatic shift of cultural power and influence is a microcosm for understanding the disestablishment of mainstream Protestantism and its own struggle to understand evangelism and mass media in light of its own ecumenical commitments and theological change.

Since the development of radio and television, Presbyterians have struggled over how their resources could best be divided among print media, radio, and television; advocates of mass media fought budget battles with other areas of the denominations' concerns. Economics played a significant role in these battles because television productions required an enormous outlay of money. But much more than money determined the final outcome of this debate.[46]

Prior to the 1960s, Presbyterians enthusiastically committed resources to communicating by means of the mass media through denominational as well as ecumenical programs. The 1950 General Assembly of the PCUSA received a seventeen-page report on a wide variety of mass media initiatives: coast-to-coast radio broadcasts, mass media evangelism efforts, radio and television production facilities, and workshops and seminary courses for church leaders throughout the country. In 1952, the PCUSA recommended that synods and presbyteries create broadcasting committees. By 1956, 36 synods and 242 presbyteries had done so. The PCUS also established with three other denominations a complete radio and television center for the development of programming, and the PCUS Women of the Church provided major financial assistance. By 1956, the Council on Theological Education of the PCUSA reported that six of the ten Presbyterian seminaries offered a range of courses in broadcast writing or broadcast production.[47]

The fragile infrastructure of mass media in the Presbyterian denominations quickly dissipated in the 1960s for several reasons. During the early years of television and radio, national broadcasting networks turned to ecumenical organizations like the Federal Council of Churches (FCC) and later the National Council of Churches (NCC) for religious programming. Federal regulations required the networks to provide free public service programming, and ecumenical agencies like the FCC and the NCC provided these broadcasting companies a single, "safe" (meaning relatively representative) partner for developing such programs. This free air time was one of the blessings of being part of mainstream Protestantism and one of the "perks" of the establishment status these denominations enjoyed.

After 1960, however, the ground rules changed dramatically. The Federal Communications Commission altered its regulations and allowed networks and local stations to charge for public service offerings. The member churches of the NCC balked at the new, enormous costs; the evangelical media ministries, previously excluded from the special arrangements enjoyed by mainstream Protestants, continued to pay for their time on the air as they had earlier.[48]

Ecumenical cooperation in mainstream Protestant programming also generated uncertainty about whether programs created by Presbyterians should be identified as Presbyterian or should instead be credited to the larger ecumenical community. Presbyterians decided upon the latter. In so doing, they seriously misunderstood the degree to

which successful use of mass media depends on name recognition.[49] They hoped, of course, that a generic Christian
message on the air waves would lead individuals to Christ
without introducing the complications of sectarian differences. But this hope overlooked the reality that accepting
Christ inevitably prompted individuals to join the body of
Christ. Joining that body was not possible through ecumenical agencies but only through particular denominations.
Ironically, the identity of these same denominational bodies was obscured when the NCC was credited as the public
source of what was Presbyterian and other mainstream
Protestant denominational programming.

Proponents of media also struggled to make a case for
television and radio, as opposed to print media. Gregg
Meister's study indicates that the late-coming mass media
fought a losing battle with more traditional programs relying on print, particularly because denominational leaders
were biased toward print. Some argued that radio and particularly television did not allow for the transmission of a
more complex or sophisticated theological message.[50]

Mass media also became a casualty of the debate over
evangelism during the 1960s and 1970s as concerns for social justice and social ministries and new theological movements caused Presbyterians to review their mission
priorities. Television and radio ministries were linked to
the older emphasis on verbal witness; as funds for denominational mission eroded in the midst of the debate, mass
media ministries suffered. The rise and popularity of
televangelists, such as Robert Schuller, Oral Roberts, Jim
Bakker, Jerry Falwell, and Jimmy Swaggart, confirmed the
Presbyterian bias against television as a means for communicating the depth and richness of the Christian faith.

But the intensity of the Presbyterian debate over evangelism and the fragmentation of denominational mission reflected a more complicated question of the church's
identity. The use of mass media depends on a message, and
amid the disruption of direction and leadership of the
1960s and 1970s, it was unclear what the church wanted to
say and who would say it.

All these factors combined to thwart the development of mass media as an integral part of Presbyterian witness, and like other mainstream Protestant denominations, the Presbyterians virtually withdrew from the airwaves and conceded prominence to evangelical and fundamentalist Protestants.

It is estimated that television is viewed daily 2.5 to 4 hours out of 5.5 hours of free time in the average American home.[51] The abdication of this means of communication is a reflection of the cultural displacement of American Presbyterianism and mainstream Protestantism. It also has long-range implications for their ability to appeal to the religious sentiments of the American people.

Indeed, as the UPCUSA Department of Radio and Television asserted in 1960, "For the church of the 20th century not to make extensive use of both television and radio would be as unthinkable as if St. Paul had refused to travel in ships or Luther and Calvin had regarded the printing press as unworthy of use."[52]

A Division of Parallel Allegiances

For many members in the Presbyterian communion and in mainstream Protestant circles after the 1960s, words of invitation to Christian faith remained the necessary complement to social action. But the ensuing decades have seen a widening polarization between those who considered themselves advocates of evangelism (i.e., verbal witness) and those who promoted a witness for social justice. As membership declined and as denominational mission fragmented, each side tended to regard the other as being willing to sacrifice either verbal witness or prophetic action from the Reformed tradition's parallel allegiances to both.[53]

Fervor for each type of Christian outreach remains vibrant, but a consensus about this enduring tension in the church's life remains elusive. Furthermore, the spirit of tolerance and the ethos of modernity have caused contemporary Presbyterians to have second thoughts about the desirability and necessity of Christian witness itself. For example, in a 1989 *Presbyterian Panel* poll, only 50 percent of Presbyterian members and 49 percent of pastors agree that "converting people to Christ must be the first step in creating a better society."[54]

In the twentieth-century debate over evangelism among Presbyterians, one can now see these representatives of mainstream Protestants slowly and painfully coming to terms with the pluralism of American society, their displacement as arbiters of culture through higher education, and the ambiguities of the denomination as an expression of Christian truth. The struggle clearly weakened these denominations as institutions. It posed as alternative choices what are in fact necessary elements of Christian witness.

The debate also reveals much about the changing character of American Presbyterianism and mainstream Protestantism's effort to redefine in constructive terms a Christian mission in a pluralistic society. In an effort to transform the world, Presbyterians sought to reform the church's mission and expand its horizons. As some concerns triumphed, others suffered. But at its roots, the debate over evangelism was an argument over what it meant to be Christian without the benefit of cultural support.

6

The Diversities of Discipleship: Mission, Racial Ethnic Ministries, Ecumenism, and Social Justice

The heart of nineteenth-century American evangelicalism and American Presbyterianism was the idea of mission, particularly missions to those who had never heard or accepted the gospel of Jesus Christ. When Old School Presbyterians founded the Board of Foreign Missions in 1838, they were clear about its evangelistic purpose: "The great object of the Board of Foreign Missions of the Presbyterian Church, is to assist in making known the Gospel, for a witness unto all nations. For this purpose the Church of Jesus Christ was established. She holds the blessings of the Gospel as the trustee for every nation and people who are without them; and it is her duty to make known the way of salvation to all the world."[1]

The missionary spirit of the age exuded both the church's confidence in the self-evident and universal truth of Christianity, its conviction that it possessed that truth, and its commission to spread it to all. For nineteenth-century evangelical Presbyterians, to be called was to be given a duty, and they undertook their missionary responsibility with devotion and seriousness. Implicit in the charter of the Board of Foreign Missions was the belief in America's own role in the civilizing and Christianizing of the world and the firm conviction of the superiority of Western culture.

By the late twentieth century, Presbyterians were still engaged in missionary work around the world. But the evangelistic task had been reinterpreted; the missionary spirit was chastened. Contact with other cultures and other religions, dialogue with other Christian traditions, massive changes in world economics and politics, the increasing pluralism of American society—these and more combined to transform the mission and missions of American Presbyterianism.

From Foreign Missions to Global Mission

The first American benevolence organization for missions, the New York Missionary Society, was founded by Presbyterians, Baptists, and Dutch Reformed in 1796. Others followed, most notably the American Board of Commissioners for Foreign Missions (ABCFM), established in 1810 and dominated by Presbyterians and Congregationalists. A year later in 1811, the ABCFM invited the PCUSA to create a foreign missions board of its own. The General Assembly declined, but it recommended the ABCFM to its membership as an acceptable avenue for Presbyterians to use in pursuing ministry to peoples overseas.[2]

Interdenominational and cooperative efforts characterized American Presbyterian and evangelical Protestant missions during the first half of the nineteenth century, despite the formation of the Board of Foreign Missions in the PCUSA in 1838. The separate PCUSA board grew out of growing doubts about the theological orthodoxy of ABCFM missionaries, and Charles Hodge of Princeton Seminary called for a denominational mission enterprise sponsored and controlled by the PCUSA. His position was opposed by Old School theologian James Henley Thornwell, who argued that mission work should be conducted by and through presbyteries rather than General Assembly agencies. New School leaders favored the ABCFM, which only accentuated Old School suspicions of the missionary agency after the Old School/New School schism in 1837.

As the benevolent empire waned in popularity during the latter half of the nineteenth century and as the corporate denomination emerged, evangelical Protestants withdrew their support from benevolence societies such as the ABCFM in favor of denominationally sponsored mission groups. New School Presbyterians followed this trend. When the northern Old and New Schools reunited in 1870, their new denomination sponsored a separate foreign missions agency. Similarly, the PCUS gradually moved from an executive committee to an identifiable Board of Foreign Missions.[3]

The purpose of nineteenth-century missions was evangelism; the goal was the conversion of "the heathen." Both in scale and results, argued Kenneth Scott Latourette, it was "the great century" of Christian expansion.[4] Presbyterian missionary activity in particular aimed at not only evangelization but also extensive educational efforts, ranging from the schooling of children to the founding of colleges, universities, and seminaries; medical work; and social and political reform. Throughout the nineteenth century, Presbyterians and other evangelical Protestants debated whether such "civilizing" efforts should precede or follow attempts to convert people to Christianity, but virtually no one argued that the two were unrelated.[5]

Furthermore, as Protestants fanned out across the globe, the supremacy in nineteenth-century foreign missions moved from Great Britain to the United States, matching the corresponding economic supremacy of the latter. Foreign missions were expensive, and women provided the bulk of funds needed to propel the missionary movement. This was especially true of American Presbyterian women, without whose dollars the foreign missionary enterprise would have floundered. Circumscribed by role and restricted from exercising power within the church, Presbyterian and evangelical Protestant women flocked to serve as missionaries, and by the late nineteenth century women comprised the majority of Protestants in world missions.[6]

The late nineteenth century brought new strains to the

theological basis of evangelical missions. Ironically, the missionaries who proclaimed the exclusive truth of Christianity were also the ones who brought back information about the complexity and richness of other cultures and other world traditions. Missionaries, who learned from their converts and from indigenous denominations as they arose, eventually raised questions about evangelization as a strategy of mission, the advantages of Western civilization, and even the exclusive truth of Christianity itself.

These questions did not have much impact until the 1920s, when fundamentalists raised suspicions about the orthodoxy of some of the PCUSA's missionaries. The evangelistic credentials of Robert E. Speer, secretary of the denomination's Board of Foreign Missions, successfully thwarted most of this critique, but the 1930s brought a frontal assault on the theological foundations and methods of Presbyterian and mainstream Protestant missionary activity.[7] The challenge was issued in a report popularly named after William Ernest Hocking, who chaired the commission that produced it. John D. Rockefeller, Jr., funded the commission's research, and seven denominations, among them the PCUSA and the UPCNA, provided directors for what was formally called the Laymen's Foreign Missions Inquiry.[8]

The Hocking Report critiqued the personnel, methods, and perspective of mainstream American Protestant missions. Describing American missionaries as mediocre, the report declared they were far too content with conventional forms of missions and overburdened by administrative responsibilities. But the Hocking commission found contemporary missionary strategies to be even more objectionable. The report suggested that missionaries did not adequately capture the spirit of liberal Protestantism, which viewed Christianity as "less a religion of fear and more a religion of beneficence." Christian proclamation, it said, should not be so focused on life in another world, and it must maintain a critical distance from the Western dominance and control which, the report insisted, had created a rising tide of reaction elsewhere in the world.[9]

The Hocking report predicted the emergence of a "religion of modern man" for a "coming world-culture." This new spirituality required greater knowledge of and cooperation with other world religions, a more generous attitude toward sincere religious seekers involved in non-Christian religions, and a more universalist approach to the salvation of humanity.[10] In this new situation, the best form of evangelism, the report argued, was quiet service. "The Christian way of life is capable of transmitting itself by quiet personal contact and contagion, and there are circumstances in which this is a perfect mode of speech," the commission declared. "Ministry to the secular needs of men [and women] in the spirit of Christ, moreover, *is* evangelism, in the right sense of the word."[11]

Initial Presbyterian reaction to the Hocking report was both defensive and antagonistic. The PCUSA Standing Committee on Foreign Missions reaffirmed its commitment to the church's doctrinal standards and to its belief that the "complete and final truth is to be found in Jesus Christ alone through the religion of which he is the center." The committee also denied that its missionaries were disrespectful of other world religions or ignored the social imperatives of the gospel, as the Hocking Report had charged. The PCUS responded with an even more biting repudiation of the Hocking Report by renaming it, "Rejecting Missions and Crucifying Our Lord Afresh."[12]

The initial Presbyterian response did not prevail, and Jack Fitzmier and Randall Balmer have demonstrated that Presbyterian missions, like those of other mainstream Protestant denominations, changed dramatically in later decades. By the 1980s, PC(USA) global mission policy closely resembled much that the Hocking Commission had recommended in 1932.[13]

Several factors contributed to this metamorphosis. First, World War II devastated the European homelands of most American Protestants. The war's destruction demanded a response of concrete relief aid, and this practical service to the Old World widened the definition of appropriate missionary work.[14]

Second, the rise of formal national and world ecumenical groups encouraged similar conversations with non-Christian religions. These consultations appeared to be a natural extension of the reconciliation of the gospel which the ecumenical movement was seeking to emulate.[15]

Third, neo-orthodoxy's dominance in American mainstream Protestantism during the 1950s emphasized a much-needed self-critical antidote to all Western and nationalistic claims to superiority. The postwar unraveling of colonialism, the assertion of independence by nations of the Third World, the struggle for equal rights by minorities in the United States, and the devastation of the Vietnam war undermined mainstream American Protestants' pretensions to know or represent the essence of Christian discipleship.[16]

A humbled mainstream Protestantism realized its past complicity in bundling Western imperialism with the transmission of the gospel. It also discovered that the missionary efforts of the nineteenth century had created, for the first time, a global Christian church, which contained diversities of discipleship that could leaven the spirituality of all Christians. Therefore, the idea of foreign missions from America to a lost world was replaced by the vision of an integrated global mission (without final "s") in partnership with domestic and overseas disciples. The perception of the missionary's role also shifted. Missionaries moved from being messengers to serving as workers and partners with indigenous churches. Rather than shaping overseas church life, Presbyterian missionaries now served at the pleasure and under the direction of churches that defined their own objectives and programs.[17]

But the older view of missions persisted. As Presbyterians and other mainstream Protestant denominations reconceived and redefined missions to be mission, evangelical Protestants clung to the nineteenth-century vision and turned independent and entrepreneurial in funding foreign missions. The result was a revolution in twentieth-century American Protestant missions. The number of missionaries exploded, more than tripling from the 1930s to the 1980s. Mainstream Protestants lost their dominance of the movement, moving from a ten-to-one majority in career missionaries to a one-to-eleven minority. The number of Presbyterian missionaries declined from 1,918 to 470 in the same half century. By the 1980s, evangelical American Protestants, most funded by "faith missions" or parachurch organizations, comprised 90 percent of all missionaries around the world.[18]

The saga of missions had come full circle. It had started as the concern of missionary-minded Protestants, was later incorporated into the organizations of the denominations, was transformed by the new realities of the twentieth-century church and the world, and finally emerged as a particular preserve of parachurch groups of the late twentieth century. Foreign missions becomes a powerful lens for viewing the contending parties of American Protestantism, its institutional adjustments, and the confrontation of mainstream Protestantism with the dilemmas of culture as well as the challenges of its faith and witness.

Ministries with Racial Ethnic Minorities

The foreign missionary movement posed the question of how American and European traditions of Christianity could be translated into other cultures. For many Presbyterians and mainstream Protestants, that issue was confronted more directly and more painfully in their attempts to evangelize people from other countries who settled—voluntarily and involuntarily—in the United States. Throughout the twentieth century, the American Presbyterian Church has increasingly recognized the pluralism represented by racial and ethnic minorities in its membership, but their participation has posed new challenges to the Anglo majority and dilemmas for the minority groups themselves.

In 1990, African American Presbyterians comprised 2.47 percent of the total membership of the PC(USA), Asian Americans 1.54 percent, Hispanic Americans 0.87 percent, and Native Americans 0.73 percent. These statistics testify to a consistent pattern in American Presbyterianism and mainstream Protestantism—the inability of these churches to invite and/or attract racial ethnic minorities into predominantly white denominations.[19]

Racial ethnic minorities' ambivalence toward American Presbyterianism is well founded in their history within the Presbyterian Church. Until the twentieth century, Presbyterians pursued a policy of supervised segregation of racial ethnic minorities. Yet it also required that racial ethnic minorities assimilate into the dominant white American culture and subscribe to the doctrinal standards of a denomination essentially shaped by the northern European experience.[20]

The civil rights movement of the 1950s and 1960s moved the church toward the ideal of integration of racial ethnic minorities into the denominational structures of American Presbyterianism. But racial ethnic minority Presbyterians soon found that formal integration submerged their particular identities at the very moment that the larger culture was finally affirming the unique value of their traditions. During the 1970s and 1980s, racial ethnic minorities have searched for structural relationships within American Presbyterianism and mainstream Protestantism that would preserve their own cultural expressions of faith while fostering inclusion of those forms of discipleship in the broader religious ethos.[21]

Although each of the racial ethnic minorities represented in the PC(USA) has its own distinctive history, the treatment of Black Presbyterians is a paradigm for understanding the Presbyterian patterns of racial ethnic minority ministries.

Africans' first contact with Christianity was "not propitious," for it produced what Vincent Harding calls "the deep ambivalence" of American Blacks toward Jesus Christ. "This ambivalence is not new," Harding writes. "For we first met the American Christ on slave ships. We heard his name sung in hymns of praise while we died in our thousands, chained in stinking holds beneath the decks. . . . When our women were raped in the cabins they must have noticed the great and holy books on the shelves."[22]

Upon reaching America's shores, Black Americans became captive subjects for evangelization. During the colonial period, Protestants engaged in only occasional and desultory attempts to convert African slaves, but in the early nineteenth century, slave holders were eventually convinced that a gospel of obedience might make better slaves. Increased efforts, such as those by Presbyterian missionary Charles C. Jones, produced more conversions and the beginnings of the Christianization of the African American people. During slavery the signs of a unique Afro-American Christianity emerged. Formed out of both African and Euro-American religious and cultural traditions, it accented freedom and community as the heart of Christian life. But even after conversion and when Blacks were permitted to attend Presbyterian churches, the slaves were relegated to the back balconies during the services.[23]

After the Civil War, Presbyterian missionaries from the PCUSA joined other northern Protestants in launching an extensive effort to educate the newly freed slaves. Their efforts were frequently greeted by resentment and hostility from Presbyterians and others in the South, but the result was some of the best Black colleges and universities in the nation, like Knoxville College, Johnson C. Smith University, and Stillman College.[24] Nevertheless, the ambivalence in Black Presbyterians continued because the model for Presbyterian fellowship with Blacks remained segregation in separate congregations and governing bodies of the church, not to speak of society itself. Throughout the nineteenth and early twentieth centuries, the pattern of segregation prevailed.

During the 1950s Black Presbyterians' call for an end to segregated structures was reinforced by the National Council of Churches and, even more important, by the civil rights movement. First Black Americans and later other ethnic groups and women demanded their inclusion and integration into the structures of the church and the society. In the PCUS, conflict over this question and the right of workers to organize, especially in the textile industry of North Carolina, was particularly bitter. Such controversy had been heating up since the 1930s. The southern Presbyterian doctrine of the "spirituality of the church" was deeply embedded in the ethos of the denomination, and in order to breach this formidable theological fortification as well as the overt racial bigotry that it sheltered, many Presbyterians suffered ostracism and hatred in the battle over civil rights in the South.[25]

The successful promotion of the principle of integration in the church during the 1960s created its own uncertainties for Black Presbyterians as they found themselves, in some cases, less visible than before. In the late 1960s, the Black Power movement encouraged a self-conscious Black Theology that prompted African American Presbyterians to question the absolute value of integration. Even though integration appeared to present the possibility of finally being accepted in the church, it also threatened to eclipse Black Presbyterian forms of worship and discipleship.[26]

In 1969 James Foreman addressed the General Assemblies of both the UPCUSA and the PCUS with a formal demand for financial reparations for the past sins of racism. This event and the work of the Black Presbyterian Caucus (PCUS) and Black Presbyterians United (UPCUSA) moved these denominations to alter their course in favor of the goal of the self-development of minority groups.[27]

Since the late nineteenth century, Black Presbyterian caucuses had provided a vehicle for the survival of Black identity and for concentrating Blacks' limited power on denominational structures. In the reunited PC(USA), caucuses for African Americans and other racial ethnic minorities have been institutionalized in a single "Racial Ethnic Ministry Unit."[28]

Even this step presented its own set of problems. The racial ethnic minorities of the PC(USA) are obviously not a monolithic, homogeneous group. A wide variety of cultural backgrounds are subsumed under names such as Hispanic American or Asian American Presbyterians. Within the Hispanic American community are at least three distinct cultural groups. The oldest and largest Hispanic constituency in the PC(USA) is located primarily in the Southwest and is linked culturally to Mexico, as well as to Central and South America. These members first became Presbyterian through home missions in the United States. Hispanic Americans from Cuba and Puerto Rico, on the other hand, are generally more recent arrivals, and they were introduced to Presbyterianism by missionaries sent in a burst of U.S. involvement in the Caribbean after the Spanish-American War.[29]

The term "Asian American" is equally all-encompassing and misleading since it stands for peoples from a multiplicity of Asian cultures who entered this country in quite different periods of U.S. history. Korean American Presbyterians are the fastest growing racial ethnic minority community in the PC(USA). Yet significant Korean immigration to the United States did not begin until the 1970s. Chinese and Japanese American Presbyterians, in contrast, are much smaller constituencies in the PC(USA), but both groups began migrating to the United States in large numbers during the mid-nineteenth century. The first formal Presbyterian mission to Asian immigrants in this country was established in 1852.[30]

Similarly, Native American Presbyterians are drawn from a number of different tribes, each with differing cultural and religious traditions that have shaped their appropriation of Christianity.[31] Thus, the tendency of Presbyterians and mainstream Protestants to describe the minorities in their membership and in American society in categorical terms seriously underestimates the character and degree of pluralism.

Each of the racial ethnic minorities has encountered white prejudice, racism, and paternalism in its relationship with the Presbyterian denominations. They share misgivings as well about the seemingly attractive policy of integration into the larger church community, but their reservations arise from quite different sources. Korean Americans provide an interesting contrast to Black Presbyterians, who have generally sought integration with occasional ambivalence. Although American Presbyterian mission work spawned a significant Presbyterian presence in Korea, first-generation Korean American Presbyterian immigrants find that the theological positions of the PC(USA) have changed dramatically since the days of early Presbyterian missionaries in Korea. Thus, the integration of Korean Presbyterian congregations into the denomination means the imposition of what some Korean American Presbyterians consider theologically questionable liberal agendas.[32] This conflict has led numerous Korean American Presbyterian congregations to join the independent Korean Presbyterian Church in America, rather than the PC(USA).[33]

What is perceived by racial ethnic minorities as denominational inflexibility, reinforced by cultural differences, often involves language and leadership. Both Asian and Hispanic American Presbyterians complain about the church's delay in translating its materials into the appropriate vernacular.[34] Strict educational standards for ordination to the ministry are also challenged. For example, in Native American culture the mantle of leadership is not acquired by education but rather by an individual's proven practical ability to serve the community over many years. Native American Presbyterians insist that this cultural criterion for leadership should be substituted for the cultural expectation of education in the appropriate racial ethnic communities. This, they insist, is not lowering standards. Instead, as one group put it: "The question is not whether we should have standards, but how standards should be set up and by whom."[35]

Those who have studied racial ethnic minorities' interaction with American Presbyterianism emphasize that the PC(USA) has not fully relinquished its commitment to the Caucasian culture from which it first arose. If the church is serious about welcoming racial ethnic minorities, they suggest, a full-bodied biculturalism must exist. Biculturalism would mean more than just the translation of denominational literature, the inclusion of a few Spanish and Korean hymns in the denominational hymnal, or even allowing racial ethnic minority congregations to pursue their own

styles of worship and organization. Instead, it would require that the dominant white, middle- to upper-middle-
class Presbyterians include regularly in their own piety,
theology, and worship the forms and practices of discipleship developed by racial ethnic minority Christians.[36]

Such biculturalism poses complex challenges to mainstream Protestantism and American Presbyterianism. At a
minimum, this relationship requires empathy and flexibility. But it also demands answers to the critical question of
boundaries. Where are current barriers to racial ethnics'
leadership in denominational families culturally bound
rather than biblically informed? What are the limits of responsible flexibility for the purposes of open fellowship?
Despite these difficulties and despite their very small numbers, the participation of racial ethnic minorities in largely
Caucasian denominations reveals some of the tensions, realities, and promise of developing a global Christian
church.

The Ecumenical Movement

Anglican Archbishop William Temple, writing in 1944,
called the ecumenical movement "the great new fact of our
era."[37] This ecumenical movement, or more accurately, the
ecumenical movements of the twentieth century, represented a dramatic shift toward cooperation and even organic unity among Protestant denominations and between
different branches of the Christian tradition.

The ecumenical impulse was made possible by the development of the idea of the church as a denomination. By
carving out a middle ground between the exclusive claims
of both the church and the sect, a denomination presupposed the right of other denominations to exist and therefore the possibility of cooperation with and among them.
But ecumenism would eventually devalue the validity of
denominations as embodiments of the diversity and unity
of Christian witness.

The Reformed tradition has been the most ecumenical of
all the branches of the Reformation. John Calvin insisted

that he did not intend the creation of a separate church, and despite the denominational squabbles that followed in Protestant history, Calvin counseled patience and understanding. "No church can be taken up with itself exclusively," he wrote. "They ought all to hold out the right hand to each other, . . . cherishing mutual fellowship. . . . Let there be nothing of pride and contempt for other churches, let there be, on the other hand, a desire to edify; let there be moderation and prudence; and in that case, amid a diversity of observances, there will be nothing worthy of reproof."[38]

American Presbyterians cooperated ecumenically with other Protestants from their first settlement in the colonies. This coordination of effort was initially limited to denominations from the same Reformed theological tradition. For example, Presbyterian revivalists like Gilbert Tennent worked in concert with the Dutch Reformed Theodore Frelinghuysen, the Anglican George Whitefield, and the Congregationalist Jonathan Edwards in promoting the First Great Awakening during the 1730s and 1740s.[39]

In 1801 Presbyterians also formulated a Plan of Union with the New England Congregationalists in order to prevent duplication of evangelistic efforts and to meet the spiritual needs of people in the Old Northwest. This pact allowed for the rapid expansion of Reformed congregations by permitting local churches to draw leadership and support from the nearest Congregationalist or Presbyterian governing body.[40]

In later decades, mainstream Protestants pursued more expansive ecumenical alliances as they created a range of interdenominational benevolent societies.[41] These ecumenical alliances were largely coalitions of individual volunteers, rather than denominationally sponsored endeavors. Nevertheless, individual contacts across ecclesiastical boundaries fostered greater appreciation of mainstream Protestant churches' common objectives.

The nineteenth-century foreign missionary movement became the principal impulse behind the twentieth-century ecumenical movement. The evangelistic challenge posed by missions to people of non-Western cultures, the difficulty in explaining the difference between various types of Presbyterians or even Protestants, and the cost of missions made an ecumenical missionary strategy compelling. Presbyterians were again among the leaders in arguing for cooperation. As early as 1838, the Old School General Assembly declared "that we regard with sincere interest, all the efforts of the different foreign missionary institutions, to make known the truth as it is in Jesus Christ to the heathen; and we recognize it as a duty binding upon all these institutions, to cultivate the best understanding with each other, in carrying forward the same great cause."[42]

Nineteenth-century Presbyterians participated ecumenically primarily through the benevolent societies. Many of these societies did not survive after the Civil War as the corporate denomination gained power and as denominational control over mission activities increased. But the corporate denomination also heightened the possibilities of ecumenical cooperation by regularizing what had frequently been only informal networks of communication and missionary activity. The nineteenth-century missionary movement set the stage for twentieth-century ecumenism and the formation in the United States of a Federal Council of Churches (FCC) in 1908.[43]

As its name suggests, the FCC represented a loose confederation of independent denominations. Early participants in the FCC hailed its potential for mission, its witness to Christian unity and, ironically, its reinforcement of denominational identities. Within the FCC, individuals learned what they shared with fellow American Christians but also what distinguished their church's theology and piety from others within the Protestant community.

The Federal Council of Churches and its successor, the National Council of Churches (NCC), were expedients for cooperation, rather than agents of planned or proposed merger. Both organizations drew their strength from the mainstream Protestant denominations, although the participation of the Greek Orthodox in the NCC broadened the base of discussions. The agenda of the FCC was focused on the need for a social gospel in American Protestantism, and the NCC continued this tradition with even more assertiveness, especially during the 1960s in the civil rights movement.[44] Indeed, the FCC and the NCC have been the ecclesiastical embodiment of social and political liberalism in twentieth-century American Protestantism.

The ecumenical movement in the United States took a dramatic new turn in 1960 when Eugene Carson Blake, stated clerk of the UPCUSA, and Episcopal Bishop James A. Pike called for a consultation on the union of mainstream American Protestant denominations. The resulting Consultation on Church Union (COCU) redefined ecumenism as neither coalition nor simple cooperation but actual merger of denominational bodies.[45] While the idea of organic union had its roots in the nineteenth century, the theological source for this redefinition was a growing conviction that denominational identities sinfully divided the greater body of Christ.[46] Although the vision of organic union in COCU eventually faltered, the emphasis on unity in the spirit and unity in fact finally contributed to the "reunion" of American Presbyterians and the forming of the PC(USA) in 1983 from its predecessors, the PCUS and UPCUSA.

The formation of the PC(USA) was the result of nearly a half-century of concerted efforts led by Presbyterians, North and South, who were determined to heal the division brought about by the Civil War. The first attempt was launched in 1937, but the committee's final plan failed to pass the requisite three-fourths of the PCUS presbyteries in 1955. Entrenched suspicion of the PCUSA, fueled by the Supreme Court's decision on desegregating schools in 1954, shaped the outcome. The PCUSA then united with the UPCNA in 1958, and the PCUS was spurned in an effort to unite with the Reformed Church in America. In the late 1960s, the PCUS and the UPCUSA formed a number of union presbyteries. In 1973, some PCUS conservatives withdrew to form the Presbyterian Church in America. Through union presbyteries and conservative defection, the balance of power in the PCUS turned toward reunion.

In 1983 in Atlanta, both General Assemblies formally dissolved and came together as the PC(USA).[47]

Conservative Protestants have been critical of mainstream Protestantism's ecumenical commitments for both theological and political reasons. The willingness to reformulate Christian faith in modern terms, the tolerance for broad understandings of doctrine, and especially the political activism in American ecumenism shaped the conservative critique. In 1943, evangelical Protestants responded by establishing their own ecumenical organization—the National Association of Evangelicals (NAE)—for common witness and work. The doctrinal basis for membership in the NAE was clearly drawn—belief in the Bible as the only infallible, authoritative word of God, the Trinity, the virgin birth of Jesus Christ, substitutionary atonement, and the "spiritual" unity of all believers in Christ.[48] Thus, even in their cooperative activity American Protestants revealed the chasm that divided them into contending ecumenical factions in the twentieth century.

The ecumenical movement in the United States coincided with the growth of global ecumenism, arising initially from Western Protestant churches but eventually including the churches of the Third World. Both the PCUSA and PCUS were founding members of a new World Alliance of Reformed Churches in 1877. The Alliance included only those churches subscribing to the Presbyterian church order and the Westminster Standards. But the practical problem of evangelizing the world generated denominational involvement in broader ecumenical associations. Just as the formidable task of Christianizing the American frontier led nineteenth-century Protestants to cooperate individually in benevolent societies, so also the daunting mission of discipling the world led missionaries to cooperate: first locally on the mission field, and later internationally in worldwide missionary conferences.[49]

The signal event marking the birth of the global ecumenical movement was the International Missionary Conference in Edinburgh during June 1910. This conference was not the first of its kind, but it was the first to produce a sustained pattern of subsequent international meetings and discussions on missions. Edinburgh spawned two significant sets of ecumenical dialogues—the "Faith and Order" talks and the "Life and Work" conferences. In 1937–38 these conversations produced a committee of the World Council of Churches (WCC), which held its initial assembly in Amsterdam in 1948.[50]

The first "Faith and Order" conference was held in 1927. Although it initially focused on the differences separating participating churches, this movement later turned to the possibilities of mutual recognition of ministries, organic church union, and discussions with non-Christian religious communities. "Faith and Order" encouraged organizations like the World Alliance of Reformed Churches to enter into dialogues with other Protestant bodies and, in the 1960s, with Roman Catholic and Orthodox churches as well. It also propelled national councils of churches to pursue consultations like COCU in the United States.[51]

"Life and Work" discussions began in 1920, ten years after the Edinburgh Missionary Conference. Unlike "Faith and Order," which considered the formal theological bases of participating churches, "Life and Work" dealt with the practical implications of the Christian gospel. The notion that "doctrine divides, service unites" attracted many to this component of the world ecumenical movement.[52] The second "Life and Work" conference in Oxford during 1937 attempted a formulation of "middle axioms" for understanding Christian social ethics. John C. Bennett, an organizer of the meeting, defined middle axioms as "those goals for society which are more specific than universal Christian principles and less specific than concrete institutions or programs of action."[53]

The confrontation with totalitarianism in World War II, the demise of colonialism, the assertion of independence by Third World governments and their churches, and the formation of the World Council of Churches brought new strains to the global ecumenical movement. At its inception, the WCC was dominated by Western churches, just as the Western nations held the balance of power in the

United Nations during the two decades after World War II. The 1960s signaled the end of Western control over the global ecumenical movement and the WCC. In 1966, only 40 percent of the delegates to the WCC Assembly came from the West. Twenty percent came from Eastern Europe; 40 percent represented churches in developing nations. As Theodore Gill has noted, this rearrangement of the power base resulted in the "middle axioms" approach to social policy falling by the "ecumenical wayside as clear-cut positions were taken on issue after issue, from patterns of economic growth to U.S. involvement in Vietnam." This, of course, fueled and in turn was fired by an already mounting cry for social witness in American churches during the 1960s and 1970s.[54]

The increasing specificity of WCC pronouncements and the direct involvement of the WCC in social justice causes around the globe generated strong negative reaction in some quarters of the Presbyterian and mainstream American Protestant community during the 1970s and 1980s. Presbyterian evangelicals and those in other denominations searched for an alternative medium, as Gill puts it, for "cooperating in a depoliticized style of world evangelization." At Lausanne, Switzerland, in 1974 an International Congress of World Evangelization was organized under the leadership of the Billy Graham organization. The PCUS, UPCUSA, and their successor, the PC(USA) have not been formally represented in this movement, though numerous individual Presbyterians have participated.[55]

Presbyterian commitment to and leadership of the ecumenical movement of the twentieth century are clear. As theologian Robert McAfee Brown succinctly put it in the 1980s, "I am a Presbyterian—therefore I am ecumenical."[56] But the ecumenical movement or movements and Presbyterian involvement also reveal patterns of world Christianity and some fascinating ironies and challenges for American Presbyterians.

First, the twentieth-century ecumenical movement was and even continues to be largely a Protestant movement, led by churches in the United States and Western Europe. Prior to Vatican II, the movement demonstrated a distinct uneasiness about contact with Roman Catholics, and the anti-Catholicism that characterized so much of American Protestant history colored twentieth-century ecumenism. The Second Vatican Council has dramatically changed this environment, particularly in congregations. More traumatic has been the shift of power in global ecumenical circles away from the West and to the churches of Africa, Asia, and Latin America, especially when a theological critique of Western theology was coupled with stinging indictments of Western political and economic influence.

Second, the global ecumenical movement has reflected the century-long division in American Protestantism—now exported throughout the world through the missionary movement. The NAE in the United States and the Lausanne movement reveal the wariness of the NCC and WCC in dealing with the evangelical, fundamentalist, and Pentecostal communities within the Protestant family, as well as the power of the ecumenical impulse to forge cooperative and conciliar structures among conservative Protestants. At the same time the so-called "third force" in twentieth-century Christianity, the Pentecostal/charismatic movement, has spread extensively, especially in the Third World.

Third, by the late twentieth century, conciliar organizations like the NCC and the WCC were in disarray. These bodies were never known as models of organizational efficiency; indeed, one supporter called the NCC "the most complex and intricate piece of ecclesiastical machinery this planet has ever witnessed."[57] But as support for the idea of the American corporate denomination began to evaporate in the 1950s and 1960s, so did financial and moral support for bodies like the NCC, WCC, and even most regional councils of churches. If the ecumenical movement is to be defined in terms of these organizations, it was largely moribund by the end of the twentieth century.

Fourth, ironically the ecumenical movement has triumphed at the local level in the United States and in many parts of the world.[58] As noted earlier, contemporary Americans move easily, if not casually, from one denomination to another and between Roman Catholicism and Protestantism, and this tendency is especially pronounced among Presbyterians. Moreover, congregations of various denominations collaborate easily in social ministries of many kinds. Contemporary Americans find nothing particularly binding about denominational identities, blurred as they have become. As organizational ecumenism has withered, popular ecumenism has triumphed. Its acceptance of religious diversity, due sometimes to theological indifference, is a striking feature of late-twentieth-century America.

Fifth, this victory produced severe dilemmas for Presbyterians and mainstream Protestants. On the one hand, these denominations have resisted formal organic union, such as the original vision of COCU; yet they declare that their mission is to bring others to Christ, not particular denominations. Leaders bemoan losses to other denominations; yet they are puzzled when lay people demonstrate declining interest or support for denominational structures and programs.

Finally, the ecumenical movement was spawned by the missionary movement, and missionaries were among the most eloquent voices crying out against injustices and exploitation of people throughout the world. Precisely because of the Western orientation of the ecumenical movement, their voices and later those of Third World Christians were directed primarily at the negative effects wrought in the West and other parts of the world by Western political and economic policy. The critique of the West frequently involved some form of Marxist theory, which further alienated and divided Western Christians. The dream of one body in Christ, which propelled the ecumenical movement, was shattered by these divisive economic and political issues, and Presbyterian efforts to find a social ethic in the twentieth century ironically contributed to an increasing division over what constitutes a meaningful and faithful Christian witness of the church in society.

From Old to New Agendas

The "Evangelical United Front" of nineteenth-century Protestantism assumed that the Christian faith should be applied to the social order. Drawing on the emphases of the Calvinist tradition, American Presbyterians also held that the church and individual Christians were responsible for translating their faith into society and its structures. What H. Richard Niebuhr described as the model of Christ transforming culture prevailed as the dominant motif of nineteenth-century evangelicalism; with the exception of the Thornwellian tradition of "the spirituality of the church" which heavily influenced the PCUS, this vocation characterized American Presbyterianism.[59]

The late-nineteenth and early twentieth-century chasm in American Protestantism left in its wake a sharp division over Christian social ethics. The evangelical-fundamentalist wing turned away from addressing social and political issues in what David Moberg calls "the great reversal." The modernist-liberal wing became committed to what came to be known as the social gospel. In the words of its foremost theologian of the early twentieth century, Walter Rauschenbusch: "We have a social gospel. We need a systematic theology large enough to match it and vital enough to back it." Rauschenbusch was convinced that "the social gospel is a permanent addition to our spiritual outlook and that its arrival constitutes a stage in the development of the Christian religion."[60] At the heart of the social gospel was an attempt to move Christian ethics away from an exclusively individualistic emphasis to a concern for institutional structures that perpetuated sin.

The social gospel movement made few inroads in early twentieth-century Presbyterianism.[61] The prevailing Princeton theology served as a buttress against a major reconsideration of the church's mission and its conception of Christian social ethics. Three powerful movements combined to transform American Presbyterians' approach to social and political issues, and by the late twentieth century the PC(USA)'s understanding of social ethics had changed dramatically.

The first of these movements was the steady increase in the function and power of government in American society. Progressive reformers and the social gospelers of the early twentieth century denounced the laissez-faire conception of the state and urged government to initiate, legislate, and monitor reforms of the economic, social, and political life of the nation. This enlarged vision for government bore fruit in the liberalism of the New Deal, but it became especially apparent as the United States mobilized for World War II and in the decades following the war. As Wuthnow has argued, the expansion of the state in twentieth-century America has effectively politicized the culture and blurred the lines between politics and religion.[62]

A second factor has been the attempt by the churches to recognize and come to terms with massive changes in individual and community life. The power of the modern industrial corporation, the disintegrating forces of urbanization, the confrontation with race and poverty, and the changes in family life—all of these and others prompted Presbyterians and other mainstream Protestants to reexamine the vision of their social witness.

A third factor was the break with fundamentalism and the rise of neo-orthodoxy. Despite the differences within the broad movement of neo-orthodoxy, its proponents were committed to two ethical propositions. First, the church must address social and political issues. Second, those issues must include an analysis of the systemic and institutional embodiment of sin in the world. Gradually and with occasional intense opposition, American Presbyterians accepted this more comprehensive understanding of Christian mission and social ethics. The debate was especially intense in the South, where social ethics inevitably posed the agonizing question of race, but the argument raged in all sectors of American Presbyterianism and mainstream Protestantism.

Benton Johnson has concluded that Presbyterians moved from an "old agenda" to a "new agenda" for social ethics during the twentieth century. Johnson studied the General Assembly pronouncements on social issues in the

PCUS, PCUSA, UPCUSA, and PC(USA) from the 1920s
through the 1980s and compared these with the articles and
editorials in the liberal magazine *The Nation*. His research
demonstrates that there has indeed been a shift from one
set of ethical concerns to another and that General Assembly pronouncements did eventually follow the patterns of
American political liberalism.

"The old agenda," Johnson writes, "included observing
the Sabbath; abstaining from alcoholic beverages and such
'worldly amusements' as dancing and card playing; uphold-
ing traditional norms governing gender roles, sexuality, re-
production, and family life; obeying the law and exercising
moral superintendency over various aspects of public life.
The new agenda [on the other hand] has much in common
with the agenda of the political left." The turn was made
gradually and relatively peacefully until the 1960s, when a
new generation of leaders "vastly" expanded the number of
issues which the denomination addressed and accented a
more aggressively liberal perspective.[63]

The only issue that shifted from the old to the new
agenda was a concern for world peace, Johnson finds. But
as Presbyterians became increasingly aware of the complexity of issues and the crises confronting not only American society but the world as a whole, they greatly expanded
their attempts to address these issues and formulated their
response in consistently liberal terms. The new agenda is
particularly noteworthy in its emphasis on four major areas: the awesome devastation of war and the threat of mili-
tarism; the growing gap between rich and poor, not only in
the United States but particularly between the West and the
rest of the world; the confrontation with racism and the
embrace of pluralism; and the reexamination of gender
roles and the family, including sexual ethics.[64]

The new agenda spawned new denominational programs
as well as a host of efforts at the local and regional levels to
educate people about these issues and to engage them in
various activities—ranging from protest movements to
support of organizations working to ameliorate these
problems.

As Johnson points out, however, several critical problems emerged from the new agenda. Though severe conflict came only after the 1960s, the new agenda was largely a result of legislation, rather than education. Leaders at every level of the church neglected to win support for the new agenda, and the chasm between the congregation and denominational structures widened. Furthermore, in the 1960s the denominations subtly shifted the function of these statements from "pronouncements" to "policies," and the change meant that what used to be designed as an educational tool now became the foundation for programs and therefore budgets. The denominations not only shifted their emphases, Johnson argues, but dropped the old agenda almost completely. The rise of the new religious right since the 1960s can in part be explained by its seizure of issues relating to individual morality and family life which Presbyterians and other mainstream Protestants no longer chose to address. Finally, as Mark Noll and Lyman Kellstedt have shown, by the 1980s the shift to the new agenda put denomination policy at odds with the predominant Republican voting preferences of Presbyterians.[65]

A 1970 overture to the PCUS General Assembly stated the problem, according to Johnson, "concisely: The denominational leadership may indeed be 'far ahead—even in the right direction—of its following,' but to 'relentlessly push for courses of action for which no widespread support exists' is a 'sign of failure to lead, i.e., to win the understanding and support of its following.' "[66]

In retrospect, the transformation of American Presbyterian social ethics and its commitments to social justice can be seen as part of a Reformed church's attempt to deal with the problem identified by the social gospel—the structural and institutional character of sin. What began as a debate about the church's mission being either evangelism or social witness has now been resolved. Even a figure such as Jerry Falwell of the new religious right recognizes the need for political involvement by Christians and the responsibility of churches to address social and political problems. What Wuthnow calls the "intrusive" character of the state in American culture has made all religious groups intensely political. The strategies may have been defective; the positions flawed; but the effort by twentieth-century Presbyterians to reformulate their social witness was part of a growing recognition of their privileged place in America and in the global economy. Ironically, as they attempted to distance themselves from their culture, they also embraced an ideology that was itself utterly American and frequently contentious.[67]

Johnson argues that the PC(USA) "needs to develop a third agenda aimed at revitalizing itself as a religious institution and to assign this task a very high priority in the critical period just ahead." He concedes that the old forms of piety, such as Sabbath observance, will be difficult, if not impossible, to restore in American Presbyterianism and mainstream Protestantism. But, he says, "attention must once again be paid to nurturing the spiritual needs of individuals, to providing moral guidance in their intimate relations, to promoting peacemaking and celebration of diversity within the church itself, and to devising new and distinctive forms of spiritual practice that can generate energies for Christian service."[68]

The missions, racial ethnic ministries, ecumenism, and social justice concerns of American Presbyterians in the twentieth century have all been efforts to reach out to the world beyond the denominational community. Contact with that outside society has brought their church new understandings of all four enterprises. But the vitality of each endeavor depends ultimately on the denomination's regular cultivation of its internal religious resources.

7

The Ecology for Nurturing Faith: Education, Disciplines, and Programs for Faith Development

Commenting on the teaching ministry of the church, John Calvin declared, "We see how God, who could in a moment perfect his own, nevertheless desires [Christians] to grow up into [adulthood] solely under the education of the church."[1] From Calvin and other Protestant Reformers has come a concern, if not an obsession, with education that has transformed Western culture and much of the world.

The commitment of Reformed Christians to education began as a theological mandate. Each person had to encounter the gospel personally. That encounter came by reading God's Word—translated into the language of the people. Therefore, everyone needed to know how to read. If a person could not read scripture and encounter the gospel personally, then the collective body of believers—the church—would have fallen short of its responsibility before God. From these theological roots grew the ideal of universal literacy—one of the most revolutionary changes in the last five hundred years. Though now secularized, this ideal was rooted in the Protestant affirmation of scripture as the source of authority and salvation, and it played a major role in the development of education in the modern world.[2]

The Reformed tradition has placed extraordinary emphasis on the educational mission of the church. The Second Helvetic Confession highlighted this calling in almost brutally frank words. "The greater part of meetings for worship," it declared, should be "given to evangelical teaching," rather than "excessively long and irksome public prayers" or "overlong sermons."[3]

Furthermore, the Reformed tradition stressed the biblical affirmation of the goodness of all creation, which meant that the entire scope of human knowledge was worthy of study. Calvin himself argued that knowledge of God and knowledge of self were inextricably linked. The Genevan Academy, established by city leaders committed to the Reformation, epitomized this broad emphasis on nurture and education. According to Calvin, it should prepare students both for the ministry and for political responsibility. Latin grammar and rhetoric, followed by more classics and Greek language study, served as the basis for professional training in theology, medicine, and law. The Genevan Academy, the model for Reformed schools in many countries, also set the standards for other educational institutions, both Protestant and Catholic.[4]

Calvinists who settled the American colonies brought with them this vision of education for the sake of the church and society. A mere ten years after their arrival in Massachusetts, Calvinist Puritans banded together to establish Harvard College. They did so because they feared a day when their present ministers would "lie in the dust," and they sought to raise another generation of leaders, both clergy and laity, "to advance learning and perpetuate it to posterity." Seventeen years later in 1647, they passed the first public education law in history. Known as "Ye Ould Deluder Satan" law since illiteracy was associated with the Devil, it was intended to ensure "that learning may not be buried in the grave of our fathers in the church and the commonwealth." The famous nineteenth-century educator Horace Mann later observed, "As a fact, it had no precedent in world history, and as a theory, it could have been refuted and silenced by a formidable array of argument and experience."[5]

Throughout the colonial period, Calvinists and other Protestants continued to establish schools and colleges, and the church remained a powerful institution of education in its own right. The family, however, supplemented by participation in congregational worship, was the principal agent for nurturing faith and knowledge of Christianity. Keeping journals, reading the Bible and manuals of spiritual instruction, as well as family devotions were hallmarks of pious Calvinist homes.[6]

These practices and commitments shaped colonial American Presbyterianism, and after the American Revolution as the denomination began to emerge, the educational mission broadened dramatically.

"What will become of the West," asked the Congregationalist-Presbyterian minister Lyman Beecher in 1835, "if her prosperity rushes up to such a majesty of power, while those great institutions linger which are necessary to form the mind, and the conscience, and the heart of that vast world." Alarmed by the infidelity and uncivilized life of the frontier, Beecher cried, "We must educate! We must educate! or we must perish by our own prosperity."[7]

Presbyterians and other evangelical Protestants answered that call during the nineteenth century by constructing an elaborate system of education and nurture—within the church and for society. Because of the Calvinist affirmation of culture as potentially redeemable rather than essentially evil, Presbyterians and other Reformed Christians participated enthusiastically in the evangelical quest for a "Christian America." Furthermore, because of their religious and cultural prominence, Presbyterians and evangelical Protestants of the nineteenth century were unusually successful at constructing a network of institutions and practices that together comprised an ecology for nurturing faith. These structures and exercises of piety not only nourished one another but also, more importantly, stimulated and sustained individual faith and discipleship, denominational identity, and a favorable environment for mainstream Protestant churches in the larger society.

During the twentieth century, this ecology changed significantly. In some cases, the transformation of mainstream Protestantism's nurturing ecology produced creative responses to the dilemmas of Christianity in the modern world. In other instances, its consequences were detrimental to faith development and spiritual vitality. However it is viewed, the story of this ecology's development in the twentieth century illumines the problems and challenges confronting contemporary Presbyterianism and mainstream Protestantism, both as institutions and as communities of faith.

The Family and the Sabbath

When American Presbyterians founded their General Assembly in 1788, they adopted a *Directory for Worship* that contained a chapter on "secret and family worship." "Besides the public worship in congregations, it is the indispensable duty of each person, alone in secret; and of every family, by itself, in private, to pray to, and worship God," the *Directory* declared. Family worship consisted of "prayer, reading the Scriptures, and singing praises." It was led by "the head of the household," presumably the father, and all were to attend, including "children and servants." Another chapter on "the sanctification of the Lord's Day" declared: "It is the duty of every person to remember the Lord's Day; and to prepare for it, before its approach." Furthermore, "The whole day is to be kept holy to the Lord; and to be employed in the public and private exercises of religion."[8]

Family worship and the Sabbath constituted two central ingredients in the nurture of American Presbyterians and evangelical Protestants throughout the nineteenth century. Worship by families was critical because the religious and political theorists of the early American republic believed that the family was the foundation for a free and moral society. As John Adams put it in 1778, "The foundations of national Morality must be laid in private families."[9]

Although the *Directory for Worship* emphasized the role of the father, evangelical Protestants of the nineteenth century increasingly turned to the mother as the embodiment and transmitter of Christianity and the home as "the sacred hearth." Thousands of sermons, tracts, books, and articles portrayed what Barbara Welter calls "the cult of true womanhood." Its attributes were "piety, purity, submissiveness, and domesticity," and women both judged themselves and were judged by their ability to fulfill this ideal. According to Nancy F. Cott, religion or piety was considered the core of woman's virtue, the source of her strength.[10]

The emphasis upon the family as the foundation of social morality and the mother as the bearer of religion was due to a shift in the economic role of the family. In colonial America, families were centers of economic production, and women played a key role in the generation of food and income. As industrialization and urbanization changed the character of American life, the family and the mother became consumers rather than producers. The "cult of true womanhood" became a form of bondage that restricted the sphere of women's activity, and yet it also forged bonds—principally through Bible study groups and women's organizations—that gave women the opportunity to share common experiences. Paradoxically, the ideas about women's role tied them to husbands, children, home, and piety, and yet the bonds linked them to one another and provided the foundation for the rise of modern feminism.[11]

It is difficult to know how pervasive the ideal of family worship was in nineteenth-century America. One of the rich and unwritten chapters in the history of American religion is in fact the discovery of the religious lives of the American people—how, in fact, people experienced their faith and transmitted it to others. What is known is that Presbyterians and other evangelical Protestants made strenuous attempts to establish family worship as an ideal. A flood of newspapers, novels, books, tracts, popular art, and music described family prayer, Bible study, and hymn singing as the necessary ingredients to prepare the individual for the critical moment of life—conversion to Jesus Christ.[12]

By contrast, the twentieth century dramatically changed the character of the modern family and the church's understanding of family worship. Sociologists and historians hotly debate whether the family is declining, but there is no disputing that it has changed. From 1960 to 1990, the divorce rate has increased by 406 percent. During the same period, the percentage of children living with only one parent rose from 9 to 25 percent. From 1965 to 1985, the rate of childbirth to unwed mothers rose from 5 to 22 percent, and the percentage of teenage mothers jumped from 15 to 58 percent. Americans who spend their adult lives with both a spouse and at least one child dropped from 62 percent in 1965, which was the highest in American history, to 43 percent in 1985, the lowest in our history.[13] Similarly, the evangelical Protestant ideal of the nineteenth-century woman has been destroyed—partly due to changes in American society but also to a broader and deeper recognition of sexual equality in the Christian faith.

The family remained a part of the ministry of twentieth-century Presbyterians and mainstream Protestants, but its focus shifted decisively. Parents had signed Family Altar pledges in the first years of the century, promising devotions with their children on a daily basis; by the second half of the century few Presbyterian families took time for daily worship together. Even so, the current *Directory for Worship* still contains pertinent direction about the practice: "Given the complexity of schedules and the separations incurred in daily occupations, it is especially important to cultivate the discipline of regular household worship."[14]

Psychology and the pastoral counseling movement had a powerful impact on the understanding of ministry with families. It had a significant influence on theological seminaries and the training of ministers, particularly after World War II. Until the 1980s, much of the pastoral counseling movement was sometimes hostile to theology and suspicious of piety, arguing that religious belief often veiled more deeply rooted problems. The changing structure of the American family and psychological understandings of family systems transformed mainstream Protestantism's approach to the family itself. To some degree, the family declined in significance in the ministry of mainstream Protestant denominations because it had fragmented into so many different forms. But the family also became less the molder of social morals and the bearer of Christian faith; rather, it became "a haven in a heartless world."[15]

The shift can also be traced in the changing character of devotional literature in the twentieth century. Early twentieth-century Presbyterian literature for private study and personal spiritual growth was remarkably uniform. It accented the Bible, the transcendence of God, and exemplary figures from church history. Gradually "a new language of spiritual life" stressing self-fulfillment and wholeness developed alongside and was interwoven with traditional categories of Christian piety. Despite the influence of neo-orthodoxy with its emphasis on the depth of human sin and the transcendence of God, the popular literature produced by Presbyterians highlighted the immanence of God and self-fulfillment. Church history virtually disappeared, and the literature increasingly reflected a diversity of images, concepts, and languages for describing the Christian life.[16]

Nineteenth-century American Presbyterians and evangelical Protestants also made Sabbath observance a centerpiece of their effort to Christianize American culture. Meeting after meeting of the General Assembly in the 1800s bemoaned the lack of proper adherence to the Sabbath, and Presbyterians joined other evangelical Protestants in protecting the sanctity of the Sabbath by protesting the delivery of mail on Sundays and by advocating other forms of "blue laws" that became common in American society. Sabbatarianism was based on the Bible, specifically the fourth commandment, and on the theological grounds of natural law. Failure to observe the Sabbath was a violation of the order of creation ordained by God; a civilized

society rested on the sanctity of the Sabbath. As the PCUS
General Assembly declared in 1908, "If the Christian sabbath goes, all is gone."[17]

In a startling about-face, Presbyterians and mainstream
Protestants in the twentieth century abandoned Sabbath
observance as a major social and religious concern. According to Benton Johnson, they simply dropped the subject. In
a review of minutes of the General Assemblies for the
PCUS, PCUSA, and UPCNA, Johnson notes that long reports on Sabbath observance continued into the early twentieth century. But by the 1930s, the subject disappeared
from view. It was, of course, a concession to the growing
pluralism and secularity of American society. Roman
Catholics, for example, never shared the Reformed obsession with Sabbath restrictions and the prohibition of
amusements and recreation. But Johnson also notes that
Sabbath observance represented a form of spiritual discipline and the creation of sacred time, which all religions
must have to maintain their vitality and appeal. The old
sabbatarianism, he acknowledges, cannot and should not
be revived; however, how individuals and churches intentionally structure their time remains a compelling challenge for Christian nurture and discipleship.[18]

The Sunday School

During the nineteenth century the Sunday school
emerged as the primary means of nurture and education
among evangelical Protestants. It has become so much a
part of the fabric of twentieth-century congregations that it
is difficult to imagine that there were no Sunday schools
two centuries ago. The movement began in late eighteenth-
century England as an effort to teach the urban poor—both
adults and children—basic literacy and the rudiments of
Christian morality and doctrine.[19] Imported to the United
States, the Sunday school movement initially operated independently of Protestant denominations, but it was
quickly incorporated into the churches and became a staple
of congregational life.

As the nineteenth century progressed, the focus of the Sunday school shifted from outreach through the education of the illiterate poor to biblical and theological study for the church's own membership. This weighty mission for the Sunday school prompted the development in the twentieth century of a new professional class of church leaders—the director of Christian education (D.C.E.) or Christian educator. In contrast to the pastoral minister, Christian educators remained members of their congregations after installation and were certified rather than ordained to their position. In 1987 the PC(USA) dramatically expanded the certification process for Christian educators, and occupants of such leadership positions were given a voice in both session and presbytery.[20]

Actual participation of church members in the Sunday school was high early in this century. The ratio of Sunday school students to church members in 1900 was .7 to 1 in the PCUS, 1 to 1 in the PCUSA and .9 to 1 in the UPCNA. High ratios for the PCUSA and the UPCNA continued through the early decades of the twentieth century, but by the end of World War II, they had dropped to levels of .8 to 1 and .6 to 1 respectively. The PCUS, in contrast, actually improved its Sunday school ratio by reaching a peak of .8 to 1 in the 1950s. However, since 1960 Presbyterians have witnessed a significant drop in Sunday school attendance. At the time of their 1983 merger, PCUS enrollment had slumped from 750,793 in 1960 to 385,256, and UPCUSA involvement had fallen from 1,936,930 in 1960 to 811,997. Currently, 1,143,506 individuals take part in their congregation's church school, even though the denomination reported 2,856,713 members in 1990.[21]

Along with staffing and participation, the content of Presbyterian Sunday school instruction has also experienced some significant changes. Nineteenth-century Sunday schools, according to Craig Dykstra and Brad Wigger, used the Bible and a vast array of tracts and pamphlets that outlined Christian faith and discipleship. This was its curriculum, but the material was noteworthy because it focused primarily on the content of the Bible and transmission of Christian doctrine. Because the material was eclectic and diverse, no one expected any uniformity or standardization of how people were nurtured in Christian faith. The key to the nineteenth-century Sunday school, they argue, was the teachers and their ability to communicate their own faith and inspire others with their example.[22]

Curriculum materials changed in the late nineteenth and early twentieth centuries. The corporate ideal of the denomination moved Presbyterians and other Protestants to regularize the lessons and standardize the curriculum. The emphasis subtly shifted away from the content of Christian faith and piety to the process of teaching itself, away from the student to the teacher. They note that the PCUSA's *Christian Faith and Life* curriculum and the PCUS's Covenant Life Curriculum partially reversed this trend by relying upon books written by theologians, but the genre of curriculum materials returned to its focus on teaching and teachers in the 1970s and 1980s.[23]

David Hester has also studied how the Presbyterian Christian education curricula have used the Bible in the twentieth century. He notes that the material mirrors theological changes and increasing pluralism, but he also analyzes the increasing sophistication of curricula as they attempted to make use of modern biblical criticism. As the material focused increasingly on the process of teaching, it also placed a heavier burden on the teacher's ability to deal with complex issues of interpretation. The corporate denomination's curriculum required professionals, expert in teaching and schooled by modern scholarship.[24] Robert Wood Lynn and Elliot Wright identify the professionalization of Sunday school teachers after World War II as a major problem.[25] Teachers with the requisite skills could not be recruited to teach the sophisticated material; congregations experimented with other, simpler material; and the fragmentation of Christian education curricula increased.

But beneath the fragmenting of Christian education curricula is not only a change in the type or genre of material. Dykstra and Wigger's survey of Presbyterian curricula suggests that the preoccupation with the problem of how to teach may obscure a deeper issue—what to teach, or our understanding of the gospel itself.[26] Christian education curricula thus demonstrate the dilemmas of American Presbyterians as they sought to fashion a Christian identity amid theological pluralism.

Congregational Worship

When people become Christians, they join congregations, and besides the Sunday school, worship has the most powerful influence on the growth of individuals in the knowledge and love of God. Contemporary worship services are, of course, notoriously diverse. Just as it is difficult to know what is happening in the minds and hearts of people as they worship today, it is equally difficult to reconstruct what the experience of worship has been historically. Similarly, the fascinating question of whether worship in the twentieth century is qualitatively better or worse than worship in some other era eludes a conclusive answer, based on historical data. However, some preliminary research concludes that American Presbyterians at least conceive of worship differently today, and their theological pluralism produces diverse ways of approaching God.

The Protestant Reformation, according to James Hastings Nichols, was actually a revolution in Christian worship. It restored the sermon to the worship life of Christians. John H. Leith has also argued that "the Protestant Reformation was born in the conviction that the church could be revived and reformed by preaching 'the most holy gospel of the glory and grace of God.' "[27] The Reformed tradition placed special emphasis on preaching, and the results have been profound and pervasive. In addition to the translation of the Bible into the vernacular, the sermon democratized Christianity, opening the mysteries of faith to the mind of each individual and making its appeal conditional not only on the work of the Holy Spirit but also the persuasive power of the preacher. Just as Protestantism and especially Calvinism played a role in the rise of democratic forms of government in the Western world, the sermon influenced democracy's dependence upon the spoken word and suasion to secure popular assent.

Worship in Calvin's Geneva did not break radically with the liturgical character of the Roman Mass, except in its emphasis on the sermon. But the later Reformed tradition, especially English Puritanism, increasingly simplified the service to purify it of "Romish" or "papist" elements. A typical American colonial Presbyterian service consisted of singing two or three psalms, the reading of scripture, a long sermon of an hour and a half to two hours, and a pastoral prayer of approximately forty-five minutes. Sermons followed a threefold plan: the explication of the text, the development of the doctrine of the text, and the application of the doctrine to the life of the believer. The Great Awakenings and the rise of evangelicalism introduced hymns—some sedate and serene, others boisterous and emotional—and a new purpose for preaching—conversion. The classic evangelical sermon of the nineteenth century called for an individual to make a decision for Christ.[28]

Even during the nineteenth century, complaints were voiced about Presbyterian preachers' sermons as "dry" and uninspiring, and measured against the more enthusiastic styles of their Methodist or Baptist counterparts, the charge was likely true.[29] The formalism of scholastic Calvinism and its uneasiness with the evangelical emphasis on free will made it difficult for many Presbyterian preachers to duplicate the intensity of revivalistic preaching. Yet the extant sermons of Presbyterian preachers of the nineteenth century display a common evangelical conviction to proclaim the truth of an infallible Bible and an identical concern for individual salvation.[30]

By the late nineteenth and early twentieth centuries, Presbyterians were among the "princes" of the pulpit of urban America. They "filled" pulpits. As John McClure declares, "No matter what the theological issue, social problem, or historical movement, the Presbyterian pulpit was widely perceived as an authoritative platform for processing information, debating perspectives, and generating interest and involvement in the first three decades of this century." Presbyterian and mainstream Protestant preachers were secure in their authority and confident of their message. As one Presbyterian minister boasted in 1932, "By reason of his training and personal equipment every preacher in our Church—from the smallest mission church to the largest city church—is prepared to do great preaching. It is not the size of the field—(is there any difference in the size of fields?)—but the size of the man that makes great preaching."[31]

As the evangelical consensus shattered and as mainstream Protestants lost their cultural dominance in the twentieth century, preachers sought to reconstruct their authority, redefine their methods, and revise their message. McClure documents the anxious twentieth-century quest for a compelling and viable method of preaching among Presbyterian and mainstream Protestant preachers and theorists of preaching. Although neo-orthodoxy temporarily gave new authority and impetus for preaching from Karl Barth's emphasis on the centrality of the Word of God, preachers found it increasingly difficult to preach authoritatively in a society that no longer accorded automatic respect for them, their office, and their message.

The single greatest challenge, argues McClure, came from modern science, which redefined truth as "subjective, situational, and verifiable only through the five human senses." As preachers struggled to make sermons more amenable to science, they employed psychology to answer the questions of self-identity or sociology to address the crises of society. The result, says McClure, has been the fragmentation of preaching theory into myriad schools of methodology, the reduction of theological substance in sermons, and competing interpretations of gospel itself.[32]

Preachers in the PCUS were less vulnerable to pluralism, according to Beverly Zink, and their sermons retained a strong evangelical concern with individual salvation well into the twentieth century. The cultural displacement of mainstream Protestantism advanced much more slowly in the South, and the dominant evangelical ethos of southern Protestantism reinforced continuity in Presbyterian preaching. Yet Zink also notes that PCUS preachers were not immune to the struggle of the denomination's debate over the spirituality of the church and the role of the pulpit in addressing social issues, such as segregation. By mid-century, PCUS preachers were also introducing the psychological and sociological themes of mainstream Protestantism, trying to articulate a gospel amid the ambiguities of increasing social conflict and cultural change.[33]

Presbyterian worship services also reveal significant alterations in the twentieth century. The earlier Puritan influence in the Reformed tradition simplified worship at the expense of liturgical richness, and nineteenth-century evangelicalism exacerbated the tendency toward simplicity and spontaneity. What was gained was exuberance, but the service inevitably depended on the gifts and talents of the individual minister. What was also lost was historical ties with the worship of Christians throughout the centuries and a broader appreciation of liturgy itself.

Beginning in the late nineteenth century, liturgical reform swept through American Presbyterianism. In 1906, the PCUSA adopted *The Book of Common Worship*, and for the first time it "recommended" forms for services and prayers for worship. Even though it predated the full-scale adoption of the corporate ideal of denominational organization, *The Book of Common Worship* and the liturgical reform movement were spurred by a similar instinct to regularize what had previously been improvised. Despite Loetscher's contention that the book "was a definite step in the direction of greater dignity and beauty of worship," it is equally true that the corporate denomination needed common manuals for its corporate worship.[34]

Subsequent worship materials in twentieth-century Presbyterianism increasingly drew from the history of the Reformed churches and ecumenically from other Protestant, Roman Catholic, and Orthodox traditions. Ronald Byars argues that this recovery recaptured the pre-Puritan attempt of the Reformers to maintain continuity with the worship of the church catholic and to avoid narrow sectarianism. Yet he

also concedes that "this remarkable ecumenical conver-
gence" in American Presbyterianism has eroded "a sense of
denominational distinctiveness, with a corresponding decrease in denominational loyalty."[35] He further believes that
Presbyterians have gained more than they have lost by worshiping in continuity with Christians in other communions,
but the predicament of ecumenical pluralism in worship is
posed in both the pulpit and the pew.

Similarly, Presbyterian hymnbooks reflect the attempt to
respond to theological and cultural currents of modern
America. At the turn of the twentieth century, only the
UPCNA held on to the Reformed tradition's practice of
singing psalms. In the PCUS and the PCUSA, hymnody
had triumphed. But in the wake of the growing cleavage in
evangelical Protestantism, many congregations sang in two
keys. For Sunday school and informal services, the denominations produced hymnbooks that retained the popular
gospel songs of late nineteenth-century evangelicalism.
Other hymnbooks with more formal hymns were developed for congregational use.[36]

Presbyterian ambivalence about its evangelical heritage
marks all the hymnals of the twentieth century. *The Hymnal*, issued in 1933, was an extraordinary work. On the one
hand, its selection of hymns kept it in print even in the late
twentieth century. On the other hand, the volume is redo-
lent of establishment Presbyterianism, with headings in
gothic type and with a careful excision of virtually all gospel songs or hymns of American evangelicalism. The 1955
Hymnbook was equally reticent about evangelical hymnody. *The Worshipbook* of 1972 attempted to capture the
growing awareness of hymns from other Christian traditions and includes a significant number of African American spirituals. Yet in the midst of the theological turmoil of
the 1960s and 1970s, the editors of *The Worshipbook* simply arranged hymns in alphabetical order, rather than trying to group them theologically or order them according to
the church year. In 1990 the PC(USA) issued *The Presbyterian Hymnal*. It is noteworthy for its ecumenical and cultural diversity, its sensitivity to inclusive language, and its

attempt to recover the earlier Reformed emphasis on singing psalms.[37]

These changes in how Presbyterian denominations ordered worship may not tell us much about the actual worship of congregations. Clearly the enduring independence
of Presbyterian congregations allows them to pick and
choose among the denominational materials. In both
Christian education curricula and worship resources, Presbyterians are eclectic in what they buy and, therefore, what
they teach and how they worship.

It should be noted, however, that just as its official publications became more ecumenical and aimed at unifying the
body of Christ, the same ecumenical spirit encouraged congregations to use materials from any other denomination
and from nondenominational sources as well. Furthermore, the richness and diversity of contemporary worship
materials, like Christian education curricula, depend on
well-informed, well-educated experts in the history of worship and Christian hymnody. The result is unquestionably
an improvement in quality. Less clear is whether these resources are accessible enough to nonexperts, or even sufficiently popular, to nurture Presbyterians in congregations
and move them to worship God in spirit and in truth.

Higher Education

The Reformed and Presbyterian love affair with higher
education began in colonial America. Harvard represented
the first of these efforts by Reformed Congregationalists,
and a host of academies and colleges, such as Princeton,
emerged as indigenous American institutions to educate
the colonial population. Most of the colonial colleges were
founded by church leaders but not as church institutions.
Woodrow Wilson once observed that Princeton was a Presbyterian institution, not because of its affiliation but because Presbyterians were "wise and progressive enough" to
found it. This pattern continued in the nineteenth century
with even state universities, such as the universities of Tennessee, Delaware, California, North Carolina, Georgia, and

South Carolina—all of which owe their origins and early development to Presbyterians. But in the nineteenth century, specifically denominational colleges appeared. Between 1780 and 1829 Presbyterians were responsible for the initiation of thirteen of the forty colleges established in the United States. By 1860, 49 of the 180 church-related colleges were Presbyterian.[38]

Presbyterian colleges at the beginning of the twentieth century numbered more than one hundred. Most of these drew students from other denominations as well as from Presbyterian families. But a Presbyterian educational atmosphere predominated, including instruction in the Bible, the strict enforcement of social regulations forbidding the use of alcohol and placing restrictions on visitations between men and women. Presbyterian colleges were intended not only for the sons and daughters of the church, for in Appalachia, the Ozarks, and among African Americans and Native Americans, Presbyterian colleges embodied a mission to reach out to young people from families without backgrounds in higher education or exposure to Presbyterianism.[39]

During the late nineteenth century, the dominance of Presbyterians and mainstream Protestants over higher education began to decline, producing a major shift in the character of these institutions—public and private—and the nature of higher education itself. The influences producing this transformation came from both the culture and the church. Government-sponsored institutions gradually expanded, particularly after World War II. Throughout the twentieth century, public institutions steadily attracted students and funds from church-related colleges' own religious constituencies, compelling schools to find students and financial support outside of the denominations. Colleges and universities, chartered by Presbyterians and other mainstream Protestants, also sought academic excellence by adhering to the secular ideals of modern universities like Johns Hopkins and by meeting the criteria of accrediting organizations and philanthropic foundations. The impulse to mitigate the influence of the church was part of an idealistic reform of church-related higher education, rooted in the desire for academic vigor and quality.[40]

Within mainstream Protestantism, other factors were working—often unwittingly—to reduce ties to the denominations and diminish the specifically Christian character of the colleges themselves. The division in nineteenth-century evangelicalism broke the momentum in founding liberal arts colleges. After the Civil War and into the early twentieth century, church-related colleges frequently offered a hospitable environment to more liberal theological perspectives. Conservatives became increasingly concerned, producing a striking shift and the development of a new and unique institution of higher education. Before the Civil War, evangelicals founded liberal arts colleges. After the war, they founded Bible schools, colleges, and institutes—the Moody Bible Institute (1886) being the most notable.[41]

The process of weakening ties between the church-related colleges and their denominations was gradual but consistent. Presidents were an early indicator—drawn less and less from the ranks of the clergy. The nature of boards of trustees also changed—with fewer ministers, less ecclesiastical control over selection, and eventually membership by people who did not belong to the sponsoring church or even to any church. Faculties followed suit. Curricula were changed to reduce, then minimize, and finally in some schools to eliminate any required instruction in Christianity or religion.

The UPCUSA's new guidelines for its colleges in 1963 represented a later stage in this development as they declared that each institution should "seek to be a learning community which in word and act will provide for intellectual advancement and religious growth, and . . . undertake to carry out the ethical implication of the faith it represents." No longer were faculty members expected to be church members; instead, they should be "dedicated to [the college's] declared institutional purpose and . . . faithfully serve the primary objective of academic excellence in a community which encourages true piety with integrity of thought and character." Rather than requiring a course in

Bible, Christianity, or even religious studies, the guidelines called for "a mature classroom encounter with the Judaic-Christian heritage."[42]

The discipline of student life was another barometer of decreasing church influence—the abandonment of required chapel services, the relaxation of rules regarding dress, alcohol, tobacco, and social activities. All were gradually loosened or abandoned in the face of student opposition, institutional tolerance, and changing cultural mores. Early in the century, church-related colleges responded to the new situation by creating campus chaplains, and these ministries flourished until the 1960s. Since then, these chaplains have often been increasingly marginalized from both students and the life of the colleges.[43]

The disengagement of church-related colleges from the Presbyterian and other mainstream Protestant denominations was strikingly peaceful and even encouraged by the denominations themselves. Part of the reason lies in the assumption of Presbyterians and mainstream Protestants that they would continue to exercise dominance over American culture and its institutions. Part of the explanation also involves the degree to which members and leaders accepted the rise of secular norms of higher education and wanted them infused into church-related institutions.[44]

Few saw the emerging secularity of higher education and the shift from private, church-related colleges to public, government-supported institutions as a threat. Even Woodrow Wilson's father and uncle, both of whom were Presbyterian ministers, encouraged him to pursue his doctorate at Johns Hopkins only a few years after its founding. But by 1990, the presidents of the sixty-nine Presbyterian colleges and universities warned that "the Presbyterian Church could be close to the point where its involvement in higher education might be lost forever."[45]

Presbyterians and mainstream Protestants were confronted with, in Robert Wood Lynn's words, "a ministry on the margin" of higher education.[46] But they also witnessed the dramatic weakening of one of the key institutions that formed the ecology for nurturing faith in American Presbyterianism and mainstream Protestantism. Church-related colleges strengthened denominational ties. They comprised an effective feeder system for candidates for ministry. They supplied several generations of lay leaders in the denominations. The Christian college is not dead; its contributions to church life will continue. But its ties to the church are frayed and its role unclear.

Theological Education

American Presbyterians of the early twentieth century, according to Lefferts A. Loetscher, were "a decidedly conservative force in theological education."[47] Dominated by scholastic Calvinism or the Princeton theology, the Presbyterian seminaries were nevertheless swept by theological and social changes later in the century that transformed their faculties, students, and curricula. Their responses altered their identity and function within the denominations and significantly shaped the idea of ministry itself.

Presbyterians and other evangelical Protestants of the nineteenth century established seminaries for two reasons: to provide ministers and to support their theological or confessional position. The founding charter of Princeton Seminary captures the vision. The Seminary "is to provide for the church an adequate supply and succession of able and faithful ministers of the New Testament; workmen that *need not to be ashamed*, being qualified *rightly to divide the word of truth*." Capturing the Reformed tradition's emphasis on the breadth of education and the unity of piety and intellect, the plan declared: "It is to unite, in those who shall sustain the ministerial office, religion and literature; that piety of the heart which is the fruit only of the renewing and sanctifying grace of God, with solid learning: believing that religion without learning, or learning without religion, in the ministers of the Gospel, must ultimately prove injurious to the Church."[48]

Nineteenth-century seminaries strongly emphasized knowledge of the Bible, and though Greek and Hebrew and sometimes Latin were required, most biblical instruction centered on the English text. Theology and church history provided the remainder of the curriculum. Courses in the practice of ministry were minimized; students sometimes taught one another, or they simply picked up the skills in area churches or after leaving seminary. Students' faith and piety were nurtured informally by the faculty and by other students; but piety was primarily treated as a private, individual matter. Faculty members were self-educated scholars in their fields. No doctoral programs in theology existed in nineteenth-century America, and few American theological students studied at European universities.

In the 1920s and 1930s, the fundamentalist controversy swept through American Presbyterianism, affecting all the seminaries and especially Princeton. After Machen's departure, the Seminary reorganized its confusing and chaotic system of two boards, and it slowly rebuilt its devastated faculty. A new generation of faculty members was appointed at all of the Presbyterian seminaries. Increasingly they held doctorates, and with them they brought the movement of neo-orthodoxy into the theological curriculum and American Presbyterianism.[49]

Presbyterian seminaries have consistently been relatively small institutions with relatively few faculty members. The faculty consequently has a tremendous influence on the character of the curriculum and on the identity of the institution.

The shift could occasionally be dramatic. For example, prior to 1936 the theology curriculum at Louisville Seminary consisted of reading the works of Charles Hodge, leavened by those of James Henley Thornwell. In 1936 Hugh T. Kerr, with a doctorate from the University of Edinburgh, was appointed to the faculty. Hodge and Thornwell disappeared from the Louisville curriculum, replaced by the theologies of Karl Barth, Emil Brunner, and other neo-orthodox thinkers.[50]

By the 1930s Presbyterian seminaries were not only feeling the influence of the modern university and its scholarly expectations; they were also leaders in forming an accrediting agency for theological schools. Two Presbyterians, Edward Roberts of Princeton and Lewis Sherrill of Louisville, and one Lutheran, Luther Weigle of Yale, played the key role in establishing the American Association of Theological Schools in 1926. The impulse to standardize educational norms and to enforce them by accreditation was a reform aimed at reducing the anarchy of seminaries' curricula and improving academic standards. It breathed the spirit of the corporate denomination's desire for standardization. It also introduced another authority for theological seminaries that potentially competed with their denominational loyalties.[51]

The resolution of the fundamentalist controversy implicitly posed a dilemma for the Presbyterian seminaries. By decentralizing theological authority and lodging it in presbyteries, the General Assembly of the PCUSA never addressed the question of the confessional standards for ordination. This raised the implicit question of the role of the seminaries as the preservers of the confessional tradition. Subtly, their role shifted from defending and imparting a particular theological perspective to helping students develop their own theologies. In the words of the Dubuque Seminary catalog in 1937, the goal of theological study was "to help students to think their way through to an adequate Christian philosophy, a comprehensive synthesis of beliefs, rather than to place the emphasis on a purely dogmatic theology."[52] The change was minor at the time, but this emphasis on the individual contributed eventually to the flowering of pluralism in Presbyterian theology and the denominations' seminaries.

Any shift in the confessional character of the Presbyterian schools was veiled by the new consensus forged by neo-orthodoxy. By the 1950s it had replaced the Princeton theology and reigned supreme at all the Presbyterian seminaries of the PCUS, PCUSA, and UPCNA. Seminary enrollments increased, riding the wave of returning and religiously inspired GIs from World War II and the Korean war, and fueled by the domestic postwar religious revival. The encouragement to critique social problems found in popular American neo-orthodox theologians like Reinhold

Niebuhr produced an explosion of courses in social ethics. The pastoral counseling movement spawned still more. The seminaries vastly expanded their offerings in the practice of ministry and developed extensive programs in field education. The vision of ministry broadened; the necessary skills multiplied; specialization and professional criteria were prized.[53]

The 1960s witnessed the arrival of the first baby boomers on Presbyterian seminary campuses and the beginning of institutional ferment. Students participated in the civil rights and anti–Vietnam war movements and turned their anti-institutional attack on the seminaries themselves. Many Presbyterian seminaries abruptly abandoned all required courses in favor of requirements in various fields, and then some just as quickly reinstituted required courses. The curriculum fragmented, with faculty competing for student time in their disciplines and with successive waves of new theological emphases. Interest in Roman Catholic theologians introduced diversity into the neo-orthodox theological instruction of the 1960s, followed by African American, feminist, and Third World theologians, as well as theologians from a diverse array of philosophical perspectives. The coherence of the biblical theology movement shattered, and in its place arose competing schools of biblical interpretation that stressed the diversity rather than the unity of scripture.[54]

The 1970s and 1980s brought increasing demands on the seminaries in the face of declining financial support from the Presbyterian denominations. Students were far less likely to be lifelong products of Presbyterian nurture, and they sought more help in strengthening their faith and deepening their piety. The seminaries responded by developing programs of spiritual formation or development. As Steve Hancock has found, the more the seminaries did, the less satisfied students were with institutional support for their spiritual journeys. However, the emphasis on social ethics in the curriculum did make students aware of the interrelationship between piety and social justice.[55]

As the corporate denomination stumbled during the 1970s and 1980s, the Presbyterian seminaries expanded the scope of their programs and began to fulfill some of functions previously exercised by denominational agencies. Continuing education programs multiplied. The new Doctor of Ministry degree brought in hundreds of students for study and certification of their professional competence. Seminaries initiated and then broadened educational offerings for lay people—courses, seminars, conferences. Facing the continued decline of denominational funding, they appealed directly to congregations and individuals, and they successfully financed their new programs. Amid the denominational revolution since the 1950s, the network of Presbyterian theological institutions became a complement to the organization of the denomination itself—virtually an *ecclesiola in ecclesia,* or a denomination within a denomination.

Beneath the surface rumbled the predicament of pluralism unleashed by the 1960s. During the 1970s and 1980s, Presbyterian seminary faculties were finally transformed from white, male bastions into groups of men and women, who included some teachers from racial ethnic minorities. The pressure to diversify came from the seminaries' own commitments and from the church, as it sought to be more representative of American society and the global church. Pluralism became an ideal, embodied in institutional and intellectual life forms of its own. Pluralism resisted attempts to forge a distinctive Reformed theological or ecclesiastical identity. As Mulder and Wyatt concluded, "Presbyterian seminary campuses were no longer bastions of scholastic Calvinism or even neo-orthodoxy but forums for diversity. A majority of faculty and students continued to be Presbyterian, but theological education became an ecumenical and increasingly cross-cultural exploration of the nature of Christian faith and witness."[56]

Denominational Programs of Nurture

Families and congregations are the primary sources of nurture for individuals, but denominations also provide programs that are an important part of their ecology for nurturing faith. Throughout the nineteenth century, most denominational programs were haphazard, experimental, even entrepreneurial. In the twentieth century, the corporate denomination regularized and even strengthened them, only to see them fragmented and weakened by changes in the denominations and in the culture. Examples of this pattern are Presbyterian sponsorship of publishing houses, denominational journals, and women's and men's organizations.

Publishing Houses

In the nineteenth century, Presbyterians understood part of their evangelistic charge to be providing books to people. Initially, they used the various benevolent societies, but later they established their own board of publication to publish and distribute the works through a system of colporteurs or traveling book salespeople. As one General Assembly declared, "One cannot lay the foundations of the Presbyterian Church without books. Other churches may do without them, but we cannot." The books ranged from sermons, tracts, and pamphlets to serious theological works, including Calvin's *Institutes*, to hymnbooks and music to inspirational literature. The strategy worked. As late as 1907 the General Assembly of the PCUSA received a report that 1,065 congregations ascribed their origins to these colporteurs, and five years later 1,500 congregations cited the distribution of literature as key to their development.[57]

In the twentieth century, the PCUS, the UPCNA, and the PCUSA established their own publishing houses—John Knox Press, Geneva Press, and Westminster Press. From the 1930s through the 1960s, the publishing houses flourished under strong leadership and with denominational blessing. Successful Christian education materials provided the income for less profitable scholarly works. Westminster published a highly successful line of children's books and even instituted an $8,000 prize for fiction in 1948. Presses increasingly saw themselves as having a mission to reach a broad public interested in religious literature, not as agencies serving only a Presbyterian constituency.[58]

That vision went largely unchallenged as long as adequate financial resources and denominational consensus prevailed. But as John Trotti and Richard Ray have shown, both UPCUSA and PCUS presses were caught in a financial and theological crossfire from the 1960s through the 1980s. Within the denominational bureaucracies, publishers competed against other agencies looking longingly at one part of the structure that generated income and enjoyed relative financial independence. Furthermore, the surpluses generated by Christian education curricula disappeared in the 1970s and 1980s as congregations increasingly rejected the denominational material. The publishers themselves captured the changes in the religious and theological worlds by publishing a few highly controversial books, which further angered opponents who wanted their editorial independence restricted. Financially strapped and politically embattled, the publishing houses merged into Westminster/John Knox Press after the reunion of 1983. Although these dilemmas endure after this union, the merged press has more recently gathered a talented staff and a significant list of titles, in addition to a large backlist, and has fostered a closer relationship with the national church's related ministry units.[59]

Denominational Journals

A comparable pattern developed for denominational magazines. During the nineteenth century, scores of Presbyterian periodicals were published, and they were invariably owned by a minister or a small group of individuals. During the late nineteenth and early twentieth centuries, Presbyterians developed their own magazines for the emerging corporate denomination. The UPCNA established the *United Presbyterian;* the PCUSA founded *Presbyterian Magazine,* buried it in the 1930s, launched the highly successful *Presbyterian Life* in 1948, and then merged it in an ecumenical venture with the United Church of Christ to form *A.D.* in 1972. The PCUS founded *Presbyterian Survey* in 1925; it alone survived into the 1990s as the magazine of the PC(USA).

Each of the three denominations struggled with the identity of its journal as "official" magazine. For some, it was a house organ, designed to build denominational loyalty. For others, it was a news publication serving to acquaint the church with its own affairs. But for the editors it was a publication that served its constituency best by using the accepted canons of journalism and by informing people about current issues in the denomination, the ecumenical church, and the world at large. The editors were usually professional journalists and were torn between their own training and the conflicting demands of the denomination.

These chronic tensions were not severe until the 1950s and 1960s. Robert Cadigan, publisher of *Presbyterian Life,* initiated the every member plan (discounted bulk subscriptions), and subscriptions soared to 400,000 in 1951. Although the idea was quickly adopted by other denominations and more subscribers did bring in added advertising revenue, the every member plan was based on the loyalties of congregations, not readers. Denominational subsidies remained the financial lifeline. Both *Presbyterian Survey* and *Presbyterian Life/A.D.* waded into controversies over race, war, and other volatile issues in the 1960s and 1970s. Membership declined, readership plummeted, and subsidies soared. The two magazines also confronted stiff competition from a proliferation of synod and presbytery newspapers and even a new denominational newspaper in the 1980s.[60]

Furthermore, print media of all kinds suffered from the video revolution of post–World War II America. When American Presbyterians and mainstream Protestants lost their privileged place on the national networks and virtu-

ally withdrew from using television, the educational and
nurturing potentials of the new medium were lost. The
changing fate of denominational magazines and the rejection of communication through television open a prism for
understanding the trials of the corporate denomination in
the twentieth century.[61]

Women's Groups

Women's organizations in American Presbyterianism
have been perhaps the most important avenue of nurture
for the majority of its members. Because women were denied full participation in the governance of the denominations, women's organizations became both a symbol of
discrimination against women and a source of freedom and
independence. Their power came from numbers and
money, for as indicated earlier, they often provided critical
funding for denominational programs, especially foreign
missions, even when they had little control over policies
and programs. These organizations also provided nurture
through congregational, presbytery, and synod chapters,
their own newsletters and magazines, their own Bible studies, and their own national conferences.[62]

But, as Joan LaFollette has shown, the nurture and mission purposes of Presbyterian women's organizations came
under attack during the 1960s as women fought for more
participation and more power in the corporate denomination. Advocacy groups were formed to advance women's
roles in congregations and throughout the denomination.
Increasing numbers of women ministers in the 1970s fueled the movement that protested entrenched male power.
Heightened consciousness among racial ethnic minority
women led them to form their own group. The General
Assembly of the PC(USA) recognized the diversity of
women's organizations and their goals by combining them
during the 1980s into one unit with inherent tensions. Presbyterian Women continued the nurture and mission emphases, but merged with it were three advocacy groups: the

Justice for Women Committee, the Committee of Women of Color, and the Committee on Women Employed by the Church.[63]

Exacerbating the problems of Presbyterian women's organizations are membership decline and the failure to attract younger women, who are often employed full time and lack the freedom to participate. As LaFollette notes, the 1988 women's meeting at Purdue University attracted a record number—5,617—but 62 percent of the participants were fifty-one or older.[64] Demographic trends, as well as internal strains, demonstrate the challenges of women's organizations and the denomination itself.

Men's Groups

Special organizations for Presbyterian men have a somewhat different history but reflect the difficulties of American Presbyterianism in the twentieth century. Dale Soden has shown how they prospered in the early decades of the century, their members' strength in numbers and social prominence bringing Presidents and other leading politicians to their meetings. They profited from the "muscular Christianity" of the era, the optimism of prewar Protestantism, and their enthusiasm for a moderate form of the social gospel, which emphasized involvement in local political movements for clean government. Between the two world wars, men's organizations declined and floundered, but they rebounded again during the 1950s, emphasizing anticommunism and patriotism as part of their appeal. The 1960s sent them into eclipse again, and by the 1990s the organization of Presbyterian Men was fighting for yet another life.[65]

Soden's analysis contains two striking ironies. Special men's organizations were always vulnerable. Men possessed power in the congregations and the denomination, so they did not need to create an alternative support network of the sort that the Presbyterian women's movement represented. When men's organizations flourished, their programs captured the spirit of the age, and when the times changed, they were doubly devastated.

Conclusion

This analysis of a Presbyterian ecology for nurturing faith should not lead to the belief that there was once some "golden age" to which it is possible to return. The present situation, like that of the past, is far more complex than that.

Significant gains that should not be lost have been made in certain elements of Presbyterian nurture and education. For example, American Presbyterians have certainly taken a wiser and more humane course by putting aside the strict Sabbatarianism of the nineteenth century that led to moralistic strictures on human behavior and coercive attempts to legislate that morality for the entire society. No one would seriously entertain the suggestion that the "cult of true womanhood" accurately captures the biblical notion of equality and mutuality between women and men. For all their difficulties, Sunday schools have access now to more material—even in its diversity—that can nurture faith and a vision of authentic discipleship. Worship services are enriched by ecumenical variety, and sermons are drawn from a broader understanding of the Christian community and the human condition. Denominational colleges and theological seminaries are arguably better academically than they have ever been. Church publications—books, magazines, newspapers—increase in number and quality, even if the denomination remains perplexed about how to use the powerful medium of television.

It was the potential of these important accomplishments that prompted many Presbyterians to support many of the changes described in this chapter.

But with these gains came concomitant losses demanding attention and remedy. It is painfully evident that the ecology of Presbyterian nurture has been critically disrupted.

Presbyterians have traditionally been parsimonious on

ritual in their personal and corporate life. Yet what few ritual rhythms formerly distinguished Presbyterian family piety, Sabbath observance, and congregational worship and life have ebbed away—lost in the first two cases from neglect, and diminished in the last instance because of theological confusion and an ecumenical blending of liturgy and song. The symbiotic relationships between Presbyterian congregations and denominational institutions like church-related colleges, seminaries, publishing houses, and journals have likewise deteriorated. Each agency has taken a separate path and now takes some pride in its individual independence as a badge of integrity.

Certainly, the corrosive effects of modernity should not be underestimated in any of these developments. But the current situation should not be simplistically credited to external, uncontrollable forces. The church participated in and in some cases encouraged these changes.

The reign of neo-orthodox theology in Presbyterian and mainstream Protestant circles in and after the 1950s introduced a strong critique of the church. A distinction between organized religion and life in the Spirit was so sharply drawn by neo-orthodoxy that institutional and ritual support of spiritual development fell in esteem. When combined with the widespread anti-institutionalism of the 1960s counterculture, this ethos tempted Presbyterians to devalue, and even disparage, those structures and disciplines that were part of their ecology for nurturing faith.

The cost of neglecting these essential components in the ecology was not appreciated until more recently when a range of signs like membership, finances, and congregational support began to falter.

There is now a need to renew the ecology of Presbyterian nurture. Such an ecology provides a vitality and order to the Christian life that distinguishes it from life without Christ. This re-formed ecology will certainly not be identical to that which provided a sacred canopy for Presbyterians earlier in the century. Indeed, many of the older institutions cannot and should not be replicated or resurrected in their previous shape. But an ecology for nurturing faith remains necessary to give shape to Presbyterian life, and its reform will not be easy. Reshaping and creating a system appropriate for modern living but faithful to the tradition and vital to spiritual development will no doubt test the discipleship and ingenuity of this and future generations of witnesses. Nevertheless, it is a task well worth pursuing, one guided and corrected by the hand of the God who continually nourishes the church.

II

The Re-Forming Church

8

The Presbyterian Predicament:
A Case of Conflicting Allegiances

The preceding analysis of American Presbyterianism in the twentieth century is a case study of the re-forming and fragmentation of this tradition, mainstream Protestantism, and American culture. It is also the story of people and institutions trying to maintain their balance amid powerful and conflicting forces. Early in our study, we began to use the term "predicament" to describe both the current situation for American Presbyterians and also their twentieth-century history. We thought that "predicament" was a particularly apt word to capture the dilemmas with which American Presbyterians have struggled, for a predicament always involves making a choice between two alternatives that are both good and often of equal value.

Contemporary Presbyterian allegiances can be characterized as several sets of dual commitments. For each one of Presbyterians' many commitments there is a complementary loyalty that competes for attention in Presbyterian discipleship. Ideally, these paired allegiances sustain a healthy tension in Presbyterian life, one that demands support of both commitments in Presbyterian proclamation and service rather than ranking them in a hierarchy of priorities. However, the twentieth-century experience has so dis-

rupted the parallel pulls of Presbyterians' coupled loyalties
that the PC(USA) finds itself now divided by its own allegiances.

The Presbyterian predicament of the twentieth century
has not been a dilemma over what options were available
to the church. If anything, the options facing the church
have been sharpened by twentieth-century events. The predicament for Presbyterians is not that of deciding which of
their longstanding commitments will be honored. It is, instead, a question of discovering how those commitments
can be integrated into a cohesive faith that gives identity,
common purpose, vitality, and flexibility to the whole communion.

Biblical Interpretation

Twentieth-century Presbyterians have tried to balance
their dependence on the authority of the scriptures with the
need to interpret the biblical message in contemporary
categories of thought. When biblical authority has been
interpreted as biblical inerrancy, fundamentalism has undermined this delicate balance. When efforts to adapt
scripture to contemporary social and intellectual changes
overshadowed the Bible's authority, a similar disruption
occurred.

In the 1920s and 1930s, Presbyterians confronted the
fundamentalist conflict over biblical authority and the attempt to define Christianity as a series of precise doctrinal
beliefs.[1] The church's decision to reject biblical inerrancy
and doctrinal precision as the litmus test for orthodoxy reflected the stance of most Presbyterians. At the same time,
the church failed to resolve its own understanding of biblical authority.[2]

The acceptance of neo-orthodox theology temporarily
created an informal consensus among mainstream Protestants about the authority of scripture. But neo-orthodoxy
provided a better critique of liberal and fundamentalist
biblical interpretation than a clear alternative key for
understanding and interpreting scripture. When neo-

orthodoxy waned in popularity, a host of valuable critiques of traditional biblical interpretation rose to prominence. Feminist, liberation, and process theologies have all contributed unique insights into the Christian gospel.

Yet they have also failed to develop a consensus on biblical interpretation. Consequently, when controversial social or ecclesiastical issues arise, an appeal to the scriptures alone seldom serves as a conclusive arbiter for settling disputes. Polls indicate that Presbyterians overwhelmingly believe that the Bible contains the written Word of God, and in that sense they remain very conservative on the issue of biblical authority.[3] But the question of how that authoritative Bible should be interpreted has been an agonizing dilemma for twentieth-century Presbyterians.

Because of the severity of the fundamentalist battles during the 1930s and the resurgence of fundamentalism in the 1970s and 1980s, many American Presbyterians have assumed that conservative forces within the denomination represented the greatest threat to the integrity of their faith. Conservatives have been equally convinced that the denomination was imperiled by liberalism in theology and politics. Neither anticipated the debilitating effect of mainstream Protestantism's disestablishment—culturally and religiously—and the secularity of American culture.

In the 1950s, rapid church growth and an apparent Protestant veneer to American laws and customs led many Presbyterians to assume that American society and its institutions were basically friendly to, if not actually informed by, their Christian faith. Neo-orthodoxy's criticism of the synthesis of American values and the Christian faith was accurate and pertinent. But social change also raised sharp questions about the character of the American faith and a presumably Christian nation. Civil rights, the Vietnam war, political assassinations, Watergate, abortion, feminism, gay and lesbian rights— these and other issues divided American society and American Presbyterians. They aroused strong emotions because they raised basic moral questions about righteousness, equality, and justice.

Since the 1960s American Presbyterians and the Christian church around the globe have been struggling with a variety of movements for independence and human rights. The common theme of justice runs through the affirmations of diverse thinkers from Third World, feminist, racial ethnic, liberationist, and gay rights groups. Because the theme of justice was and is prominent in the biblical account, justice has become for many the key for determining the central message of the scriptures. This has created its own problems as Presbyterians, along with other mainstream Protestants, debate whether definitions of justice drawn from secular culture are more determinative in modern biblical interpretation than the Bible itself. Equally important is the issue of whether justice itself is adequate as the single interpretive lens for understanding the gospel of Jesus Christ.[4]

Witness

Two more sets of parallel allegiances have been intimately related in Presbyterians' struggle to understand discipleship. One includes their commitments to the salvation of individuals while also supporting efforts to redeem and transform society. The other involves the conviction that not only verbal declarations of God's grace but also deeds of service are essential to Christian witness.

Concentrating on individual salvation at the expense of social reform abandons people to injustice and oppression in institutions and social systems. Attacking the evil of social systems can be equally futile when it neglects individuals who are seeking forgiveness, redemption, and answers to the meaning and purpose of life.

The church's struggle to find a proper mix of these two concerns has been connected with and complicated by different methods of outreach. Verbal witness devoid of physical evidence of Christian love and grace has made some Presbyterian proclamations little more than a loud noise signifying nothing of the good news of Christ. Yet a witness with limbs but without voice masks the Christ behind

Christian service. Indeed, like the fabled Cheshire cat in Alice's Wonderland, Presbyterian discipleship itself has often disappeared from public consciousness and even the church's awareness.[5]

Particularly since the 1960s, the magnitude, scope, and urgency of contemporary social problems prompted Presbyterian churches and their mainstream Protestant counterparts to question the efficacy, propriety, and motivation of past evangelism efforts. Such programs had focused largely on person-to-person contacts, and many believed that this emphasis ignored serious social ills for too long in an effort to bolster the membership and financial strength of ecclesiastical institutions.

Seeking to correct this imbalance, some Presbyterians advocated that actions must take priority over words. Actions would embody what had too often become empty words of concern for others' spiritual and temporal welfare. Where this involved muting Christian motivations in order to cooperate with non-Christians, the example of Christ's fellowship with publicans and prostitutes was invoked. When membership totals dropped precipitously, Presbyterians were reminded of Christ's injunction that one must lose one's life in order to find it. The church's mission was witness, not self-preservation.

This shift in perspective coincided with significant membership loss. There was no simple cause-and-effect relationship between these two events. But when some expressed alarm over membership loss, their concern was frequently discounted as a problem of institutional maintenance, not worthy of serious attention in a self-sacrificial, service-oriented church.

Few saw the fragility of the church as an institution and the changing character of American denominations. The debate over membership loss has led to the unfortunate assumption that verbal witness, evangelism, and church growth are contrary to social witness, or vice versa. The resulting conflict has meant that neither has received the necessary, coordinated attention that both require.

Power and Authority

Two further sets of parallel allegiances illustrate the intimate interplay of theology and polity in the Presbyterian community. In theological matters, Presbyterians have consistently honored the integrity of the individual conscience. Presbyterians believe that all Christians are called to read and study the Word of God in order to determine for themselves what is essential in belief and practice. This respect for the individual conscience has prompted the denomination in recent years to include more individuals in decision making as well as to seek a more diverse pool of people for service in decision-making bodies.

While affirming individuals' perspectives on God's will, the Presbyterian communion has also assumed that the scriptures reveal certain essential beliefs and practices that all Christians can and should acknowledge in common. These consensus doctrines and disciplines have, at their best, provided a general basis for denominational unity and a shared vision of the church's mission. This expectation of a fundamental consensus represents the traditional theological foundation for Presbyterian connectional systems where congregational policies and programs are coordinated and even directed by regional and national governing bodies in the interest of common Christian piety, witness, and social justice.

There are, of course, dangers to both sides of these allegiances when inordinate attention is given to one concern at the expense of the other. Individual conscience and participatory democracy can, at their worst, lead to a loss of cohesion and direction, while the imposition of theological vision through executive decision making can result in intolerance and a loss of common support.

Controversy over the "right of private judgment" versus the church's theological standards first erupted in American Presbyterianism over the Westminster Standards. During the 1700s, the subscription controversy was resolved by honoring the principle of conscientious objection and making the presbytery the final arbiter over individuals' theological scruples.[6] That verdict was reaffirmed in 1927 by the PCUSA General Assembly during the fundamentalist controversy. The UPCUSA's rejection of the Westminster Standards as the sole confessional basis of the church and the adoption of the Confession of 1967 and the *Book of Confessions* expanded the church's boundaries for diverse beliefs. The PC(USA) has ratified this move in the adoption of the *Book of Confessions* and "A Brief Statement of Faith" in 1991. The multiconfessional stance of American Presbyterianism is based on the recognition that all creeds are time-bound and subject to reformulation. Therefore, no one creedal statement could serve as the standard for all Presbyterians in all times and in all places.[7]

Just as Presbyterians were revising the understanding of the confessional character of the church, another powerful movement raised questions about unity and diversity. African American Presbyterians initially and later other racial ethnic minorities and women have since the 1960s insisted on increased participation in all denominational decision making. Gradually the cry for participation turned into an attack on the ideal of assimilation into structures based on white, male conceptions of the Christian faith. A new definition of the church was needed that allowed for individual and group diversity without actually dividing the denomination into a host of subdenominations.

The reorganization of the administrative structures of the UPCUSA and the PCUS during the early 1970s only exacerbated the problem of diversity and unity. As Richard Reifsnyder makes clear, both denominations virtually ground to a halt amid myriad meetings called in the name of consultation and communication. The structural changes in American Presbyterianism in the 1970s and 1980s vastly expanded the range of diversity in decision making. But these shifts frequently came at the cost of emphasizing management over leadership and the process of decision making over the actual accomplishment of the mission of the church.[8]

As the denomination moved to make room for diversity, the definition of diversity expanded beyond differences of race, sex, or cultural background to include age, physical condition, and sexual orientation, as well as a host of particular causes espoused by special-interest groups. Even though the so-called "Chapter 9" organizations lost formal constitutional recognition in the PC(USA) in 1991, their growth has multiplied the potential claims on Presbyterians' attention and allegiances. These groups do provide outlets for Presbyterian commitment and energy, but they also make even more difficult the task of affirming and renewing denominational identity and a sense of common purpose.[9]

Leadership

A related set of loyalties reflecting the contemporary struggle over diversity focuses on leadership. Church leadership is an ancient problem in Christianity. It has been a perplexing question for at least two reasons. First, the biblical notion of vocation suggests that God, not the people or the church hierarchy, ultimately calls forth people to lead the fellowship of believers. Christians have long puzzled over how that divine call could be mediated through the institution of the church and how the church could ensure that those called by God are actually discovered and placed in leadership positions. When churches fail in this endeavor they can very well end up with a leadership that has no following.

A second source of the church's dilemma over leadership is that all leaders are human. The divine call and the *charisma* imparted by the Holy Spirit have tempted many leaders to assume that their authority rests on divine right rather than divine donation. Likewise, leaders' election or appointment by people makes them susceptible to the tendency to curry favor with their finite constituency rather than be obedient to God. Every church organization has attempted to create safeguards against these dangers.

Presbyterians and other Calvinists developed a republican model of leadership for the church to guard against human fallibility. They rejected both the hierarchical structures of episcopacy and the democratic organization of congregationalism. Ministers, elders, and deacons are chosen by the people formally. But after they are elected, most Presbyterians believe they are responsible first to God, rather than the people who actually voted for them. As a further precaution, Presbyterians circumscribe the power of individual leaders by locating decision making in governing bodies where groups of representative leaders not only share but also counterbalance each other's authority.

This republican pattern of representation continued in force even after the church was awakened to the equality of men and women under the gospel. But the civil rights movement and the simultaneous assertion of the value of pluralism and diversity provided new impetus for Presbyterian racial ethnic minorities and women to call for greater representation in congregations, presbyteries, synods, and the General Assembly. The restructuring efforts of the 1970s followed this path. The UPCUSA changed its constitution in 1981 to require that every congregation shall elect "men and women from among its active members, giving fair representation of all ages and of all ethnic minorities of that congregation," to the office of ruling elder and to the office of deacon.[10] Other mechanisms were established in the UPCUSA to ensure greater distribution of leadership, a more inclusive process for selecting ministers, and diversity on committees.[11]

The new model of leadership emphasized that church courts and committees should be composed of representative leaders, but the concept of representation subtly changed. Representation was now understood to mean people from particular racial ethnic, gender, and special-interest constituencies in the church. The latest sign of this effort to institutionalize diversity is the creation of committees on representation, which monitor whether adequate numbers of individuals from constituent groups in a governing body are actually represented on committees.[12]

These provisions expanded the number of voices heard in decision-making bodies, but it also generated new imbalances. First, it limited the selection of leaders who might arise from the white membership which was the majority. In addition, because these moves were in part a protest against the dominance of male pastors and male lay leaders from large churches, the political climate shifted. Formally and informally, these pastors and lay leaders from large churches were often excluded from arenas of decision making. In 1985, 75 percent of all Presbyterian congregations had fewer than 250 members, but approximately half of all Presbyterians belonged to congregations of more than 500 members. Thus, the equitable distribution of leadership across constituent groups has sometimes meant inequities in representation for nearly a majority of Presbyterians.[13]

A second difficulty has been that leaders chosen in this system of distributed leadership feel dual obligations, which, at least in theory, the older republican leadership did not bear. Distributed leaders must seek God's will for the entire people of God, but they also feel duty-bound to advocate for the particular constituency that provided for their selection in the first place. Ironically, distributed leadership, which aims at the ideal of greater wholeness through broadened participation, may compound the impact of partisan politics within the church.

Reform

Presbyterians place an extraordinary emphasis on the teaching role of the church. They are equally committed to the principle that the church should be governed by laws, rather than by individual whim. John Calvin declared that the two marks of the true church were the faithful proclamation of the Word and the administration of the sacraments. To that John Knox added a third—the proper exercise of church discipline—and American Presbyterians ever since have attempted to use the legislative power of the church to order and organize a life of grace.[14]

The educational task of the church became increasingly critical as denominations developed during the nineteenth century. Because they were voluntary organizations, denominations depended on the willingness of individuals to join a congregation and support it. Denominational loyalty had to be taught, earned, and inspired. Individuals and society could be changed, but when the church was legally disestablished and separated from the power of the state, denominations were compelled to rely on education and persuasion to influence their members and to reform society through legislation.

During the twentieth century, the broad movement of political progressivism looked to the state as the initiator of social change and the guarantor of social justice. Presbyterians were modest participants in the early social gospel movement, but throughout the century they have shared in the confidence that legislation was a means of creating a just society. Political liberalism relied on its ability to win support from diverse coalitions for programs of reform. Likewise, the corporate denomination owed its vitality to its capacity to win the allegiance of congregations in support of the denomination's mission.

Both the liberal state and the corporate denomination suffered damaging blows from the fragmentation of American culture and pluralism. The corporate denomination assumed that the ecology for nurturing faith that supported denominational loyalty would remain in place, but it did not. As it dissipated, Presbyterians and other mainstream Protestants turned their denominational energies toward regulating and monitoring mission and the church's life. In deemphasizing or ignoring the task of educating people to change, they turned instead to legislating. This *rule by rules*, rather than by education and persuasion, bruises the voluntary relationship of individuals with congregations and denominations. It also generates divisive tensions between congregations and national denominational structures.[15]

The Congregation and the Denomination

A sixth area of balance for Presbyterians in the twentieth century involves the congregation and its relationship to the larger denomination. Here two quite different types of tensions had to be addressed in the twentieth century. The first is not unique to contemporary American religious life. The question of how congregations should associate with one another through regional, national, and international structures has been addressed repeatedly in American religious history. Connectional denominations like the PC(USA) have always assumed that Christian congregations, like individual Christians, must sustain close fellowship among themselves to reflect more faithfully the church universal.

The organizational revolution of the mid-twentieth century has hit the PC(USA) and other connectional denominations especially hard. Membership and giving trends indicate that the theological rationale behind connectional churches has diminished appeal and persuasive power. All but one of the mainstream Protestant denominations that have experienced significant membership loss in the last thirty years have had connectional forms of government.[16]

Similarly, giving patterns illustrate a dramatic shift away from denominational structures. In the PC(USA), the dollar amount of donations per giving unit has actually increased faster than inflation since 1983. But giving to the General Assembly has dropped dramatically since the 1950s and 1960s as congregations increasingly designate their benevolence gifts and allocate more to local and regional causes.[17] The individualistic ethos of American culture no doubt affects congregations as they allocate more for their own needs than for the larger denomination and as they insist on determining where their donated funds will be used. But these financial patterns are part of a broader and deeper process of alienation between congregations and denominational structures.

As Wulff and Marcum have found, the gulf between Presbyterian clergy and laity may not be as significant as the chasm both groups perceive between themselves and the General Assembly.[18] The evidence suggests that at least in terms of financial support, this alienation began as early as the 1950s—in the decade of the postwar "revival" and significantly before any signs of membership decline. This disengagement also affects virtually every national organization in American culture; corporations, for example, bemoan the loss of "company loyalty."

Cormode discovered no direct and immediate correlation between declining General Assembly financial support and specific social and political controversies, increasing pastoral salaries, or the reorganization of General Assembly agencies to move mission to the local and regional levels. Even so, the controversies that have engulfed American Presbyterians over the last three decades—often focused in the General Assembly—have taken a gradual and debilitating toll. Similarly, congregational irritation has been exacerbated by the regulatory behavior of denominational structures when they rely too heavily on legislation to achieve goals.[19]

In short, the national structures of mainstream Protestant denominations are far more fragile and vulnerable than they may appear. For Presbyterians and other connectional Protestants, this should be cause for concern; as critical as the congregation may be, it will never be able to capture the fullness of the biblical conception of the body of Christ or to carry out the mission of the church in its breadth and depth.

Ecumenism and Denominational Identity

A final difficult balance for Presbyterians concerns ecumenical cooperation and denominational identity. During the twentieth century, Presbyterians have participated in an unprecedented movement of cooperation among Protestant denominations, Eastern Orthodoxy, and the Roman Catholic Church.

Early ecumenical efforts led denominational leaders to hail such cooperation as a spur to denominational identity. Contacts in ecumenical circles, they argued, taught individuals what they shared with other American Christians but also their own unique emphases. It was assumed that participants already knew their own tradition sufficiently well to recognize the differences and the value of their own and others' faith.

As the ecumenical movement developed in the twentieth century, it moved from dialogue to actual merger talks. But with some exceptions, organizational mergers came to a halt along denominational lines. The result has been a deep ambivalence about denominational identity in American Presbyterianism and mainstream Protestantism. On the one hand, leaders proclaim the vision of unity in Christ (John 17) and express chagrin at the persistent divisions within Christianity; on the other hand, leaders affirm the particular insights and piety carried by their denomination's theological tradition and promote programs to strengthen denominational loyalty and self-understanding.

The ecumenical movement's effects at the local level are also ironic. Members of ecumenical churches like the PC(USA) exhibit significant indifference to denominational particularities when they choose a church home, donate funds, or select programs for their local congregation. Yet they also are apathetic toward the institutional embodiments of the ecumenical movement, such as local councils of churches, the National Council of Churches, and the World Council of Churches, which wither because they lack financial support.

Balancing Parallel Allegiances

This chapter has outlined typologies of various strains and dual allegiances that bring stress to the PC(USA) at the close of the century. One response to Presbyterians' present predicament would be to acknowledge that the church has fragmented much like the larger society. Some would argue that since significant issues divide us and since it seems unlikely that any new consensus will unite us, we should make a virtue out of the current situation and applaud this pluralism. As in James Madison's vision of the American political order, contending interests will ultimately produce a common good. Some Presbyterians will emphasize certain aspects of the faith, while others will promote their counterparts.

The longstanding Presbyterian allegiance to the sovereignty of the individual conscience and the twentieth-century debate over the need for racial ethnic groups to phrase the gospel with their own accents would suggest that there is ample historical warrant for such a position. This concept of the church would also emphasize individual freedom—a highly prized value in modern American life. Perhaps it would even lead to the union of all mainstream Protestant denominations when they relinquish their unique differences in the interest of a common denominator of Christian convictions.

This solution, however, is troubling and unsatisfying. It assumes that the complementary emphases of the Christian faith cannot be embodied in the same person or corporate body. Therefore, it suggests that a holistic faith is a modern impossibility.

Because their dual allegiances represent a genuine predicament for American Presbyterians and mainstream Protestants, they do not lend themselves to an easy "either-or" solution. In each instance, the gravity and allure of the scriptural warrant for each choice calls for a balancing of the options.

One way of envisioning the Presbyterian predicament is to imagine these dualities as parallel allegiances. The two concerns in each set of allegiances are different but related because they run parallel to each other in the Christian understanding of faithful discipleship.

In a stable world the church might pursue both concurrently with equal emphasis and energy given to each. But the Christian church has never known such a world. Historical circumstances have always shaped its witness. One way of understanding the changes in American Presbyterianism is to recognize the denomination's need to shift emphases in order to either redress past imbalances or address new winds in the culture.

The twentieth century has made this task especially difficult, if not daunting. The tragic internecine war in American Protestantism has deeply scarred American Presbyterianism. Because of the Presbyterian desire to inform and reform society, the social and political upheaval of this century left Presbyterians particularly vulnerable to the fragmentation of American culture. The trajectories of the allegiances have diverged so sharply that they are often viewed as mutually exclusive forms of Christian discipleship. The point of equilibrium within each set of loyalties is likewise difficult to decipher at any one point in time. But even more troubling, the polarization of American Protestantism has become so deep that the very idea of equilibrium is disparaged as a moral and spiritual compromise.[20]

Historians initially gave the name "mainstream Protestantism" to churches like the PC(USA) because they embodied the theological convictions of the majority of at least the powerful in American society, if not most of the general populace. More recently, the term "Establishment Protestantism" has been used for these denominations. This terminology reflects the historical awareness that American religious life has always been marked by astounding diversity ever since the first settlements. "Establishment" denominations are those that comprised a subculture of Americans, a minority in actual numbers. But this minority exercised inordinate power in shaping American culture.[21]

It is time now for these churches to redefine "mainstream" in terms of *neither* their relative popularity in the culture *nor* their members' predominance in the seats of power, but instead in terms of the essential component parts of the Christian faith. In short, these denominations should seek to redefine "mainstream" theologically, rather than socially or culturally.

Mainstream Protestantism defined in this way would mean two things. First and foremost, it would stand for a brand of Christian spirituality that is unwilling to abandon any element of the Christian gospel in the interest of furthering parallel and complementary concerns.

This form of reconstructing a theological mainstream

will not be easy. The deeply divisive issues that confront these churches and American culture encourage the tendency toward single-issue politics and single-minded approaches to complex problems. This re-visioning of a theological mainstream will run counter to these already strong trends in the society. But it is, nonetheless, the more holistic approach and, therefore, one more faithful to the Christ who died to make us all whole once again.

This redefinition of the mainstream will also be difficult because it requires the sobering acknowledgment that the mainstream's "predicament"—i.e., being caught between competing, though complementary, allegiances—is a permanent condition and its unique calling.

The taut pull between each of the parallel allegiances is not an accident of twentieth-century history. All of the mainstream's paired commitments have ample biblical warrant. Therefore, their complementary pressures on mainstream piety are inherent in a Christian life informed by scripture.

A second theme in the redefinition of the mainstream would follow from the first. An equilibrium *among* all the parallel allegiances would comprise the substance of true Christian discipleship. There is a model for what such an equilibrium might resemble and, like so much of religious experience, it involves a metaphor that captures only part of the richness of the Christian life. The metaphor is a mobile.

On every mobile there is a set of balanced polarities. Each pole within the set requires an offsetting force, and together the several polarities contribute to a collective equilibrium. The key to a mobile is equilibrium, not a perfect and equal balance among options. The various ends of a mobile have different weights, and even those weights are altered as the wind currents change.

Imagine each of the parallel allegiances we have described as components of an overarching denominational mobile. Each holds opposing, but complementary, values or allegiances at its ends, and a basic equilibrium must be maintained by the church between each set of dual allegiances *and* among the several sets of complementary allegiances in the denominational mobile.

Events within the church and society represent variable winds that can buffet the denomination's equilibrium, just as they have during the twentieth century. This will force members and leaders to alter their weighing of priorities on any one of Christianity's many polarities in order to maintain the necessary tension between its poles and among the several polarities, thereby sustaining the church's basic spiritual equilibrium. The key here is *flexible equilibrium, not balance or stasis*. Circumstances have required and will require that the denomination lean its resources toward one or several of its parallel allegiances. *But* if the church leans too far and too long in any one direction, the fundamental stability of its spiritual life is threatened. This produces extremes that are ultimately unfaithful to the tradition, but, what is more important, they do not capture the breadth of the gospel of Jesus Christ.

When the Presbyterian predicament is viewed in terms of equilibrium, its current difficulty in addressing its problems can be better understood. On all of the polarities that challenge contemporary Presbyterians, they are caught between two equally valuable loyalties that now conflict either because of unexpected events or because of past imbalance in emphasis.

Troubled by this conflict and not understanding its inevitability, the church has not supported its parallel allegiances so much as it oscillated widely between them. These rough gyrations—such as Benton Johnson's description of the shift from an "old" to a "new" agenda in social ethics—leave confusion, uncertainty, and frustration in their wake.

The problem is not oscillation as much as it is the dramatic reversals of direction in twentieth-century Presbyterianism and mainstream Protestantism. These radical shifts arise from a mistaken notion about the character of Christian discipleship, understood as single-mindedness toward a single goal. But the single-mindedness of the Christian faith is not emphasis on a simple set of singular concerns. Rather, its unique focus should be the overall equilibrium of a number of parallel, intimately related concerns embedded in the Christian gospel.

When such equilibrium becomes the mark of the church's movement in mission, shifts of personnel and resources will still occur. Tensions between allegiances will and must remain. But the readjustments will look less like the extreme swings of a pendulum and more like the modulated movements of a mobile in the wind.

The balancing act required by this metaphor is anything but a moral compromise. Maintaining equilibrium across a range of parallel allegiances is much more than fence-straddling. It is, instead, a strenuous and ever vigilant effort to sustain a steady tension between the competing accents of the Christian faith, even as the church attempts to rectify the imbalances of the past and adjust to the challenges of the future.

Presbyterians' strong sense of their own finite nature leads them to expect, at least in theory, a never-ending process of readjustment and reform: *Ecclesia reformata, semper reformanda*—the church reformed and always to be reformed. The task remains constant. Despite all the vicissitudes that the church has experienced, its primary calling is to search God's word and the prevailing currents of culture to discern where the Spirit of God is leading people to lean their weight in service to the good news of Jesus Christ.

Two final observations must be noted. First, as with all religious metaphors, the illumination provided by the mobile is limited. While the image evokes a proper sense of the complementary tensions in Christian discipleship and the much-needed equilibrium that those tensions dictate, it lacks the energy and propulsion that the gospel of Jesus Christ infuses into a Christian life of love and service. Christians are called to balance their actions, but they are likewise commissioned to act so that the body of Christ not only is witnessed by the world but also witnesses to the world. For this reason, the metaphor of the mobile must itself be balanced by a constellation of other equally rich symbols like a bicycle, a gyroscope, or a ship of faith. These images share with the mobile the critical notion of equilibrium, but they suggest further the essential movement of a mainstream Christian community into, through, and around the world.

Second, human effort is certainly required to keep the church in equilibrium, but it is ultimately not sufficient to read the times. The church must continually call upon God. Through the Holy Spirit, the foresight and understanding required to decipher a righteous equilibrium will come.

Every mobile has a plumbline, whether visible or invisible, that runs through its gravitational center. So too any truly mainstream Christian community must have a plumbline. That center in the Reformed tradition is a radical devotion to a sovereign God. The Lord showed the prophet, Amos, a man standing by a wall with a plumbline in his hand. And the Lord said to Amos, "What do you see?" Amos answered, "A plumb line." And the Lord said, "I am setting a plumbline in the midst of my people Israel; I will never again pass them by" (Amos 7:7–8).

All of the parallel allegiances confronting contemporary Presbyterians are secondary to and revolve around this center of spiritual gravity, which is our plumbline—our creator, redeemer, and sustainer. Without this plumbline, Christians can be "tossed to and fro and blown about by every wind of doctrine" (Eph. 4:14). But with that plumbline, the church can be righted by God and become right with God in an equilibrium that testifies to the breadth and depth of Christian discipleship which is in but not of this world.

9

The Re-Forming Church:
An Agenda for Reform

This book has argued that American Presbyterians and other mainstream Protestants are living through a significant re-forming, reshaping, and redefinition of their churches. Likewise, their relationship not only to American culture but also to the global Christian church is changing. The formative period of American Protestantism extended from the mid-eighteenth through the mid-nineteenth centuries. It was followed by perhaps as much as a century of consolidation. But even as mainstream Protestantism reached its apogee of influence and dominance, it was fragmenting from within and facing new challenges from society.

Throughout the twentieth century and especially since World War II, these churches have confronted the re-forming of American mainstream Protestantism and American religion. That process has brought considerable pain and anguish to these denominations. The transformation of American Presbyterianism and mainstream Protestantism is so great that their situation bears a striking similarity to that of their counterparts of the formative period 200 years ago. What was formed then is now being re-formed.

The question is whether there is anything these churches—and specifically the PC(USA)—can do to make the process of re-forming an occasion for reformation. This chapter is designed to set out an agenda for discussion about issues that we think are critical for recreating the equilibrium of a faithful church. This agenda is clearly not exhaustive, and it is intended as a corrective to current trends. As such it will be short-term and will need its own corrections. The agenda is rooted in concerns arising out of our research and our own judgment about how these issues have shaped and will affect the future of American Presbyterianism.

Reform Begins with Repentance

Repentance is central to the biblical concept of conversion–new life in God's grace. For us as Presbyterians, repentance begins with the recognition that we do, indeed, have a set of problems that we can no longer avoid. From congregations to the General Assembly, the PC(USA) has been extraordinarily adept at denying that problems existed or at redefining them in less threatening terms.

One example illustrates the mood of the denomination. In 1976, after ten years of steady membership decline, the UPCUSA General Assembly received a long and superbly researched report on the reasons for the loss of members. Another decade and a half of further research has filled in additional details, but the 1976 report identified virtually all the major causes of membership decline. The report brought forth little commentary at the 1976 Assembly meeting. A year later, an *A.D.* magazine editor commissioned a separate article on the report to highlight its findings. Even then, the article prompted only one published letter to the editor. Although one committee member hoped the report would be "required reading for presbyteries and local churches," it was lost—its findings known to only a few in the church and to specialized researchers.[1]

Part of the explanation for the pattern of denial in the

PC(USA) and mainstream Protestant denominations lies in embarrassment and guilt over membership loss. It was the rare congregation that did not experience a decline in membership or a plateau in growth. Furthermore, the fact that demographics played a critical role in membership decline may have provided solace to some who saw the drop as something beyond their control.

But as the research on American Presbyterianism suggests, membership decline is only one—albeit very noticeable—aspect of the challenges confronting the church. Although the Louisville research on American Presbyterianism may be incomplete, it is part of a growing body of literature that will help interpret the transformation of American Presbyterianism and mainstream Protestantism. The PC(USA) can no longer ignore its findings. The denomination's challenges are complex; they are also real. One historian flatly concludes that by the end of the 1980s "the mainline clearly [was] in far more trouble concerning its survival than even the critics were projecting."[2]

But repentance involves more than simply acknowledging that problems exist. This research calls into question the current values and priorities of the denomination. It challenges the validity of both the categories and the contentions of competing groups within the church. For example, the discovery that membership decline is due to the loss of people to no religious affiliation can scarcely be comforting to either liberal or conservative camps.

Repentance will mean confessing that we have distorted the meaning of the Christian faith and the church's mission. In accenting some part of the biblical message, we have failed to understand and proclaim the breadth of God's word. The fragmentation of American Presbyterianism is a product of forces which shaped us; it is also a result of self-inflicted wounds and ideological rigidity.

God's intention for the church and the world is reconciliation and wholeness. God summons us to reexamine our presumptions and presuppositions, to repent of our divisions, and to ask forgiveness. God summons us to be the church—one body in Christ.

Reform Means Openness to Growth and Evangelism

The Opposition to Growth

One of the striking features of the PC(USA) is a pervasive anti-growth attitude and ideology. Apathy and hostility to growth are characteristic of congregations, as well as of governing bodies. One presbytery executive, Ferdinand Pharr, declared in 1991, "Most of the congregations I know believe they have enough members." In a 1991 *Christian Century* article, a newly retired couple told of moving to a town where they visited eleven Protestant churches. In each case, they made a contribution with a check so that someone knew their address. The congregations offered little or no welcome; practically none of the churches encouraged them to become members. All they were looking for, they plaintively said, was "a friendly church."[3]

Despite a loss of one-third of its membership and despite targeting evangelism as one of the two priorities of the denomination, the PC(USA)'s rhetoric about growth surpasses its behavior. When asked by the *Presbyterian Panel* what the church's priorities should be, Presbyterian members placed the following statement ninth among fourteen options: "Encouraging church members to make explicit declarations of their personal faith to friends, neighbors and co-workers." A Gallup study of Episcopalians indicated that only one in eleven regularly invited people to church; four in ten never did. The proportions for Presbyterians are similar. Only one in ten invites people to church "to a great extent" while almost three in ten do so "very little." This is the case despite the fact that studies demonstrate most people join churches because a friend or relative invited them. Presbyterians' reticence in this regard is a disturbing signal of the church's spiritual health.[4]

When Presbyterian congregations receive new members, they frequently fail to retain their loyalties. As they gain some members through the front door, they lose even more through the back door. Many congregations find themselves unwilling or unable to adjust to new people and the sharing of responsibility and leadership.[5]

The anti-growth mentality characterizes the policies and programs of governing bodies as well. As Coalter has found, the deemphasis on verbal evangelism, which began in the 1960s, produced a vehement debate over Presbyterian priorities. Attempts to reemphasize evangelism were criticized as the abandonment of social justice. Furthermore, the popularity of the "church growth" school of thought, prominent in the 1970s and 1980s, fueled the charge that growth should be achieved through the creation of homogeneous congregations.[6] To be in favor of growth, it seemed, was to be intentionally exclusivist and therefore unethical, even though most Presbyterian congregations were homogeneous and behaved as the church growth school predicted.

The popularity of televangelists, the scandals surrounding their ministries, the shallow and treacly piety portrayed in popular evangelical literature, the alliance of the religious right with the political right—all these and more contributed to the suspicion of evangelicalism and evangelism and the spread of an anti-growth ethos in both the PCUS and the UPCUSA since the 1960s.

The 1960s also marked the decade when presbyteries reduced their involvement in new church development.[7] When new churches were proposed for growing suburban areas, many presbyteries found themselves locked in a struggle over the needs of the inner city versus suburban church growth. Or small congregations in or near a growing populace felt threatened by the proposed new church. Or the presbytery developed sufficiently cumbersome policies for studying and evaluating a plan for planting a new congregation that the advocates lost interest. By emaciating new church development, Presbyterians effectively eliminated one means of partially offsetting the negative demographic trends since the 1960s.[8]

In the 1960s and 1970s, both the PCUS and the UPCUSA shifted General Assembly priorities, even as their own resources declined. Offices for handling denominational evangelism programs lost their previous public visibility. The redefinition of mission criticized the concern to bring new people into the church community as mere number-counting for institutional maintenance and the desire to found new churches as antiecumenical. In the 1980s, the PC(USA) declared that evangelism and doing justice are the two priorities of the denomination, but no significant reassessment of budget allocations has occurred since the new denomination was founded in 1983. In fact, despite the 1988 General Assembly's decision to allocate an additional $15 million to evangelism, the denomination neutralized that message by designating the $15 million as money to be raised outside the normal denominational operating budget through the Bicentennial Fund campaign. The PC(USA) still lives with the policies and programs forged in the crucible of the 1960s and 1970s.

As both implicit attitude and explicit ideology, the opposition to growth must be reexamined. It is highly unlikely that the denomination will be able to return to the membership levels of the mid-1960s; in fact, because of declining birth rates among Presbyterians, it may even be difficult to stabilize membership at the current level of 2.9 million members.

However, the membership decline in American Presbyterianism and mainstream Protestantism is the loss of people, particularly young people, to no religious affiliation at all. That is a spiritual and religious challenge to the PC(USA) which calls into question our willingness to be witnesses to the good news in Jesus Christ.

Focus on Three Groups

If the PC(USA)—from the congregation to the General Assembly—reassesses its attitudes toward growth, it should focus on the unchurched, who comprise 10 percent of the American population and are the most rapidly growing segment. Three groups warrant particular attention:

Mental Members. Kirk Hadaway's research and Gallup polls indicate that there is a significant population of

Americans who identify in some way with the Presbyterian tradition but do not belong formally to any Presbyterian church.[9] These inactives, or people tied by family connections to the Presbyterian communion, should be approached and invited to participate in the denominational community more intimately. No doubt some old scars from former congregational or denominational conflict will need to be healed. But reconciliation is now an integral part of the Presbyterian vocabulary for discipleship, and that language must be confirmed through active reunion with the disgruntled, the disenchanted, and the disenfranchised.

The Youth of the Baby Boom Generation. The disaffiliation of the baby boom generation cannot be ignored. But it should not be allowed to obscure the less populous but important future generations that followed or were spawned by the baby boomers. The Hoge/Johnson/Luidens study suggests that even disaffiliated baby boomer parents are concerned that their children receive moral and/or religious training. In the increasingly secularized public life of America, the church remains one of the few institutions where such training is a continuing, central part of its mission. Sociological studies indicate that Americans do not tend to become more religious as they age.[10] Therefore, the likelihood of the baby boom generation returning en masse on its own is minimal. But their children of elementary, junior high, high school, and college age are an urgent concern of the church, and they may provide a potentially strong connection between baby boomer parents and the church.

Pursuing programs for youth may attract some of the baby boomers back to church, but whether it does or not, it will nevertheless address those youthful populations of the next generation(s) who have not as yet indicated whether they will join or reject the Christian community. Bolstering youth ministry would also redress a neglect of several decades during which the young people of Presbyterian and mainstream Protestant churches have received little sus-

tained and focused attention and where the ministries of
nurture through church camps and campus ministries have
atrophied.

Racial Ethnic Ministries.   In 1990, racial ethnic minorities comprised only 5.7 percent of the PC(USA)'s membership of approximately 2.9 million. Blacks, Asians, and
Hispanics are increasing more rapidly than other portions
of the American population. As we have noted, Presbyterians have resisted bringing racial ethnic minorities into the
life of the church. When they have attempted it, they have
been notoriously ineffective. Race and class have proved to
be nearly impenetrable barriers to minority participation.
Presbyterian modes of worship and education have not
been appealing; requirements for ordination have been
burdensome. One encouraging sign is the fact that African
American Presbyterian membership has increased mod-
estly from 58,442 in 1985 to 64,183 in 1990.[11]

If present trends continue, the Caucasian portion of the
American population will be a minority by the middle of
the next century. Given Presbyterian birth rates, the denomination cannot hope to grow by continuing to rely
upon its Caucasian constituency. New efforts to reach out
to racial ethnic minority groups not only make practical
sense; what is far more important, such efforts would also
redress centuries of exclusion and represent a renewed
quest to be faithful to the Pauline vision of the body of
Christ.

However, as various studies in the Louisville research
make clear, the denomination cannot hope to appeal to
these racial ethnic minorities without expanding and
changing present policies and programs. Adjustments in
educational processes and requirements must be made to
facilitate the completion of theological studies by members
of Presbyterian racial and ethnic minorities. Affirming
their different understandings of leadership is equally
important. Presbyterians in predominantly Caucasian congregations need to keep open avenues to minority membership and leadership.

Even when it may be impossible to bridge the chasm created by race and class and bring minorities into full membership, Presbyterian congregations could at least develop working relationships with minority congregations. In many urban areas, Presbyterians have no presence in minority communities; if it is impossible to create a distinctively Presbyterian image, then we should build alliances with existing congregations.

The suggestion of these three groups for special attention does not mean that groups like older adults should be ignored by the church. The three groups mentioned do not exhaust the possibilities for outreach. However, the case of older adults is an example of why we selected the groups that we did. Older adults are one of the few age groups where Presbyterians have experienced positive growth.[12] Denominations like the PC(USA) do address—even if imperfectly—the spiritual needs of the over-forty-five population better than those of their younger counterparts.

Beyond the question of target populations, the first and most critical step in evangelism will be the decision to want to grow. The expectation that growth will come automatically or easily is rooted in sloth and in an elitist, establishment mentality that assumes the perpetual appeal of Presbyterianism. The PC(USA) and its congregations cannot expect growth without effort or intention.

Furthermore, the reluctance to be open to growth through new people and new ideas is a denial of Christ's call to proclaim a message that is good news and that summons us in ministry to others outside the church.

Focus on Faith, Witness, and Service

The evangelistic impulses in Presbyterianism have been stifled in the twentieth century for a variety of reasons. Presbyterians have drunk deeply at the well of modernity, which has made them acutely aware of the relative and conditional character of all human knowledge. The civil war in American Protestantism has raged with particular intensity in American Presbyterianism. Since the liberal wing of the

church has exercised dominant influence for the last half
century, evangelism has often been misconstrued or sup-
pressed. Few Presbyterians are even aware of their rich
evangelistic and evangelical heritage, which at its best emphasized not only the individual conversion to Jesus Christ
but also the transformation of unjust structures of society.
The 1923 PCUSA Board of Home Missions said as much
when it declared "our [church's] purpose must be a saved
soul in a saved body in a saved community."[13]

The recovery of that evangelistic and evangelical tradition is the subject of another Louisville Seminary research
project.[14] But based on our study of American Presbyterianism in the twentieth century, the outlines of evangelism
for congregations and the denomination in the future can
at least be sketched.

Faith. Evangelism comes from the Greek word *euange-
lion,* which means "good news." The word "gospel" derives
from the Anglo-Saxon word, "godspell," which also means
"good news." This good news is that God loves us and offers us forgiveness and new life. We know the good news in
Jesus Christ. The sixteenth-century translator of the English Bible, William Tyndale, beautifully captured the joy
of the good news that people know in Jesus Christ: "Euage-
lio (that we cal gospel) is a greke worde, and signyfyth good,
mery, glad and joyfull tydings, that maketh a mannes hert
glad, and maketh him synge, daunce and leepe for ioye."[15]

In recent American Presbyterian history there has been a
confusion about the primacy of faith in the Christian life.
Faith is not knowledge of either the Bible or Christian doctrine, although it obviously includes that. Faith is the experience of knowing God's grace in Jesus Christ. As John
Calvin put it, faith is "a firm and certain knowledge of
God's benevolence toward us, founded upon the truth of
the freely given promise in Christ, both revealed to our
minds and sealed upon our hearts through the Holy
Spirit."[16]

People come to church because they are seeking faith—
an experience of God. The church is the primary arena for

acquiring and nurturing faith, but for mainstream Protestants and American Presbyterians this challenge presents a predicament. Their denominations have been key contributors to and proponents of the growth of American liberalism and a liberal society.

As political scientist Robert Booth Fowler has argued, liberalism and a liberal society have three basic characteristics: "1) a commitment to skeptical reason, an affirmation of pragmatic intelligence, an uneasiness about both abstract philosophical thinking and nonrational modes of knowledge; 2) enthusiasm in principle (and increasingly in practice) for tolerance not only in political terms but much more obviously in terms of lifestyle and social norms; 3) affirmation of the central importance of the individual and individual freedom." However, despite their commitment to liberalism, American Presbyterians and mainstream Protestants have been touched by, and in turn are called to affirm, the experience of God that transcends skepticism, pluralism, and individualism. The church thus becomes a "refuge," according to Fowler, from the spiritual emptiness and moral diversity of American culture.[17]

Without sacrificing its social witness or its prophetic vision of reforming unjust structures, the church should recognize its critical role in guiding and inspiring people as they inquire into the knowledge and love of God in Jesus Christ. People come to church seeking faith in God.

Witness. What was often lost in the emphases of both the scholastic Calvinism of the Princeton theology and neo-orthodoxy was Calvin's insight into faith as the experience of God. In reacting against the emphasis on conversion and experience in American evangelicalism, contemporary American Presbyterians and mainstream Protestants still have profound experiences of God's grace and presence. However, congregations frequently inhibit discussion of such depth encounters because they are considered too private to share or too personal to be held in common. The result is that congregations are less intimate. Their members are unaccustomed to expressing their faith with one another and therefore uncomfortable with communicating their faith with others outside the church.

Presbyterians are overwhelmingly well-educated, articulate people. The beginning of an evangelism program for the PC(USA) must start with the people themselves. It means reopening the category of religious experience. Congregations should create different contexts for people to talk about their encounters with God. It is likely that a wide variety of religious experiences will emerge. These are the raw materials of theological reflection, and they can begin to shape a new ethos in which people will learn, from the Bible, the church's teaching, and one another, what authentic faith can be.

Only after creating communities where faith is expressed can Presbyterians be articulate witnesses to others. They will need help. They will need models from ministers and lay leaders who are themselves articulate about their experiences of God, their faith, their understanding of what the good news is. At the heart of Christianity is the affirmation of the incarnation: God became human in Jesus Christ. Central to the understanding of evangelism is the recognition that faith is mediated through human beings.[18] If Presbyterians find new freedom to express their faith, they will then be able to witness to others.

Service.   Despite all the signs of individualism, materialism, and consumerism in American society, there remains a deep and powerful strain of idealism that summons people to prophetic and sacrificial service in charities, social service agencies, and a host of organizations for social reform. This is even true of many baby boomers. They came of age amid severe social strains over deep moral problems in American society, and they are both willing and eager to try to change the conditions that breed inequity and injustice in society.

Congregations should find ways to allow this idealism to be expressed and to nurture and communicate their Christian motivations for service in the world. The act of service without a motivation for it will frequently breed discouragement and disillusionment. Why, after all, should someone become involved in building low-income housing, helping battered women, caring for the victims of AIDS, protesting polluting industries, or other causes through the church? A host of other organizations compete with the church for the time and financial support of committed people. The church can offer what they do not provide: a vision of service to the world that is grounded in God's grace in Jesus Christ. Because God first loved us, we are freed to proclaim that salvation in word and deed to others.

These three dimensions—faith, witness, service—have been captured by Grayson Tucker in an image of a vital congregation. After studying several congregations that moved from severe internal problems to new health, Tucker observed how each was "a two-armed church with a strong heart." Their "two arms are the mission of evangelism and social action" while their "strong heart is the mission of worship and preaching, nurture, and education."[19] Such an image embodies the equilibrium of a faithful church.

Focus on Denominational Priorities in Evangelism

So far, we have discussed evangelism in terms of what congregations can do, but the research suggests three areas that should be reemphasized in the evangelism program of the PC(USA). All three have been important parts of the outreach of American Presbyterians during the twentieth century, but all three have been gravely neglected in recent decades. They are new church development, ministries on college campuses, and mass media. In identifying these as denominational priorities in evangelism, we do not assume that they will be carried out exclusively by the General Assembly, synods, or presbyteries. But since they involve considerable amounts of money and coordinated planning, they will inevitably require cooperation beyond individual congregations.

New Church Development.   As we have seen, American
Presbyterians suffered two blows in the 1960s. Demographic trends that supported growth after World War II
turned against Presbyterian churches as the baby boom
came to an end. Simultaneously, the church reduced its
commitment to new church development. One blow came
from society; the other was self-inflicted. The evidence suggests that *denominational* growth is directly related to the
founding of new churches, rather than increases in existing
congregations.[20]

Throughout the nineteenth and most of the twentieth
century, Presbyterians recognized that the American population is constantly moving. They moved with the population, albeit somewhat more slowly and deliberately. But
since the 1960s, the denomination's attention to new
church development has plummeted. Even the recent call
to create 1,000 new churches by the year 2000 will not
equal the rate of new church starts during the 1950s.[21]

Critics complain about the expense of new church development, but several points need to be made. There are
many models for starting new churches. Some are more expensive than others. The PC(USA) has access to sophisticated demographic studies and people skilled in urban
planning. Through these resources, fairly accurate predictions can be made about the potential success or failure of a
new congregation. Some congregations will fail because
new church development is risky. But there is more than
one way to lose the church's life only to find it.

Furthermore, an ever-diminishing membership base is
related to the decline in denominational income for the
General Assembly and other governing bodies. New church
development is one specific step the denomination as a
whole could take to address declining membership and diminished financial support for denominational mission
programs.

Ministries on College Campuses.   Perhaps the most important mission field of the church in contemporary
America is the college campus. College years are usually the

time when young adults drift away from previous church involvement. At the same time, increasing numbers of young people in American colleges have no previous church involvement but share both altruistic impulses and a deep hunger for the experience of God. And yet, the secularization of American society is amply evident in American higher education.

Robert Wuthnow concludes that people with higher levels of education are more likely to leave the church.[22] His data conflict with findings in the Presbyterian baby boomer study, which found no correlation between higher education and disaffiliation from the church.[23] However this dispute is resolved, the fact remains that some disaffection with the church often occurs during college.

PC(USA) ministries on college campuses are a means to maintain ties to the church and to nurture a maturing Christian faith.[24] The denomination recognized this fact historically when it created and supported its sixty-nine colleges and universities. The ties between the denomination and these colleges have been gradually weakened during the twentieth century. But these institutions remain a vital resource for the PC(USA) in its evangelism program, and the denomination must take the steps necessary to strengthen these institutions as an integral part of its program of nurturing faith. As a result of the vast expansion of public higher education in the twentieth century, over 80 percent of the college population are in state-supported colleges and universities. Thus, PC(USA) ministry on college campuses must also focus on the opportunities to be found in these institutions.

Conservative denominations have already recognized the importance of ministries on college campuses as part of the denominational evangelism program. The PCA sponsors more campus ministers in Mississippi alone than the PC(USA)'s Synod of Living Waters supports in Kentucky, Tennessee, Mississippi, and Alabama. Campus ministries are often the largest budget items in state conventions of the Southern Baptist Convention.[25]

There are many models of ministry on college campuses,

and the PC(USA) should recognize that no one model will
be appropriate everywhere. For example, the denomination may need to experiment and look at cooperating with
parachurch groups, such as InterVarsity, to find effective
ways of recreating a presence on college campuses. But it is
equally critical for the denomination to understand that
campus ministry must be redefined and reconceived as
evangelism—the persuasive communication and embodiment of the Christian faith in the midst of a highly secular
environment. In recovering a commitment to ministry in
higher education, Presbyterians will reaffirm a classic Reformed conviction: the life of the mind and the life of faith
are fundamentally one.

Mass Media. American Presbyterians and mainstream
Protestants dominated religious programming in the mass
media during the height of their cultural influence. After
the Federal Communications Commission ended their
privileged status, mainstream Protestants generally withdrew from mass media in the 1960s. Evangelical and fundamentalist entrepreneurs stepped into the breach, since
they had been paying for their air time all along. Just as
they began to suffer membership declines, mainstream
Protestants and American Presbyterians virtually abandoned the most powerful form of communication available
in the twentieth century.[26]

Television is only part of the communications revolution
of the twentieth century, and the speed of technological
change through computerization far outpaces the resources
of the denomination. The costs of media production are
enormous, and in the face of declining funds for General
Assembly causes, it seems impossible to imagine a major
commitment of denominational funds for mass media
projects. But the denomination could help by coordinating
the work of individuals and organizations that have greater
flexibility and freedom. Furthermore, the vast expansion of
VCRs and cable television in homes and congregations offer avenues of mass media that can target audiences effectively and inexpensively.

How the PC(USA) should use mass media ought to be the primary question as the denomination studies its evangelistic challenge in the twenty-first century. To ignore its potential is to hide the light of the gospel under a basket.

Reform Means Revitalizing
Education and Nurture

The re-forming of American Presbyterianism and mainstream Protestantism in the twentieth century has left these denominations seriously weakened as communities of faith. As we have seen in chapter seven, the ecology for nurturing faith has been disrupted. Programs and organizations that educated Presbyterians in the Christian faith and helped bind individuals and families to the church were essential parts of this ecology, but it no longer functions with the same vitality and power.

The central challenge to the PC(USA) is the summons to renew and strengthen the ecology for nurturing faith. This will require a major emphasis on nurture and education. Four areas of concern emerged from our research—families, congregations, governing bodies, and leadership.

The Household of Faith

The shift from the old to the new agenda in American Presbyterianism since the 1960s, documented by Benton Johnson, meant that the family virtually disappeared as a central denominational concern. Since the 1960s, the family has undergone dramatic and epochal changes. Scholars may debate whether the family is in decline, but it clearly faces a crisis. The 1960s marked the beginning of the rising rate of divorce in American society. The feminization of poverty in America in the last three decades has created a new class of impoverished women and children. Out-of-wedlock births have soared from 5 percent in 1960 to 25 percent of all births in 1988. From 1960 to 1990, the number of children living with a single adult jumped from 7 percent to approximately 25 percent. As Don S. and Carol

Browning note, these facts "point to a situation that the mainstream Protestant churches have not wanted [to] face. For the past thirty years these churches have been timid and inarticulate about the growing family crisis. They have let the family issue fall into the hands of reactionary political and religious forces to the right or radical cultural forces to the left."[27]

The Brownings' call for renewed attention to the family and its critical role in raising children is based on what they describe as a "new love ethic," one that emphasizes equality and mutuality in families, in contrast to subservience and self-sacrifice.[28] This welcomed emphasis recognizes how distorted understandings of familial love contribute to a kind of family life that can be destructive for parents and children. But what is particularly urgent is to place the family back on the agenda of social and theological concern in mainstream Protestantism and American Presbyterianism—from the congregation to the policies and programs of governing bodies.

Recovering a concern for family life will be controversial, for any discussion of the family inevitably raises difficult issues regarding divorce, gender roles, gay and lesbian life-styles, and singles in the life of the church. But these vexing questions should be debated within the context of a commitment by the church to sustain and strengthen diverse types of families and households. The family constitutes a critical part of the ecology for nurturing faith in American Presbyterianism, and despite increasing rates of divorce, especially among younger members and clergy, the family is still the heart of Presbyterian membership. The 1991–1993 sample of Presbyterians polled by the *Presbyterian Panel* revealed that the vast majority are married (79 percent of the members, 84 percent of the elders, 90 percent of the pastors, and 86 percent of the specialized clergy). Furthermore, more than 80 percent of each group are parents.[29]

Congregations can play an important role in the nurture and sustenance of family life and in creating family relationships for those who are not married or who do not have children. Particularly given the fragmentation of American society and the powerful forces undermining family life, the church has a unique ministry in fostering an ethos of health and wholeness for adults and children.

"Without wallowing in false nostalgia, there has been a fundamental shift," declares columnist Ellen Goodman. "Americans once expected parents to raise their children in accordance with the dominant cultural messages. Today they are expected to raise their children in opposition." Goodman captures the mood of contemporary parents fighting the materialistic and inhumane values inherent in much of the media and the culture. "It's what makes child-raising harder," she writes. "It's why parents feel more isolated. It's not just that American families have less time with their kids, it's that we have to spend more of this time doing battle with our own culture." She concludes: "It's rather like trying to get your kids to eat their green beans after they've been told all day about the wonders of Milky Way. Come to think of it, it's exactly like that."*

That is an authentic cry for help; the church must listen to its anguish and respond.

One way congregations can support families is to help them learn to worship together again. Before the development of the Sunday school, family piety and worship, along with congregational worship, were the primary means of transmitting the faith. It should come as a considerable shock that a recent study revealed that 63 percent of a group of Presbyterian adolescents have never or rarely had family devotionals, and only half have participated with their parents in a service project. Thirty percent of these adolescents have never or rarely heard their mothers speak about their faith, and 58 percent of their fathers have never or rarely broached the subject with them.[30] Presbyterians not only do not worship as families; they are amazingly inarticulate about religion.

---

*The *Holland* (Mich.) *Sentinel,* August 17, 1991. © 1991, The Boston Globe Newspaper Company/Washington Post Writers Group. Reprinted with permission.

The PC(USA)'s *Directory for Worship* emphasizes the importance of family worship, but the call is rarely heard in congregations. The *Directory* places special responsibility for family worship on "the parent(s) or the one(s) exercising parental responsibility." They "should teach their children about Christian worship by example, by providing for household worship, and by discussion and instruction." Children, it continues, join in household worship through "praying and singing, listening to and telling Bible stories, reading and memorizing, leading and sharing, enacting and responding."[31]

The recovery of family worship will not solve the crisis of the American family, but it will help families tap the resources of Christian faith and discipleship to resist the forces eroding the vitality of family life. Furthermore, it is one specific step each family and congregation can take to renew and rebuild the ecology for nurturing faith.

Congregations

The Louisville research project points to an arresting conclusion about the PC(USA) as a denomination—namely, that the power and vitality of American Presbyterianism rest largely in congregations. As denominational structures have weakened, congregations are emerging as the key place where Christian faith and Presbyterian identity are forged and where diverse forms of mission take place. This was, of course, the way Presbyterianism began in America, and historically and theologically one could argue that the congregation is the irreducible core of Presbyterian life.

As Barbara Wheeler has noted, however, the congregation "has not been systematically investigated," and despite mountains of books of advice and exhortation about what congregations can do, the diversities and dynamics of congregations raise fascinating questions that new research is attempting to answer.[32] Some of the projects in the Louisville research did focus on congregations,[33] and clearly the congregations of disestablished Protestant denominations

confront significant challenges. Unable to rely on religious
or cultural reinforcement in American society, congregations now find themselves competing for their members'
time, values, and allegiances. The problem of membership
decline, as we have seen, is primarily that of the retention
of members, many of whom drift "out the back door" to
nonaffiliation with any church.

Congregations foster faith and allegiance in many different ways, and we offer only two suggestions to strengthen
their role in the ecology for nurturing faith: a new understanding of the Sabbath and congregations as educating
communities.

Earlier we have seen how the nineteenth-century Presbyterian obsession with Sabbath observance, with all its inherent moralism and legalism, finally gave way to a more
tolerant understanding of the fourth commandment. By
the 1930s, what had been a concern of Presbyterians for
more than a century had virtually ended; the subject was
quietly dropped. The difficulty, however, is that something
very fundamental to the religious character of American
Presbyterianism was also lost.

Benton Johnson concedes that Sabbath observance may
look trivial when compared to, for example, the need for
justice in southern Africa. "But it is not a trivial thing when
we remind ourselves that spiritual practice is one of the
three pillars of a religious tradition, the other two being its
teachings and its morality," he writes. "Spiritual practice
waters the roots of the soul and thereby enlivens the spirit.
When done by members of a community, it recreates the
energy to sustain its morality, which means that it is able to
sustain both itself and its various missions. Without teaching and spiritual practice the will to live by the moral code
of a faith fades away."[34]

Sabbath observance as spiritual practice—this is at least
one way to renew the ecology for nurturing faith. Obviously, it cannot be reconstructed on the basis of blue laws,
nor should it be rebuilt on the basis of the old Victorian
strictures against enjoyable recreation. What the Sabbath
issue raises for contemporary Christians is the allocation of

time, which is an ethical and theological question, especially in an age and a culture where time can be more precious than money. Presbyterian minister Stephen P. McCutchan declared in 1991, "I have been convinced for some time now that the major theological issue at the end of the twentieth century is the meaning of the Sabbath." With a multiplicity of choices and with the pace of modern life escalating, McCutchan argues, the church must help people recover the Sabbath for worship and rest as a way of nurturing faith and providing distance from the tyranny of "busyness" in contemporary life.[35]

Nineteenth-century Sabbatarianism was based on enforcement of the fourth commandment and appeals to natural law. In the twentieth century those justifications are undoubtedly less persuasive. Yet in teaching and practice, congregations can help people make the choice to "remember the Sabbath and keep it holy" as a way of reclaiming a rhythm to life that affirms God's claim on and call to human re-creation as well as renewing and refreshing their relationship with God and others in worshiping communities of faith.

The ecology for nurturing faith has also been disrupted by the travail of the Sunday school. Craig Dykstra and Bradley Wigger have demonstrated how church school curricula became preoccupied with teaching teachers how to teach; David Hester has shown the problems of interpreting the Bible in twentieth-century Presbyterian church school resources.[36]

These and other studies point to a painful conclusion for mainstream Protestants. The Sunday school, which has been vested with virtually the entire responsibility for Christian education, cannot carry this burden. A noble and exciting experiment of the early nineteenth century, the Sunday school is simply no longer capable of fulfilling the vast scope of its educational mission.[37]

Mainstream Protestants, according to C. Ellis Nelson, have three options. They can try to renew all the ways in which congregations nurture and educate members; or, as a second possibility, they can establish parochial schools.

Nelson believes that neither of these options is feasible. Instead, he proposes that "the congregation must become conscious of itself as a community in which teaching and learning are going on incessantly and must organize itself to be the center for interpreting faith." In *How Faith Matures*, Nelson calls for mainstream Protestant congregations to consider themselves communities committed to educating and nurturing people in the Christian faith. Sunday school classes do not disappear in his strategy, but they are subsumed by an intentional effort, initiated by the minister and adult leaders, to transmit and reinforce Christian discipleship through worship and mission. The congregation as an educating and nurturing community, he argues, will take on some characteristics of a sect as it intentionally seeks to "become a Christian community where members receive inspiration and guidance to orient their lives toward God and not toward the values of a secular society."[38]

In perhaps no other area of congregational life is the role of nurture and education more critical than in ministry to youth. The "new agenda" of American Presbyterianism since the 1960s reduced the emphasis on nurturing the allegiance and deepening the faith of youth and young adults. What Robert Bellah has described as a contemporary American rite of passage—leaving home and leaving the church—is not a biological necessity. Therefore, it cannot and should not be taken for granted in the future.[39]

Governing Bodies

Research on American Presbyterianism, supplemented by other studies, confirms the fact that the denomination is undergoing a revolution. This dramatic reconfiguration has introduced significant stress to every area of the church. The character of the contending interests varies, but the level of friction in late twentieth-century American Presbyterianism is disturbing and debilitating.

One kind of friction is the gap between congregations and the governing bodies of the PC(USA)—presbyteries, synods, and the General Assembly. As we have seen, this perceived conflict pits pastors *and* laity against governing bodies, and it may be even more pervasive than the widely discussed differences between conservatives and liberals or ministers and lay people. It is certainly equally pernicious and tragic.

Governing bodies have always passed laws to order the life of American Presbyterians. That is not at stake. Rather, what roils the waters of American Presbyterianism today is what Dykstra and Hudnut-Beumler call the denomination as regulatory agency or what McCarthy and Moorhead see as the ascendance of polity over theology.[40] It is actually the increasing tendency of the governing bodies of the PC(USA) to substitute legislation for education, to impose policies rather than persuade people to change. The result is alienation between the "two churches" of American Presbyterians—the one centered in the congregation, the other focused in governing bodies. Each is often seriously at odds with the other.[41]

It is important to recognize that there are deeply committed Christians and intensely devoted Presbyterians in both groups, and that the regulatory or legislative mentality is characteristic of not only governing bodies but also congregations and many other institutions in American society. It is particularly noticeable in voluntary organizations because it often causes sharp conflict and alienation. In our experience, few people intend to use the church as a regulatory agency, and when their behavior is perceived as coercive, they are shocked and surprised.

Consider an anecdotal example: One of us was invited to a presbytery to interpret the results of our research. The issue before the presbytery was a fifteen-page, single-spaced report from the personnel committee, recommending a policy for presbytery employees who acquired AIDS. The debate raged for hours. Approximately two-thirds of the presbytery supported treating the victims of AIDS with compassion. The remaining minority was divided equally, half condemning and half supporting the proposed policy because of their differing views of homosexuality. Fortunately, our presentation was marked as an order of the day; when we left at 8 P.M. the issue had not yet been resolved.

Here is a wonderfully human and perfectly Presbyterian illustration of the denomination as a regulatory agency and the triumph of legislation over education. The laudable intent of the policy was obviously to help congregations understand better the critical need to minister to victims of the AIDS epidemic—in other words, education. The means became legislating a new personnel policy for the presbytery. The result was intense concentration on a document that consumed hours in preparation and additional hours in debate, and it left behind a legacy of frustration and anger.

What is so unfortunate about the regulatory ethos of denominations like the PC(USA) is that it is largely unconscious and motivated in most cases by idealism. This study has shown how a mentality of establishment has pervaded mainstream Protestantism, and how that consciousness has failed to appreciate the fragility of the church's hold on its own membership. Thus, one consequence has been the erosion of the ecology for nurturing faith. The regulatory mentality of contemporary American Presbyterianism also fails to recognize the limits of legislation in voluntary organizations like the church. Theologically, it substitutes law for grace in the life of the church, and it bruises the church's long-standing affirmation of the right to follow the leadings of one's conscience.

At one time, the organization of American Presbyterianism was described as a set of church courts or judicatories. Interestingly, today they are known as "governing bodies." Ironically, the more they govern the weaker they become.

We believe there is another model—transforming "governing bodies" into "educating bodies." This is an extension of Nelson's vision of the congregation as an educating community, for it would involve the self-conscious decision by presbyteries, synods, and the General Assembly to see their primary role as that of educators and nurturers of congregations. Some presbyteries are already experimenting with this new model. Large amounts of business are dispensed with quickly through "consent agendas," and the remainder of the meeting is devoted to educational programs on the Christian faith and key issues confronting the church. In this new model, the prized qualities of "educating body" leadership would be the ability to communicate, teach, persuade, and inspire.

The PC(USA) will always need laws, policies, and procedures to live "decently and in order." But the contemporary turmoil unleashed by the organizational revolution in American denominationalism will not be contained and will only be exacerbated by taking refuge in legislation. Denominations and denominational structures must recover their roles as teachers and nurturers of Christian faith and discipleship.

Leadership

One sign of the organizational problems of contemporary mainstream Protestantism and American Presbyterianism is confusion about leadership and the disillusionment of leaders themselves. Both are powerful trends affecting every institution in American culture. The confusion about leadership is rooted in a long-standing ambivalence toward leadership in American society. In nearly every generation, people long for leaders and yet often disparage and undermine them when they appear.

In American Presbyterianism, the 1960s and 1970s brought new leaders to prominence amid a wave of reaction against the highly visible white male leadership that had exercised the dominant influence during the heyday of the corporate denomination. The new structures opened the doors to more women and members of Presbyterian racial ethnic minorities, male and female. But they also placed new restrictions on the latitude that leaders enjoyed. The new leaders, as we have seen, were intended to be managers of conflict, capable of building consensus.

They were also anonymous, hidden from view by complex processes for communication and reaching common agreement.

The organizational revolution in American Presbyterianism has been devastating to these leaders who cannot lead. As denominational ties frayed and as alienation between congregations and governing bodies grew, these individuals frequently found themselves increasingly alienated and alone. Similarly, the conflict and turmoil in American society have taken an enormous toll on pastors and professionals in congregations. Expectations of ministers have soared as their own morale has suffered. Forced terminations of pastoral staff have increased. One layperson, observing the struggle of a new pastor in his congregation, observed, "There just isn't much margin for error in the ministry any more."

A *Presbyterian Panel* poll in 1989 surprisingly revealed that two-thirds of the members and elders of the PC(USA) were highly optimistic about the future of the denomination. Ominously, pastors were less optimistic, and specialized clergy were even less hopeful.[42] There is enough circumstantial evidence to indicate that a crisis of leadership and morale grips the PC(USA) and mainstream Protestantism. What can be done?

First, the PC(USA) should nurture the leaders it already has. Amid opposition to him during the Vietnam war, Lyndon Johnson was criticized for his arrogant comment: "I'm the only president they've got!" But the remark is apt for Presbyterians and their leaders today. They are the only leaders Presbyterians have. Rather than bemoaning their weaknesses, we ought to nurture their strengths. Rather than blaming them for an organization that is not working, we ought to begin to see that we are trapped by structures and forces that are not necessarily of our own making. One elder made a practice of writing his minister a note every time he appreciated something in a sermon or benefited from some act of ministry. Every leader longs for at least one or two individuals like that. In short, we need to recognize that bureaucrat bashing and pastor baiting are self-destructive. We are all in this together.

Second, we need to identify and nurture the next generation of leaders. One of the victims of the weakened ecology for nurturing faith has been an informal network of lay people, pastors, college professors, campus ministers, and others who conscientiously identified and encouraged people to consider the ministry. Some did enter the ministry; others did not but became significant lay leaders. The collapse of that network of leadership recruitment has been debilitating. Most students preparing for ministry today are self-selected, rather than called forth by others for leadership in the church. Furthermore, American theological educators are deeply troubled but rarely able to talk about the volatile issue of the quality of students entering ministry today.[43]

John Calvin distinguished between the inner call and the outer call, one from God and the other mediated through the church.[44] Presbyterian churches—its ministers and lay leaders—are strangely silent today about enlisting the leadership that can give life and vision to the denomination in the future. We need to look for and invite individuals to consider devoting their lives to a unique and challenging vocation of service to God through the church. Furthermore, we should create new networks to nurture the leadership that will give definition and direction for future Presbyterian witness.

Third, leaders should see themselves as educators and their task as nurture and persuasion. The fragmentation of mission and the weakening of the ecology for nurturing faith in American Presbyterianism mean that the role of leadership must change. The corporate denomination relied on high levels of trust between different parts of the church, forged by a common vision of the denomination's values and goals. Both trust and consensus have fragmented, but they can be reconstructed, at least in part. What passes for "prophetic leadership" is often not leadership at all but a refusal to spend the necessary time and energy to educate and persuade, rather than legislate or direct.

The nature of leadership and the task of leaders have been perpetual challenges for the church, but they have an immediacy and urgency for contemporary Presbyterians as we negotiate our way through the tumult of the organizational revolution sweeping American denominations.

Reform Means Recovery of Theological Vision

The calls for a renewal of theology in mainstream Protestantism come from nearly all directions. Sydney Ahlstrom has argued that "in the seventies, for reasons that are not easily diagnosed, creative theology virtually passed from the scene, though one can surmise that this dearth can be attributed to the swirling social events that agitated the nation as a whole. That lack of theological concern—whatever its cause—can only be regarded as a tragedy."[45] Theologians and the discipline of theology are often marginalized in the life of the church, and this has impoverished both the church and the theological task.[46]

"The only weakness for which a recovery course [for mainstream Protestantism] cannot now be charted is the churches' theological predicament," Benton Johnson has concluded. "The problems standing in the way of theological renewal are formidable. Not only must such a renewal pass today's strict tests of intellectual credibility; it must be able to energize large numbers of lay people as well."[47]

Johnson, a sociologist, is accurate in emphasizing the important role that theology must play in the reform of American Presbyterianism and mainstream Protestantism. One can turn the kaleidoscope of mainstream Protestantism in many directions and see it as a crisis of membership, or a crisis in organization, or a crisis of cultural and religious disestablishment. But we believe that theology is the most important ingredient in the Presbyterian predicament and that the recovery of theological vision is also crucial for the reform of American Presbyterianism and mainstream Protestantism. Our research leads us to propose four areas where Presbyterians need to devote their attention in the future.

The Predicament of Pluralism

Pluralism is the most prominent characteristic of Christian theology in the late twentieth century and a central key to the theological predicament of American Presbyterianism. Pluralism is not only a description of the variety of belief, doctrine, and practice in global Christianity but also an accepted ideal for many theologians.

Pluralism has many roots. Obviously, the history of the church demonstrates that Christianity has been conceived and reconceived in very different ways during two thousand years, and the development of historical theology and church history during the nineteenth and twentieth centuries has made contemporary Christians keenly aware of the pluralism of interpretation and practice within the Christian tradition. Similarly, the nineteenth-century missionary movement awakened Christians to the pluralism of religions in the world and posed basic questions about the universal and transcendent truth of Christianity itself.

In the twentieth century, pluralism has erupted with enormous power due to the assertiveness of Third World churches, racial ethnic minority groups in American culture, and women. The diversity of American culture and the disestablishment of mainstream Protestantism—culturally and religiously—have meant that American Presbyterians and their mainstream Protestant counterparts now embrace as a fact of life not only racial, cultural, and gender diversity but ideological pluralism as well. They have "discovered America," to use William M. Hutchison's phrase;[48] to put it perhaps more sharply, they have discovered the world.

Pluralism is both the product of and a peculiar predicament for Protestantism and Presbyterianism. It represents the result of what Paul Tillich called "the Protestant principle"—the insistence that nothing is ultimate except God, and therefore everything is relative. In Presbyterianism, the sovereignty of God, the recognition that "all synods and councils may err," and the affirmation that "God alone is Lord of the conscience" all underscore the time-bound and relative character of any formulation of the mystery of God's grace in Jesus Christ.[49]

Furthermore, twentieth-century Presbyterians have been particularly eager to embrace pluralism as a way to escape the doctrinal rigidities of scholastic Calvinism and as an alternative to the American, WASPish, masculine, middle-class character of their own tradition. Pluralism for many represents the reform of the church.

There is no question that pluralism has enriched and enlivened the life and theological discussion of American Presbyterianism and mainstream Protestantism. It has broadened the community of discourse to include a much broader array of Christians from different cultures and both sexes. It has made Christians aware of the cultural character of Christian thought. It has expanded the methods by which theology is conceived. Barbara Brown Zikmund explored some of the theological implications of the ordination of women, for example, and concluded that the biblical witness is more fully represented when both women and men exercise leadership.[50]

Few Presbyterians propose rejecting pluralism in favor of narrowly defined precise formulations of the Christian faith. In this sense, Edward Farley is right in describing American Presbyterians as critical modernists, who accept the principal categories of modern thought and remain critical and open to changing their understanding of God's revelation in Jesus Christ.[51]

But pluralism is a predicament as well because it poses agonizing problems for American Presbyterians and the entire Christian church. It is an especially poignant dilemma for a denomination, which is dependent upon distinctive features to distinguish itself from other denominational options and to justify theologically its existence as a fragmented member of the body of Christ. Furthermore, for a denomination like the PC(USA) which claims to stand in a confessional tradition, pluralism poses the question of the limits or boundaries of Christian faith in a very penetrating form.

Despite its great value, Barbara Brown Zikmund argues

that the elevation of pluralism as a positive principle has created its own set of problems in American Presbyterianism and mainstream Protestantism.[52]

One problem is theological authority. The twentieth-century experience of American Presbyterians makes this an especially vexing issue. During the 1920s the PCUSA defined itself as a denomination with a centralized, national administrative structure; it also reaffirmed the right of presbyteries to determine the standards of orthodoxy, thus decentralizing theological authority. The neo-orthodox consensus temporarily obscured the dilemma of a centralized, national organization with decentralized theological authority. But the adoption of a multiconfessional base for American Presbyterianism in the 1960s, as well as the explosion of theological pluralism since the 1960s, now makes it difficult for any American presbytery to exercise the authority it has wielded for nearly three centuries.

Furthermore, the acceptance of pluralism has been part of the identity crisis of American Presbyterians. It has rendered them confused about the nature of Presbyterian doctrine and, even more seriously, made both clergy and laity uncertain about the character of Christianity itself. If Presbyterians find it difficult to witness to their faith, it is partially due to the corrosive nature of pluralism. As Dean Hoge has written, "The question Who are we? or What do we believe? is not satisfactorily answered by a recitation of diverse viewpoints current in the church. Evangelism is barely possible when the identity of the church and its gospel are difficult to state clearly. Today it is no accident that many middle-class Protestants are hesitant to discuss their own Christian beliefs with other persons."[53]

When diversity of culture, race, and gender is institutionalized as it is in the PC(USA), it guarantees access to decision making by groups who were previously excluded. Such diversity has advantages but also poses problems. For example, if one's physical and/or cultural identity (sex, race, ethnic background, age, disability, etc.) become the controlling factors in determining representation, there is virtually no limit to the categories of possible representation.

But an even more serious problem arises when acceptance of diversity requires an equally warm reception to the full plurality of theological perspectives within the church. If different cultural, racial, and gender experiences generate their own distinct and separate versions of the Christian faith, the variety of representation multiplies exponentially. All shades of theological persuasion must not only be represented and heard; they must also be given equal weight. The church then finds itself virtually powerless to utter a discerning theological word amid a cacophony of competing voices.

The Mistaken Challenge

The Presbyterian embrace of pluralism is only a partial hug. In dethroning scholastic Calvinism and in combating fundamentalism, American Presbyterian theologians have been far more open to liberal than to conservative formulations of the Christian faith, especially the Pentecostal-charismatic movement. Denominational positions—whether theological or political—have been predominantly liberal in content and spirit, although the nature of that liberalism changed considerably during the last fifty years. The hegemony of the liberal party in American Presbyterianism is due partly to the genuinely liberal tendencies of American Presbyterians and their appreciation of the bracing liberal theological critique of America's serious social problems in the late twentieth century. Liberalism also prevailed because two schisms drained away the most conservative elements in the denomination, and theological liberals eventually won control of the educational and political structures of the denomination. But theological supremacy won through political power can be illusive, as the struggle in the Southern Baptist Convention during the 1980s clearly demonstrates.[54] Furthermore, on political issues, the membership of the PC(USA) has never been as liberal as its leadership, and that is one explanation of the continuing strife within American Presbyterianism.[55]

The liberal suspicion of conservatism, spawned by the

fundamentalist movement, has had several unfortunate,
even tragic, consequences. It made Presbyterians view conservatism as a monolith, and when conservative Christianity changed after the 1930s, Presbyterians were blinded to
the development and the differences among fundamentalists, Pentecostals, charismatics, and evangelicals. All four
were misperceived as simply the old fundamentalist wolf.

It also prompted conservative Presbyterians to respond in
kind, and since many were skilled polemicists, the rhetoric
frequently became vehement and at the least uncharitable.
Conservative Presbyterians have been equally defensive and
uncritical about twentieth-century liberalism, which itself
changed during the course of the twentieth century. In light
of the decline of political liberalism since the late 1960s, the
liberal wing of American Presbyterianism is both embattled
and an attractive subject for criticism and ridicule.

To some degree, this polarization of Presbyterianism is
understandable because of the harshness and bitterness of
the fundamentalist controversy and the critical nature of
the issues debated by liberal and conservative American
Presbyterians. But the preferential option for liberalism
and the suppression of conservative alternatives are ironic
in a denomination which takes pride in its openness and
tolerance.

The degree of polarization and division may also be ex-
aggerated by the forceful views of contending interest
groups. For example, Rogers and McKim suggest that Presbyterians and mainstream Protestants are overwhelmingly
"moderate." Most of them comprise a "moderate middle"
in a bell-shaped curve, with small minorities of liberals and
conservatives at each end. This is particularly true, they
argue, about Presbyterian convictions about biblical authority. The overwhelming majority of Presbyterians affirm
that the Bible is authoritative for Christian faith and life.
What does divide Presbyterians is the question of how that
authoritative Bible should be interpreted—particularly in
divisive moral issues dealing with families, gender roles,
and human sexuality.[56] In this regard, Presbyterian disputes over biblical interpretation have a long historical lin-

eage and are not unique to the late twentieth century. But it is important to recognize that these debates still center on the question of how the Bible continues to inform and shape the church's life, not whether it should.

The civil war in American Presbyterianism is a striking example of the church's preoccupation with the wrong challenge. If liberals and conservatives have stalked each other warily throughout the century, their obsession with combating each other has weakened themselves and depleted their resources for addressing a deeper and more fundamental problem: the challenge of secularity.

The Real Challenge

The question of secularization and secularity in American culture is fascinating. As we have seen, polls suggest that there has been virtually no change in religious belief during the last half-century. What has changed is religious affiliation and behavior, although even that remains fairly constant after some of the peaks and valleys are smoothed out. Church membership over the last fifty years has not shifted dramatically. However, since the 1960s American Presbyterians and mainstream Protestants have suffered disproportionate losses, and many conservative churches have grown. Why?

This book has attempted to outline the complexity of this phenomenon and to emphasize that membership decline is part of a broader problem for American Presbyterians and mainstream Protestants. But a concise answer would run as follows.

Presbyterians have suffered significant membership decline because of demographic factors, principally a decline in the birthrate as the postwar baby boom came to an end. Baby boomers became disaffected with the church. More generally, Presbyterians have failed to foster the faith and commitment in their members and have deemphasized programs of outreach. This is why renewing the ecology for nurturing faith in the PC(USA) is the critical issue before the denomination.

The erosion of nurture and the defection of Presbyterians to no church affiliation are in part testimony to the allure of secularity in American society, both within and outside the church. A classic theme of the Reformed tradition has been the affirmation of the goodness of culture, but in the twentieth century that affirmation has frequently deteriorated into an embrace of secular culture. Furthermore, there is no question that a secular society has both impoverished and enriched the character of life in late twentieth-century America. As Martin E. Marty has written, "Whoever writes the history of these decades [1960s–1980s] without doing justice to both the oppressive and liberating aspects of secularity . . . will certainly not be recognizably dealing with modern America."[57]

The disaffiliated Presbyterian baby boomers illustrate the peculiar character of secularity in American society and its effect on American Presbyterianism. The disaffiliated represent almost half (48 percent) of all Presbyterian baby boomer confirmands. Within this group, approximately 80–85 percent are residually religious since they continue to hold to Christian beliefs. Some even attend church. However, 15–20 percent have no religious beliefs at all.[58]

In short, as Presbyterians have praised pluralism and fought each other over what constituted proper Christianity, the real challenge for them was the gradual disaffection of somewhat religious young people. While battling perceived heresies of various kinds, American Presbyterians and mainstream Protestants failed to see that the threat to Christianity in the twentieth century was not heresy, but idolatry.

The idolatry of this age takes various forms. What we see as secularity is described by Lesslie Newbigin as the "paganism of the West." In Europe and elsewhere it has taken the form of totalitarianism. The technological faith that shapes so much of the world's values today is yet another manifestation of what is ultimately the true threat to the church—the attempt to define life apart from God.[59]

A recovery of theological vision in American Presbyterianism and mainstream Protestantism must begin with a

mutual recognition by the contending parties in the internecine Protestant civil war that the threats each represent
to the other are minor in comparison to the corrosive effects of secularity. As Wuthnow has suggested, surely reconciliation between these camps would be an elementary
Christian response.[60] But reconciliation is also a theological
imperative for these churches in order to be faithful witnesses to the Christian gospel.

The recovery of theological vision for American Presbyterians also begins with listening to the vital and spirit-
filled Christianity of newer communions. Though this
particular study focuses primarily on the American Presbyterian experience, the fresh insight of Newbigin is just one
example of the insight and wisdom available as a new theological agenda forms.

A Theological Agenda for the Church

In struggling to understand the re-forming of American
Presbyterianism and mainstream Protestantism, we began
to formulate some of the theological questions posed by
these epochal changes. They arise not only out of research
and study but also from our conversations with Presbyterians and others who are deeply concerned about the future
of the PC(USA) and other mainstream Protestant denominations. We propose these as questions for theological reflection on reconstructing a Reformed vision of Christian
witness.

1. Who is Jesus Christ? The only requirement for membership in the PC(USA) is that an individual must acknowledge Jesus Christ as Lord. In every era of reform in
the history of the church, Christology has been a central
question. It is especially urgent today.

What affirmations about the uniqueness of Christ can we
make in the midst of the pluralism of American culture and
world religions? What does it mean to confess that Jesus
Christ is savior of the world? What do we mean when we
say that in Jesus Christ God became human and that in
Jesus Christ God forgives human sin and reconciles the

world? How does this good news change the way we live
and the structures of society?

In short, the renewal of theology begins with a focused
attention to the heart of the Christian faith—Jesus Christ
and the gospel he proclaimed.

2. What is the authority for the Christian life? The Reformers insisted upon the authority of scripture as the supreme revelation of God's grace in Jesus Christ. For
centuries, this doctrine was virtually unquestioned in the
Reformed tradition, but beginning with the Enlightenment
and at an escalating rate in the nineteenth and twentieth
centuries, biblical authority has been subjected to penetrating challenges.

Questions about the authority of scripture have come
from biblical scholars employing new methods of historical
and literary criticism. These have enriched our knowledge
of the Bible, but they have also raised troubling issues
about how the Bible should be interpreted. For American
Protestants, the debate over slavery and abolition was
waged in large measure on biblical grounds. Similarly, controversy over women's full participation in the church's life
revolved around interpretive differences over strictures
against women in some biblical passages and numerous
scriptural disclosures of the fundamental equality of all
humans under Christ. In the contemporary church, the authority and interpretation of the Bible again play a major
role in the discussion of homosexuality.

Perhaps the greatest contemporary challenge to the authority of scripture comes from the general acceptance of
relativism in American culture and American education.
The idea of transcendent truth—truth that is not dominated by history or culture—is one that many persons find
impossible to accept, being tempted instead to retreat into
a form of tolerant individualism that finally regards truth
as a matter of personal taste.

The church must recognize the urgent need to recover
the authority of scripture as the Word of God, and it must
regain its ability to interpret biblical authority in a way that
will give life and meaning to Christian teaching. For Ameri-

can Presbyterians, there is no recourse to simple formulas of inerrancy or infallibility, but the rejection of such inadequate formulas for scriptural authority does not solve the problem. The key to the renewal of American Presbyterianism and mainstream Protestantism is a recovery of theological insight and biblical wisdom, and it must include a reaffirmation of the Bible as the authoritative guide to Christian faith and witness.

3. What can we hope for in a world that is increasingly paralyzed by both personal and communal despair? Nineteenth-century evangelicalism exuded the optimism of American expansionism, but American Presbyterianism and mainstream Protestantism have found optimism and hope difficult in the twentieth century. The concept of hope rings discordantly in the hallways of this century with its destructive warfare, holocausts, famines, and other horrors. Mainstream Protestant theologians have relentlessly attacked the presumptions of utopian Christianity which assumed that there would or could be some realization of the kingdom of God in this world. History, they advised, is tragic, and only through the work of God is tragedy transformed into irony.[61] While this may be true, irony alone does not capture the breadth and depth of Christian hope; it is also a thin reed on which to anchor one's life amid such crises as death, illness, divorce, and the injustices of society. What hope do we as Christians offer to this world?

4. Why, after all, is there a church—an ordered community of Christians? Why is faith a communal experience, rather than a private one? Swirling beneath the sociological trends in American society is not only the institutional crisis of American Presbyterianism and mainstream Protestantism but the haunting query of individuals about the need for and purpose of the church. Why must individual disciples of Christ seek intimate person-to-person companionship in congregations, particularly in an age of mass media? Are community, refuge, praise, service, sacrifice, and invitation all part of the diverse mission of the church? If so, how are they linked in mutual support and nurture of human souls and societies? If it is true that the large num-

bers of Presbyterian baby boomers retain a rudimentary
Christian faith but do not attach themselves to congregations; if it is true that religious belief in American culture
has not significantly declined; and if it is true that Americans commonly develop their beliefs without recourse or
reference to the church's guidance, then the church's community must have a forthright and compellingly persuasive
vision of what the church is and should be for Christian
witness.

5. What do we as Reformed Christians offer as our contribution to Christian life and witness? This fifth question
comes last—intentionally. This question is not subsidiary
to the four previous ones nor does it take precedence over
them. Reformed Christianity at its best has not sought to
be different from other traditions of the faith simply to be
different. It recognizes that the central questions for all
Christians are, What does it mean to be saved? What is
Christian hope? and Why and how are Christians to be the
body of Christ, the church? Reformed Christianity has
strived to provide the *clearest* explication and embodiment
of the answers found to these questions in biblical revelation. As the *Book of Order* suggests, Presbyterians affirm
with all Christians God's incarnation in Jesus Christ and
the Trinity. We join with all Protestants in acknowledging
the authority of scripture and justification by grace through
faith. But we also affirm that the fullness of Christ's good
news is not made completely transparent in disciples unless
they take with utter seriousness "the majesty, holiness, and
providence of God who creates, sustains, rules, and re-
deems the world in the freedom of sovereign righteousness
and love."[62]

From this follow four other distinctives that Presbyterians believe uncover the full potential and responsibilities of a Christian discipleship informed and enfolded by
the divine revelation. According to the *Book of Order*,
these are:

1. The election of the people of God for service as well as
salvation

2. Covenant life marked by a disciplined concern for order in the Church according to the word of God

3. A faithful stewardship that shuns ostentation and seeks proper use of the gifts of God's creation

4. The recognition of the human tendency to idolatry and tyranny, which calls the people of God to work for the transformation of society by seeking justice and living in obedience to the Word of God.[63]

This is a mere outline of what an ecumenical Presbyterian credo might be. We took it from an unlikely source—the *Book of Order*—only to suggest that the resources for reconstructing the theological identity of American Presbyterianism may be more accessible and familiar than many acknowledge.

The last of these distinctives require Presbyterians to be in intimate ecumenical relationship with other Christian traditions. The Reformed recognition of our finite nature and limited vision as well as our habitual surrender to idolatry and tyranny requires that we remain open to conversation and correction from other Christian groups. It is only in that struggle together that the Reformed goal of disclosing the deepest implications of the Word made flesh will be furthered.

If we understand more clearly the breadth and depth of our own tradition as well as the refining value of our ties with Christians who span continents and centuries, we will recover a theological vision that could indeed lead a re-forming church to be a reformed church.

Conclusion

Perhaps the most difficult task for us is to recognize the opportunity that the church confronts in this confusing era. The successive disestablishments of American Protestantism—legally, religiously, culturally—mean that mainstream Protestantism has lost its dominance over American culture. All churches must recognize that they now stand in competition with a secular culture. If there is a mainstream any longer, it is not defined by religious or

cultural hegemony but by the willingness of these churches
to proclaim, without being ashamed, the wholeness of the
Christian faith, rather than accent any of its extremes.

American Presbyterians have been central actors in the
drama of mainstream disestablishment in the twentieth
century, and they could be major figures in the reforming of
this tradition. Central to this task will be the recognition
that this dark night of the Presbyterian soul offers us a new
freedom, a liberation from the need and desire to establish
a Christian America or Christendom again. The challenge
is to become a church that remains open and responsive to
the needs of the age but does not lose its bearings—a
church with equilibrium.

The experience of disestablishment in American history
is, of course, not unprecedented, and perhaps a chapter
from the first disestablishment might serve as a guide for
Presbyterians and mainstream Protestants. In the Connecticut election of 1811, the Democrats defeated the Federal-
ists. Congregationalist/Presbyterian Lyman Beecher knew
that this spelled the end of establishment Congregationalism in Connecticut. The church lost its privileged position
and had to compete with every other denomination. His
son Charles recalled his father's reaction: "I remember see-
ing father, the day after the election, sitting on one of the
old-fashioned, rush-bottomed kitchen chairs, his head
drooping on his breast, and his arms hanging down. 'Father,' said I, 'what are you thinking of?' He answered, solemnly, 'THE CHURCH OF GOD.' "[64]

Lyman Beecher recollected later of this time, "It was a
time of great depression and suffering. It was the worst attack I ever met in my life. . . . I worked as hard as mortal
man could, and at the same time preached for revivals
with all my might, and with success, till at last, what with
domestic afflictions and all, my health and spirits began to
fail. It was as dark a day as ever I saw. The odium thrown
upon the ministry was inconceivable. The injury done to
the cause of Christ, as we then supposed, was irrepara-
ble."[65]

Then Beecher noted the unexpected consequences of the

disestablishment that he had at first bewailed. He wrote, "For several days I suffered what no tongue can tell *for the best thing that ever happened to the State of Connecticut.* It cut the churches loose from dependence on state support. It threw them wholly on their own resources and on God."[66]

What Beecher and the Congregationalists lost was legal recognition. What mainstream Protestants have lost is cultural and religious hegemony.

The central challenge before mainstream Protestants is to recognize our cultural and religious displacement and the need to recover our identity as Christians and bearers of particular traditions that contribute to the richness of the Christian family. We are being thrown back on our own resources and on God, who steadfastly sustains and guides us through all the predicaments in which we find ourselves. If we are attentive to God's leadings and faithful to our tradition's understanding of God's will, the re-forming of American Presbyterianism and mainstream Protestantism may also become the moment of the reforming of the church.

Notes

Series Foreword

1. Arthur M. Schlesinger, Sr., "A Critical Period in American Religion, 1875–1900," first appeared in the *Massachusetts Historical Society Proceedings* 64 (1930–32) and is reprinted in John M. Mulder and John F. Wilson, eds., *Religion in American History: Interpretive Essays* (Englewood Cliffs, N.J.: Prentice-Hall, 1978), pp. 302–317.

2. Robert T. Handy, "The American Religious Depression, 1925–1935," *Church History* 29 (1960): 3–16, reprinted in Mulder and Wilson, *Religion in American History,* pp. 431–444; Handy, *A Christian America: Protestant Hopes and Historical Realities,* 2nd ed. (New York: Oxford University Press, 1984), pp. 159–184.

3. Sydney E. Ahlstrom, "The Radical Turn in Theology and Ethics: Why It Occurred in the 1960s," *Annals of the American Academy of Political and Social Science* 387 (1970): 1–13, reprinted in Mulder and Wilson, *Religion in American History,* pp. 445–456; Ahlstrom, "The Traumatic Years: American Religion and Culture in the 1960s and 1970s," *Theology Today* 26 (1980): 504–522; Ahlstrom, *A Religious History of the American People* (New Haven, Conn.: Yale University Press, 1972), pp. 1079–1096.

4. Wade Clark Roof and William McKinney, *American Main-*

line Religion: Its Changing Shape and Future (New Brunswick, N.J.: Rutgers University Press, 1987); Robert Wuthnow, *The Restructuring of American Religion: Society and Faith Since World War II* (Princeton, N.J.: Princeton University Press, 1988).

5. John V. Taylor, *The Primal Vision: Christian Presence Amid African Religion* (Philadelphia: Fortress Press, 1964), chapter 13, "The Practice of Presence," pp. 196–205.

Introduction

1. Quoted in C. Vann Woodward, *Origins of the New South, 1877–1913* (Baton Rouge, La.: Louisiana State University Press, 1951), p. viii.

2. Dean R. Hoge and David A. Roozen, eds., *Understanding Church Growth and Decline: 1950–1978* (New York: Pilgrim Press, 1979); Robert Wuthnow, *The Restructuring of American Religion: Society and Faith Since World War II* (Princeton: Princeton University Press, 1988); Robert Wuthnow, *The Struggle for America's Soul: Evangelicals, Liberals, and Secularism* (Grand Rapids: Wm. B. Eerdmans Publishing Co., 1989); Wade Clark Roof and William McKinney, *American Mainline Religion: Its Changing Shape and Future* (New Brunswick, N.J.: Rutgers University Press, 1987); Robert S. Michaelsen and Wade Clark Roof, eds., *Liberal Protestantism: Realities and Possibilities* (New York: Pilgrim Press, 1986); William R. Hutchison, *Between the Times: The Travail of the Protestant Establishment in America, 1900–1960* (Cambridge: Cambridge University Press, 1989).

3. The results of the Disciples of Christ study are reported in Newell Williams, ed., *A Case Study of Mainstream Protestantism: The Disciples' Relation to American Culture, 1880–1989* (Grand Rapids: Wm. B. Eerdmans Publishing Co., 1991).

4. Address by Dorothy Bass, conference at Louisville Presbyterian Theological Seminary, October 1990.

5. Peter Berger, Brigitte Berger, and Hansfried Kellner, *The Homeless Mind: Modernization and Consciousness* (New York: Random House, 1973).

6. Robert T. Handy, *A Christian America* (New York: Oxford University Press, 1984), pp. 159–184.

7. Barbara W. Tuchman, *The March of Folly: From Troy to Vietnam* (New York: Alfred A. Knopf, 1984), p. 383.

1: Religion and American Culture

1. *Addresses delivered at the Celebration of the Centennial of the General Assembly of the Presbyterian Church in the Academy of Music and Horticultural Hall, Philadelphia, on May 24th, 1888* (Philadelphia: MacCalla & Co., 1888), p. 23.

2. Ibid., pp. 176, 177.

3. Seymour Martin Lipset, *The First New Nation: The United States in Historical and Comparative Perspective* (New York: Doubleday & Co., Anchor Books, 1967), pp. 159–192.

4. John K. Wilson, "Religion Under the State Constitutions, 1776–1800," *Journal of Church and State* 32 (Autumn 1990): 753–773.

5. Winthrop S. Hudson, *Religion in America*, 4th ed. (New York: Macmillan Publishing Co., 1987), pp. 96–103; and Lefferts A. Loetscher, *A Brief History of the Presbyterians*, 4th ed. (Philadelphia: Westminster Press, 1983), pp. 75–76.

6. Bernard Bailyn, *The Ideological Origins of the American Revolution* (Cambridge, Mass.: Harvard University Press, 1967); Gordon S. Wood, *The Creation of the American Republic, 1776–1787* (Chapel Hill, N.C.: University of North Carolina Press, 1969); and Handy, *A Christian America*, pp. 27–37.

7. Roger Finke and Rodney Stark, "How the Up-Start Sects Won America: 1776–1850," *Journal for the Scientific Study of Religion* 28 (1989): 27–44.

8. Anson Phelps Stokes, *Church and State in the United States* (New York: Harper & Bros., 1950), vol. 3, p. 453.

9. Robert T. Handy was the first to name this shift in religious forces as a second disestablishment. *A Christian America* (New York: Oxford University Press, 1984), pp. 165–166.

10. Will Herberg, *Protestant-Catholic-Jew: An Essay in American Religious Sociology* (Garden City, N.Y.: Doubleday & Co., 1956), pp. 272–273.

11. Herberg, *Protestant-Catholic-Jew*, pp. 274–281.

12. Quoted in Sydney E. Ahlstrom, *A Religious History of the American People* (New Haven, Conn.: Yale University Press, 1972), p. 954.

13. Roof and McKinney, *American Mainline Religion*, pp. 33–39.

14. Richard J. Neuhaus, *The Naked Public Square: Religion and Democracy in America* (Grand Rapids: Wm. B. Eerdmans Publishing Co., 1984); and Lesslie Newbigin, *Foolishness to the*

Greeks: The Gospel and Western Culture (Grand Rapids: Wm. B. Eerdmans Publishing Co., 1986), pp. 34–41, 75–94.

15. Robert N. Bellah et al., *Habits of the Heart* (New York: Harper & Row, 1985), pp. 275–296.

16. Robert N. Bellah, *The Broken Covenant: American Civil Religion in Time of Trial* (New York: Seabury Press, 1975), pp. 13–20; Jonathan Edwards, "Some Thoughts Concerning the Present Revival of Religion in New England," *The Works of President Edwards* (New York: S. Converse, 1830), vol. 4, pp. 128–133; and Conrad Cherry, ed., *God's New Israel: Religious Interpretations of American Destiny* (Englewood Cliffs, N.J.: Prentice-Hall, 1971), p. 85.

17. Cherry, *God's New Israel*, p. 90.

18. Bellah, *Broken Covenant*, p. 53.

19. Edward Bradford Davis, "Albert Barnes—1798–1870: An Exponent of New School Presbyterianism" (Th.D. diss., Princeton Theological Seminary, 1961), pp. 147–153, 169–174, 357–392, 434–438, 492; and *The Life of Ashbel Green* (New York: Robert Carter & Brothers, 1849), pp. 193–197.

20. Schlesinger, "A Critical Period in American Religion," pp. 307–317.

21. William R. Hutchison, *The Modernist Impulse in American Protestantism* (Cambridge, Mass.: Harvard University Press, 1976); George M. Marsden, *Fundamentalism and American Culture: The Shaping of Twentieth-Century Evangelicalism, 1820–1925* (New York: Oxford University Press, 1980); Ernest R. Sandeen, *The Roots of Fundamentalism: British and American Millenarianism, 1800–1930* (Chicago: University of Chicago Press, 1970); Timothy J. Weber, *Living in the Shadow of the Second Coming: American Premillennialism, 1875–1925* (New York: Oxford University Press, 1979); Vinson Synan, *The Holiness-Pentecostal Movement in the United States* (Grand Rapids: Wm. B. Eerdmans Publishing Co., 1971); Donald W. Dayton, *Theological Roots of Pentecostalism* (Metuchen, N.J.: Scarecrow Press, 1987); and Edith W. Blumhofer, *The Assemblies of God: A Chapter in the Story of American Pentecostalism* (Springfield, Mo.: Gospel Publishing House, 1980).

22. Lefferts A. Loetscher, *The Broadening Church: A Study of Theological Issues in the Presbyterian Church Since 1869* (Philadelphia: University of Pennsylvania Press, 1954); and Bradley J. Longfield, *The Presbyterian Controversy: Fundamentalists, Mod-*

ernists, and Moderates (New York: Oxford University Press, 1991).

23. George M. Marsden, *Understanding Fundamentalism and Evangelicalism* (Grand Rapids: Wm. B. Eerdmans Publishing Co., 1991), pp. 62–82. See also George M. Marsden, *Reforming Fundamentalism: Fuller Seminary and the New Evangelicalism* (Grand Rapids: Wm. B. Eerdmans Publishing Co., 1987).

24. Wuthnow, *Restructuring of American Religion*, pp. 71–99; Wuthnow, *The Struggle for America's Soul*, pp. 68–96; and Wuthnow, "The Restructuring of American Presbyterianism: Turmoil in One Denomination," in *PP*, pp. 27–48.

25. *The Letters of Henry Adams (1892–1918)*, ed. Worthington Chauncey Ford (Boston and New York, 1938), vol. 2, pp. 279–280; cited in Robert S. Michaelsen, "The Protestant Ministry in America: 1850–1950," in *The Ministry in Historical Perspectives*, ed. H. Richard Niebuhr and Daniel D. Williams, rev. ed. (San Francisco: Harper & Row, 1983), p. 250.

26. For an extensive account of the impact of incorporation on American life, see Alan Trachtenberg, *The Incorporation of America: Culture and Society in the Gilded Age* (New York: Hill & Wang, 1982); see especially the bibliographic essay, pp. 235–250. Also see Herbert Gutman, *Work, Culture and Society in Industrializing America* (New York: Alfred A. Knopf, 1976); and Robert Bellah et al., *Habits of the Heart*, pp. 42–44.

27. Trachtenberg, *Incorporation of America*, pp. 101–139; Arthur M. Schlesinger, *The Rise of the City 1878–1898* (New York: Macmillan Co., 1933); Blake McKelvey, *The Urbanization of America 1860–1915* (New Brunswick, N.J.: Rutgers University Press, 1963); and Kenneth T. Jackson, *Crabgrass Frontiers: The Suburbanization of the United States* (New York: Oxford University Press, 1985).

28. Roof and McKinney, *American Mainline Religion*, pp. 63–67.

29. Alfred D. Chandler, *The Visible Hand: The Managerial Revolution in American Business* (Cambridge, Mass.: Harvard University Press, 1977); Bellah et al., *Habits of the Heart*, pp. 44–46; Louis B. Weeks, "The Incorporation of the Presbyterians," in *OR*, pp. 39–43; Craig Dykstra and James Hudnut-Beumler, "The National Organizational Structures of Protestant Denominations," in *OR*, pp. 311–317.

30. Leonard Dinnerstein and David M. Reimers, *Ethnic Ameri-*

cans: A History of Immigration, 3rd ed. (New York: Harper & Row, 1988), pp. 15–16.

31. Ibid., pp. 91–98.

32. U.S. Bureau of the Census, *Statistical Abstract of the United States: 1990*, 110th ed. (Washington, D.C.: U.S. Government Printing Office, 1990), pp. 14, 17; and Gallup and Castelli, *People's Religion*, p. 18.

33. For information on future ethnic composition in the United States, see Leon F. Bouvier and Cary B. Davis, *Immigration and the Future Racial Composition of the United States* (Alexandria, Va.: Center for Immigration Research and Education, 1982), pp. 7–19.

34. Ibid., p. 19; U.S. Bureau of the Census, *Statistical Abstract of the United States: 1975*, 96th ed. (Washington, D.C.: U.S. Government Printing Office, 1975), p. 14; and U.S. Bureau of the Census, *Statistical Abstract . . . 1990*, pp. 14, 17, 19–20.

35. Roof & McKinney, *American Mainline Religion*, p. 131.

36. Ibid., p. 57.

37. Lyle E. Schaller, *Reflections of a Contrarian: Second Thoughts on the Parish Ministry* (Nashville: Abingdon Press, 1989), pp. 68–69.

38. Roof and McKinney, *American Mainline Religion*, p. 131.

39. Quoted in Robert T. Handy, *The American Tradition of Religious Freedom: An Historical Analysis* (n.p.: National Conference of Christians and Jews, n.d.), p. 7.

40. Albert J. Raboteau, *Slave Religion: The Invisible Institution in the Antebellum South* (New York: Oxford University Press, 1978); Eugene D. Genovese, *Roll, Jordan, Roll: The World the Slaves Made* (New York: Pantheon Books, 1972); and Lawrence W. Levine, *Black Culture and Black Consciousness: Afro-American Folk Thought from Slavery to Freedom* (New York: Oxford University Press, 1977).

41. Bellah et al., *Habits of the Heart*, pp. 250–274.

42. Alexis de Tocqueville, *Democracy in America* (1835; reprint New York: Vintage Books, 1954), vol. 2, p. 104.

43. Bellah et al., *Habits of the Heart*, pp. 142–163.

44. Ibid., p. 221.

45. *Religion in America 1990*, p. 8.

46. Newbigin, *Foolishness to the Greeks*, pp. 43–51, 75–94.

47. Ibid.

48. R. Laurence Moore, "Secularization: Religion and the So-

cial Sciences," in William R. Hutchison, ed., *Between the Times* (New York: Cambridge University Press, 1989), pp. 233–252.

49. Neuhaus, *The Naked Public Square.*

50. Dorothy C. Bass, "Ministry on the Margin: Protestants and Education," in Hutchison, ed., *Between the Times*, p. 50.

51. Thomas Huxley was the principal speaker at the opening exercises. John M. Mulder, *Woodrow Wilson: The Years of Preparation* (Princeton: Princeton University Press, 1978), p. 75.

52. George M. Marsden, "The Soul of the American University," *First Things* 10 (January 1991): 34–35.

53. James Turner, "Secularization and Sacralization: Some Aspects of the Teaching of Humanities in American Colleges, 1850–1900" (paper presented at a conference on Christianity and the University sponsored by the Pew Charitable Trust, Duke University, June 1–2, 1990).

54. Ibid. See also James Turner, *Without God, Without Creed: The Origins of Unbelief in America* (Baltimore, Md.: Johns Hopkins University Press, 1985).

55. Bass, "Ministry on the Margin," in Hutchison, ed., *Between the Times*, p. 49; Wuthnow, *Restructuring of American Religion*, p. 155; and U.S. Bureau of the Census, *Statistical Abstract . . . 1990*, p. 129.

56. Wuthnow, *Restructuring of American Religion*, p. 155.

57. Bass, "Ministry on the Margin," in Hutchison, ed., *Between the Times*, p. 49; Wuthnow, *Restructuring of American Religion*, p. 155; and *Statistical Abstract . . . 1990*, p. 129.

58. Marsden, "Soul of the American University," pp. 36–38.

59. Ibid., pp. 38–39.

60. Ibid., pp. 39–40.

61. Ibid., pp. 39–41.

62. Wuthnow, *Restructuring of American Religion*, p. 162.

63. Ibid., p. 158.

64. Ibid., p. 158, 160.

65. For a thorough examination of the current state of the secularization thesis, see David Lyon, *The Steeple's Shadow: On The Myths and Realities of Secularization* (Grand Rapids: Wm. B. Eerdmans Publishing Co., 1985), pp. 24–63. See also Jeffrey K. Hadden and Anson Shupe, eds., *Secularization and Fundamentalism Reconsidered* (New York: Paragon House, 1989).

66. *Religion in America 1990*, pp. 6, 21; Gallup and Castelli, *The People's Religion* (New York: Macmillan Publishing Co., 1989), pp. 4, 56–58, 61, 68.

67. Berger, Berger, and Kellner, *The Homeless Mind.* See also Richard D. Brown, *Modernization: The Transformation of American Life, 1600–1865* (New York: Hill & Wang, 1976); and S. N. Eisenstadt, ed., *The Protestant Ethic and Modernization: A Comparative View* (New York: Basic Books, 1968).

68. John F. Wilson, "The Sociological Study of American Religion," in *Encyclopedia of the American Religious Experience*, ed. Charles H. Lippy and Peter W. Williams (New York: Charles Scribner's Sons, 1988), pp. 27–28.

69. William G. McLoughlin, *Revivals, Awakenings and Reform: An Essay on Social Change in America, 1607–1977* (Chicago: University of Chicago Press, 1978), pp. 7–24.

70. W. B. Yeats, "The Second Coming," *The Collected Poems of W. B. Yeats* (New York: Macmillan Co., 1942), p. 215.

2: Membership Growth and Decline

1. Figures for denominational membership were drawn from Lauris B. Whitman, ed., *Yearbook of American Churches* (New York: Council Press, 1968), pp. 195–201; and Constant H. Jacquet, ed., *Yearbook of American and Canadian Churches 1990* (Nashville: Abingdon Press, 1990), pp. 248–255. Wade Clark Roof and William McKinney, *American Mainline Religion* (New Brunswick, N.J.: Rutgers University Press, 1987), pp. 155, 175.

2. Dean R. Hoge and David A. Roozen, eds., *Understanding Church Growth and Decline, 1950–1978* (New York: Pilgrim Press, 1979), pp. 21–159, 179–223, 315–333; Roof and McKinney, *American Mainline Religion*, pp. 106–185.

3. Dean Kelley has insisted that theological content is irrelevant in attracting members and sustaining church affiliation. Instead, he claims that people respond to religious groups that take what they believe seriously, whatever that belief might be, and discipline those members who do not carefully practice what the group preaches. See Dean Kelley, "Is Religion a Dependent Variable?" in Hoge and Roozen, eds., *Understanding Church Growth and Decline*, pp. 334–343.

4. Edwin Scott Gaustad, *Historical Atlas of Religion in America,* Revised Edition (New York: Harper & Row, 1976), pp. 87, 165, 166; Roger Finke and Rodney Stark, "Turning Pews Into People: Estimating 19th Century Church Membership," *Journal for the Scientific Study of Religion* 25 (1986): 180–192. See also Jon But-

ler, *Awash in a Sea of Faith* (Cambridge, Mass.: Harvard University Press, 1990), pp. 257–288.

5. Ibid.

6. Finke and Stark, "How the Up-Start Sects Won America, 1776–1950," pp. 27–44; and Gaustad, *Historical Atlas*, p. 108.

7. Donald A. Luidens, "Numbering the Presbyterian Branches: Membership Trends Since Colonial Times," in *MPD*, pp. 32–33; and Gaustad, *Historical Atlas*, p. 92.

8. William R. Hutchison, "Past Imperfect: History and the Prospect for Liberalism," in *Liberal Protestantism*, pp. 65–82.

9. Luidens, "Numbering the Presbyterian Branches," in *MPD*, pp. 63–64.

10. Ibid., pp. 58–65.

11. *Religion in America 1990*, p. 29.

12. Ibid., p. 33.

13. Ibid., p. 29, 43.

14. George Gallup, Jr., and Jim Castelli, *The People's Religion* (New York: Macmillan Publishing Co., 1989), pp. 31–32, 111–112.

15. Dennison Nash, "A Little Child Shall Lead Them: A Statistical Test of the Hypothesis That Children Were the Source of the American 'Religious Revival,' " *Journal for the Scientific Study of Religion* 7 (1968): 238–240.

16. Luidens, "Numbering the Presbyterian Branches," in *MPD*, pp. 61–62.

17. Roof and McKinney, *American Mainline Religion*, p. 161.

18. Ibid., pp. 151–157.

19. Gallup and Castelli, *People's Religion*, p. 111.

20. Dean R. Hoge, Benton Johnson, and Donald A. Luidens, *Vanishing Boundaries: The Religion of Protestant Baby Boomers* (forthcoming).

21. Ibid.

22. Ibid.

23. David A. Roozen, William McKinney, and Wayne Thompson, "The 'Big Chill' Generation Warms to Worship," *Review of Religious Research* 31 (March 1990): 314–322. Also see Jack Marcum, "Baby Boomers: In the Church or Far Out?" *Monday Morning* (June 1990), 18–19.

24. Roozen et al., "The 'Big Chill' Generation," pp. 320–321; Marcum, "Baby Boomers," pp. 18–19.

25. Roozen et al., "The 'Big Chill' Generation," p. 320.

26. Mark Chaves, "Secularization and Religious Revival: Evi-

dence from U.S. Church Attendance Rates," *Journal for the Scientific Study of Religion* 28 (1989): 464–477.

27. H. Richard Niebuhr, *The Social Sources of Denominationalism* (Cleveland: World Publishing Co., 1929), p. 259; Roof and McKinney, *American Mainline Religion*, pp. 141–143.

28. Presbyterian Church (U.S.A.), General Assembly, *Minutes*, 1990, pt. II (Louisville, Ky.: Office of the General Assembly, 1990), p. 544.

29. Niebuhr, *Social Sources of Denominationalism*, pp. 77–105. The exception is the American Baptist Churches, with their Black, dually aligned congregations.

30. Roof and McKinney, *American Mainline Religion*, p. 111.

31. Ibid., pp. 110, 114.

32. Ibid., pp. 165, 166, 167.

33. Ibid., pp. 117–126, 166.

34. An early and prominent proponent of this position was Dean M. Kelley, *Why Conservative Churches Are Growing* (New York: Harper & Row, 1972).

35. Roof and McKinney, *American Mainline Religion*, p. 170.

36. Rick Nutt, "The Tie That No Longer Binds: The Origins of the Presbyterian Church in America," in *CM*, pp. 236–256.

37. Roof and McKinney, *American Mainline Religion*, pp. 154, 172, 175–176.

38. Ibid., pp. 171, 174. The data on this finding is not precise since it does not indicate conclusively whether persons over forty-five switched denominations before or after they reached that age.

39. Ibid., pp. 173–174, 178.

40. *Religion in America 1990*, p. 29.

41. Roof and McKinney, *American Mainline Religion*, pp. 171–172.

42. C. Kirk Hadaway, "Denominational Defection: Recent Research on Religious Disaffiliation in America," in *MPD*, pp. 104, 106; and Hoge, Johnson, and Luidens, *Vanishing Boundaries*.

43. Hadaway, "Denominational Defection," in *MPD*, pp. 105, 107, 109.

44. Roof and McKinney, *American Mainline Religion*, p. 242; their italics. See also Hadaway, "Denominational Defection," in *MPD*, pp. 102–121; and Donald P. Smith, "Closing the Back Door: Toward the Retention of Church Members," in *MPD*, pp. 86–101.

45. Hadaway, "Denominational Defection," in *MPD*, pp. 109–111.

46. *Religion in America 1990*, p. 32. Population statistics were drawn from *Statistical Abstract . . . 1990*, p. 7. PC(USA), G.A., *Minutes*, 1988, pt. II, p. 493. Exact statistics for all Presbyterian denominations are not available because they are either not collected or not reported annually. However, *The Yearbook of American and Canadian Churches* provides statistics for some of the more prominent Presbyterian churches and lists the year that a particular membership statistic was reported. *The Yearbook of American and Canadian Churches* lists the Associate Reformed Presbyterian Church, General Synod, with 36,949 members in 1988; the Cumberland Presbyterian Church with 91,491 members in 1988; the Evangelical Presbyterian Church with 33,000 members in 1988; the Korean Presbyterian Church in America with 24,000 members in 1986; the Orthodox Presbyterian Church with 19,094 members in 1987; the Presbyterian Church in America with 208,394; the Reformed Presbyterian Church of North America with 5,174 members in 1988, and the Second Cumberland Presbyterian Church with 30,000 members in 1959. Jacquet, ed., *Yearbook of American and Canadian Churches 1990*, pp. 248–255; and Constant H. Jacquet, Jr., ed., *Yearbook of American and Canadian Churches 1989* (Nashville: Abingdon Press, 1989).

47. Jon R. Stone, "The New Voluntarism and Presbyterian Affiliation," in *MPD*, pp. 122–149.

48. Ibid., pp. 134–145.

49. Ibid., pp. 146–149.

50. Gallup and Castelli, *People's Religion*, p. 145; Roozen et al., "The 'Big Chill' Generation," pp. 320–321; Wade Clark Roof, "Return of the Baby Boomers to Organized Religion," in Jacquet, ed., *Yearbook of American and Canadian Churches 1990*, pp. 284–289.

51. *Religion in America 1990*, p. 29.

52. Roof and McKinney, *American Mainline Religion*, pp. 168–169; and Hoge, Johnson, and Luidens, *Vanishing Boundaries*.

53. Norval D. Glenn, "The Trend in 'No Religion' Respondents to U.S. National Surveys, Late 1950s to Early 1980s," *Public Opinion Quarterly* 51 (1987): 293–314.

54. Roof and McKinney, *American Mainline Religion*, p. 181.

55. Hadaway, "Denominational Defection," in *MPD*, p. 113.

56. Roof and McKinney, *American Mainline Religion*, pp. 164–165; Jon Stone, "The New Voluntarism and Presbyterian Affiliation," in *MPD*, pp. 128–129; and Warner, "Mirror for American

Protestantism: Mendocino Presbyterian Church in the Sixties and Seventies," in *MPD*, pp. 198–224.

57. Robert H. Bullock, Jr., "Twentieth-Century Presbyterian New Church Development: A Critical Period, 1940–1980," in *DD*, pp. 73–82; Jerrold Lee Brooks, "Reaching Out: A Study of Church Extension Activity in Mecklenburg Presbytery, North Carolina, 1920–1980," in *MPD*, pp. 177–197; and Phillip Barron Jones, "An Examination of the Statistical Growth of the Southern Baptist Convention," in Hoge and Roozen, eds., *Understanding Church Growth and Decline*, pp. 160–178.

58. Milton J Coalter, "Presbyterian Evangelism: A Case of Parallel Allegiances Diverging," in *DD*, pp. 46–54.

59. Andrew M. Greeley, *Religious Change in America* (Cambridge, Mass.: Harvard University Press, 1989), pp. 112–128.

3: Denominationalism and Leadership

1. Peter Drucker, *The New Realities: In Government and Politics, in Economics and Society, in Business, Technology, and World View* (New York: Harper & Row, 1989), p. 3.

2. The most notable exception to the neglect of denominations as organizations is Paul M. Harrison, *Authority and Power in the Free Church Tradition* (Princeton, N.J.: Princeton University Press, 1959). See also Ben Primer, *Protestants and American Business Methods* (Ann Arbor, Mich.: UMI Research Press, 1979). The term "organizational revolution" was used by Kenneth Boulding in *The Organizational Revolution* (New York: Harper & Brothers, 1953). See also Robert Presthus, *The Organizational Society* (New York: Vintage Books, 1962); and Russell E. Richey, "Institutional Forms of Religion," in *Encyclopedia of the American Religious Experience*, ed. Charles H. Lippy and Peter W. Williams (New York: Charles Scribner's Sons, 1988), pp. 31–50. For examples of the sparse literature on the economics of religious institutions, see William Bassett and Peter Huizing, eds., *The Finances of the Church* (New York: Stichtling Concilium-Seabury, 1979); Loyde Hartley, *Understanding Church Finances: The Economics of the Local Church* (New York: Pilgrim Press, 1982); and Virginia A. Hodgkinson and Robert Wuthnow, eds., *Faith and Philanthropy in America: Exploring the Role of Religion in America's Voluntary Sector* (San Francisco: Jossey-Bass, 1990). For the best historical survey of charitable giving, see Robert H.

Bremner, *American Philanthropy* (Chicago: University of Chicago Press, 1960).

3. Winthrop H. Hudson, "Denominationalism as a Basis for Ecumenicity: A Seventeenth Century Conception," in *Denominationalism*, ed. Russell Richey (Nashville: Abingdon Press, 1977), pp. 21–49.

4. Leonard J. Trinterud, *The Forming of an American Tradition: A Re-examination of Colonial Presbyterianism* (Philadelphia: Westminster Press, 1949), pp. 38–52.

5. Gordon Donaldson, *Scottish Church History* (Edinburgh: Scottish Academic Press, 1985), pp. 45–52. For a treatment of how complex the relationship was, see Michael Lynch, "From Privy Kirk to Burgh to Church: An Alternative View of the Process of Protestantization," in Norman MacDougall, ed., *Church, Politics, and Society: Scotland, 1408–1929* (Edinburgh: John Donald, 1983), pp. 85–96.

6. For an explanation, see Louis Weeks and William Fogleman, "A 'Two Church' Hypothesis," *Presbyterian Outlook* 172 (March 26, 1990): 8–10.

7. Trinterud, *The Forming of an American Tradition*, pp. 144–165; and Milton J Coalter, Jr., *Gilbert Tennent, Son of Thunder* (Westport, Conn.: Greenwood Press, 1986), pp. 55–136.

8. Handy, *A Christian America*, pp. 21–26; and Martin E. Marty, *Righteous Empire: The Protestant Experience in America* (New York: Dial Press, 1970), pp. 35–45, 67–77.

9. William R. Hutchinson, *Errand to the World: American Protestant Thought and Foreign Missions* (Chicago: University of Chicago Press, 1987); R. Pierce Beaver, "Missionary Motivation Through Three Centuries," in *Reinterpretation in American Church History*, ed. Jerald C. Brauer (Chicago: University of Chicago Press, 1968), pp. 113–152; Charles I. Foster, *An Errand of Mercy: The Evangelical United Front, 1790–1837* (Chapel Hill, N.C.: University of North Carolina Press, 1960); and Kenneth Scott Latourette, *The Great Century, 1800–1914*, vols. 4–6 in *A History of the Expansion of Christianity*, 7 vols. (New York: Harper & Bros., 1938–46).

10. Donald G. Mathews, "The Second Great Awakening as an Organizing Process, 1780–1830," *American Quarterly* 21 (1969): 23–43, reprinted in John M. Mulder and John F. Wilson, eds., *Religion in American History: Interpretive Essays* (Englewood Cliffs, N.J.: Prentice-Hall, 1978), pp. 199–217.

11. Nathan O. Hatch, *The Democratization of American Chris-

tianity (New Haven, Conn.: Yale University Press, 1989) points to the way in which all evangelical Protestantism shared in this enterprise. See also Daniel Walker Howe, "The Evangelical Movement and Political Culture in the North During the Second Party System," *Journal of American History* 77 (March 1991): 1216–1239.

12. John W. Kuykendall, *The Southern Enterprise: The Work of National Evangelical Societies in the Antebellum South* (Westport, Conn.: Greenwood Press, 1982); and Foster, *Errand of Mercy.*

13. Robert W. Lynn and Elliot Wright, *The Big Little School* (New York: Harper & Row, 1971); and Anne M. Boylan, *Sunday School: The Formation of an American Institution, 1790–1880* (New Haven, Conn.: Yale University Press, 1988).

14. See Harve Geiger, *The Program of Higher Education of the Presbyterian Church in the United States of America* (Cedar Rapids, Iowa: Laurance Press, 1940), pp. 40–102; and Donald G. Tewksbury, *The Founding of American Colleges and Universities Before the Civil War* (New York: Arno Press, 1969), p. 91.

15. See Timothy L. Smith, *Revivalism and Social Reform*, rev. ed. (Baltimore: Johns Hopkins University Press, 1980); Peter Brock, *Pacifism in America* (Princeton: Princeton University Press, 1968); Ronald Wells, ed., *The Wars of America: Christian Views* (Grand Rapids: Wm. B. Eerdmans Publishing Co., 1982); Gayraud S. Wilmore, *Black Religion and Black Radicalism*, rev. ed. (Maryknoll, N.Y.: Orbis Books, 1983); David Brion Davis, *Slavery and Human Progress* (New York: Oxford University Press, 1984); Foster, *Errand of Mercy*; Eleanor Flexner, *Century of Struggle: The Women's Rights Movement in the United States* (Cambridge, Mass.: Harvard University Press, 1959); Barbara Leslie Epstein, *The Politics of Domesticity: Women, Evangelism, and Temperance in Nineteeth Century America* (Middletown, Conn.: Wesleyan University Press, 1981); Anne M. Boylan, "Women in Groups: An Analysis of Women's Benevolent Organizations in New York and Boston, 1797–1840," *Journal of American History* 71 (1984): 497–522; and W. J. Rorabaugh, *The Alcoholic Republic: An American Tradition* (New York: Oxford University Press, 1979).

16. "The United Presbyterian Church in Mission," *Journal of Presbyterian History* 57 (1979): 183–423; "Women in Mission," *American Presbyterians* 65 (1987): 1–70; "150 Years of Foreign Missions," *American Presbyterians* 65 (1987): 71–172; Ashbel Green, *Presbyterian Missions* (1820; New York: A. D. F. Ran-

dolph & Co., 1893); Earl Ronald MacCormac, "The Transition from Voluntary Missionary Society to the Church as a Missionary Organization among the American Congregationalists, Presbyterians, and Methodists" (Ph.D. diss., Yale University, 1961); Michael C. Coleman, *Presbyterian Missionary Attitudes Toward American Indians, 1837–1893* (Jackson, Miss.: University Press of Mississippi, 1985); and David Irwin Craig, *A History of the Development of the Presbyterian Church in North Carolina, and of the Synodical Home Missions* (Richmond: Whittet & Shepperson, 1907).

17. Bremner, *American Philanthropy*, pp. 20–57.

18. Jack P. Maddex, "From Theocracy to Spirituality: The Southern Presbyterian Reversal on Church and State," *Journal of Presbyterian History* 54 (1976): 438–457; Ernest Trice Thompson, *The Spirituality of the Church* (Richmond: John Knox Press, 1961).

19. Dykstra and Hudnut-Beumler, "National Organizational Structures of Protestant Denominations," in *OR*, pp. 306–330.

20. Robert H. Wiebe, *The Search for Order, 1877–1920* (New York: Hill & Wang, 1967).

21. Louis Weeks, "The Incorporation of the Presbyterians," in *OR*, pp. 37–54.

22. Ibid.; and Craig Dykstra and J. Bradley Wigger, "A Brief History of a Genre Problem: Presbyterian Educational Resource Materials," in *PV*, pp. 180–204.

23. Ronald P. Byars, "Challenging the Ethos: A History of Presbyterian Worship Resources in the Twentieth Century," in *CM*, pp. 134–61.

24. PCUSA, G.A., *Minutes*, 1902, pt. I, p. 166.

25. Richard W. Reifsnyder, "Managing the Mission: Church Restructuring in the Twentieth Century," in *OR*, pp. 55–60.

26. Ibid., pp. 55–65; Joan C. LaFollette, "Money and Power: Presbyterian Women's Organizations in the Twentieth Century," in *OR*, pp. 198–231.

27. Lewis L. Wilkins, Jr., "The American Presbytery in the Twentieth Century," in *OR*, pp. 103–111.

28. Reifsnyder, "Managing the Mission," in *OR*, pp. 63–65.

29. Dykstra and Wigger, "A Brief History of a Genre Problem," in *PV*, pp. 180–204; David C. Hester, "The Use of the Bible in Presbyterian Curricula, 1923–1985," in *PV*, pp. 205–234; Coalter, "Presbyterian Evangelism," in *DD*, pp. 33–54; John R. Fitzmier and Randall Balmer, "A Poultice for the Bite of the Co-

bra: The Hocking Report and Presbyterian Missions in the Middle Decades of the Twentieth Century," in *DD*, pp. 105–125; James A. Overbeck, "The Rise and Fall of Presbyterian Official Journals, 1925–1985," in *DD*, pp. 83–95; John B. Trotti and Richard A. Ray, "Presbyterians and Their Publishing Houses," in *PV*, pp. 148–179; Theodore A. Gill, Jr., "American Presbyterians in the Global Ecumenical Movement," in *DD*, pp. 126–148; and Erskine Clarke, "Presbyterian Ecumenical Activity in the United States," in *DD*, pp. 149–169.

30. Herman C. Weber, *Presbyterian Statistics Through One-Hundred Years* (Philadelphia: General Council, PCUSA, 1927), p. 141.

31. Scott Brunger and Robin Klay, "A Financial History of American Presbyterian Giving, 1923–1983," in *OR*, pp. 122–131; and D. Scott Cormode, "A Financial History of Presbyterian Congregations Since World War II," in *OR*, pp. 170–181.

32. Robin Klay, "Changing Priorities: Allocation of Giving in the Presbyterian Church in the U.S.," in *OR*, pp. 132–152; and Stewardship and Communication Development Ministry Unit, Presbyterian Church (U.S.A.), "Plan to Challenge the Church for Increased Financial Support," October 1988, pp. 1–2.

33. Brunger and Klay, "A Financial History of American Presbyterian Giving," in *OR*, pp. 122–131; and David G. Dawson, "Mission Philanthropy, Selected Giving and Presbyterians," *American Presbyterians* 68 (1990): 121–132.

34. Klay, "Changing Priorities," in *OR*, pp. 132–152; Scott Brunger, "Global and Local Mission: Allocation of Giving in the Presbyterian Church in the U.S.A. and the United Presbyterian Church in the U.S.A., 1923–1982," in *OR*, pp. 153–169; and Cormode, "A Financial History of Presbyterian Congregations Since World War II," in *OR*, pp. 170–197.

35. Reifsnyder, "Managing the Mission," in *OR*, pp. 65–84.

36. Klay, "Changing Priorities," in *OR*, pp. 132–152; and Brunger, "Global and Local Mission," in *OR*, pp. 153–169.

37. Cormode, "Financial History of Presbyterian Congregations," in *OR*, pp. 170–197.

38. Bellah et al., *Habits of the Heart*, pp. 142–166.

39. Robert Wuthnow, *The Restructuring of American Religion* (Princeton, N.J.: Princeton University Press, 1988), pp. 133–172; Wuthnow, *The Struggle for America's Soul* (Grand Rapids: Wm. B. Eerdmans Publishing Co., 1989), pp. 3–94; and

Wuthnow, "The Restructuring of American Presbyterianism," in *PP*, pp. 27–48.

40. Jeffrey K. Hadden, *The Gathering Storm in the Churches* (Garden City, N.Y.: Doubleday & Co., 1969); R. Stephen Warner, *New Wine in Old Wineskins: Evangelicals and Liberals in a Small-Town Church* (Berkeley, Calif.: University of California Press, 1988); R. Stephen Warner, "Mirror for American Protestantism: Mendocino Presbyterian Church in the Sixties and Seventies," in *MPD*, pp. 198–223; and Jon R. Stone, "The New Voluntarism and Presbyterian Affiliation," in *MPD*, pp. 122–149.

41. Peter Berger, "The Class Struggle in American Religion," *Christian Century* 98 (February 25, 1981): 194–199; and Peter Berger, "Different Gospels: Social Sources of Apostasy," in *American Apostasy: The Triumph of "Other" Gospels* (Grand Rapids: Wm. B. Eerdmans Publishing Co., 1989), pp. 1–14; James Davison Hunter, *Culture Wars: The Struggle to Define America* (New York: Basic Books, 1991).

42. *Presbyterian Panel*, March 1989, p. A-3; Keith M. Wulff and John P. Marcum, "Cleavage or Consensus: A New Look at the Clergy-Laity Gap," in *PV*, pp. 308–326; and Dean Hoge, *Division in the Protestant House* (Philadelphia: Westminster Press, 1976).

43. Reifsnyder, "Managing the Mission," in *OR*, pp. 55–95; Reifsnyder, "Changing Leadership Patterns in the Presbyterian Church in the United States During the Twentieth Century," in *PV*, pp. 249–250.

44. Lois A. Boyd and R. Douglas Brackenridge, "Presbyterian Women Ministers: A Historical Overview and Study of the Current Status of Women Pastors," in *PV*, pp. 289–307.

45. Ibid.

46. Barbara Brown Zikmund, "Ministry of Word and Sacrament: Women and Changing Understandings of Ordination," in *PP*, pp. 134–158.

47. Dale S. Soden, "Men and Mission: The Shifting Fortunes of Presbyterian Men's Organizations in the Twentieth Century," in *OR*, pp. 231–252.

48. Gary S. Eller, "Special-Interest Groups and American Presbyterianism," in *OR*, pp. 253–277.

49. See chapter 4, as well as the essays in *CM* and *PV*.

50. Barbara G. Wheeler, "Uncharted Territory: Congregational Identity and Mainline Protestantism," in *PP*, pp. 67–89; Warner, "Mirror for American Protestantism," in *MPD*, pp. 198–223; Warner, *New Wine in Old Wineskins* (Berkeley, Calif.: University

of California Press, 1988), pp. 23–65; Mark N. Wilhelm, "Membership Decline and Congregational Identity in Yonkers, New York: A Case Study in the Presbyterian Church (U.S.A.)," in *MPD*, pp. 150–176.

51. Lewis L. Wilkins, Jr., "The American Presbytery in the Twentieth Century," in *OR*, pp. 118.

52. Weeks and Fogleman, "A 'Two Church' Hypothesis," pp. 8–10; Wade Clark Roof, *Community and Commitment: Religious Plausibility in a Liberal Protestant Church* (New York: Elsevier/North-Holland, 1978); and Wulff and Marcum, "Cleavage or Consensus," in *PV*, pp. 308–326.

53. Wuthnow, "The Restructuring of American Presbyterianism," pp. 46–48; Eller, "Special-Interest Groups and American Presbyterianism," in *OR*, pp. 253–277; and Berger, "Different Gospels," pp. 1–14.

54. Wuthnow, *Restructuring of American Religion*, pp. 125–131.

55. Dykstra and Hudnut-Beumler, "National Organizational Structures of Protestant Denominations," in *OR*, pp. 306–330.

56. David B. McCarthy, "The Emerging Importance of Presbyterian Polity," in *OR*, pp. 278–305; and James H. Moorhead, "Redefining Confessionalism: American Presbyterians in the Twentieth Century," in *CM*, pp. 78–83.

4: Theology and Confessions

1. Charles Hodge, *Systematic Theology*, 3 vols. (New York: Charles Scribner's Sons, 1872–73), vol. 1, pp. 10, 11, 13.

2. Albert Barnes, *Lectures on the Evidences of Christianity in the Nineteenth Century* (New York: Harper & Brothers, 1879), pp. 352–353, 354.

3. Schlesinger, "A Critical Period in American Religion, 1875–1900," pp. 302–317; Ahlstrom, *A Religious History of the American People* (New Haven, Conn.: Yale University Press, 1972), p. 11; Paul A. Carter, *The Spiritual Crisis of the Gilded Age* (DeKalb, Ill.: Northern Illinois University Press, 1971).

4. See, for example, George M. Marsden, *Understanding Fundamentalism and Evangelicalism* (Grand Rapids: Wm. B. Eerdmans Publishing Co., 1991), pp. 62–82.

5. Mark A. Noll, ed., *The Princeton Theology, 1812–1921* (Grand Rapids: Baker Book House, 1983), pp. 11–48.

6. Ibid.; Mark Noll, ed., *Charles Hodge: The Way of Life* (New York: Paulist Press, 1987), pp. 1–49; John M. Mulder and Lee A. Wyatt, "The Predicament of Pluralism: The Study of Theology in Presbyterian Seminaries Since the 1920s," in *PV*, pp. 37–70, especially n. 12; Lefferts A. Loetscher, *Facing the Enlightenment and Pietism: Archibald Alexander and the Founding of Princeton Theology Seminary* (Westport, Conn.: Greenwood Press, 1983).

7. Winthrop S. Hudson, "Denominationalism as a Basis for Ecumenicity," in *Denominationalism*, ed. Russell E. Richey (Nashville: Abingdon Press, 1977), pp. 21–44; Moorhead, "Redefining Confessionalism," in *CM*, p. 82; and "Presbyterians and Biblical Authority," *Journal of Presbyterian History* 59 (1981): 95–284.

8. Lefferts A. Loetscher, *A Brief History of the Presbyterians*, 4th ed. (Philadelphia: Westminster Press, 1983), pp. 128–131.

9. William R. Hutchison, *The Modernist Impulse in American Protestantism* (Cambridge, Mass.: Harvard University Press, 1976). Lefferts H. Loetscher, *The Broadening Church: A Study of Theological Issues in the Presbyterian Church Since 1869* (Philadelphia: University of Pennsylvania Press, 1954).

10. Loetscher, *The Broadening Church*, pp. 90–156; Ernest R. Sandeen, *The Roots of Fundamentalism: British and American Millenarianism, 1820–1925* (New York: Oxford University Press, 1980), pp. 188–269; George M. Marsden, *Fundamentalism and American Culture: The Shaping of Twentieth-Century Evangelicalism, 1820–1925* (New York: Oxford University Press, 1980), pp. 109–175; Bradley J. Longfield, *The Presbyterian Controversy: Fundamentalists, Modernists, and Moderates* (New York: Oxford University Press, 1991), pp. 77–180.

11. Mark A. Noll, comp., *The Princeton Theology: An Anthology* (Grand Rapids: Baker Book House, 1983), p. 19.

12. Quoted by Martin E. Marty, *The Noise of Conflict, 1919–1941*, vol. 2 of *Modern American Religion* (Chicago: University of Chicago Press, 1991), p. 157. The same point is made by Longfield, *The Presbyterian Controversy*, pp. 209–230.

13. Quoted in Marty, *The Noise of Conflict*, p. 181.

14. Loetscher, *The Broadening Church*, pp. 130–156.

15. Ibid., p. 151.

16. Ibid., p. 135.

17. Jack B. Rogers and Donald K. McKim, "Pluralism and Policy in Presbyterian Views of Scripture," *CM*, pp. 39–41; Marty, *The Noise of Conflict*, pp. 303–340.

18. Ahlstrom, *A Religious History of the American People*, p. 934. The phrase is Karl Adam's.

19. Mulder and Wyatt, "The Predicament of Pluralism," in *PV*, pp. 37–70.

20. Ibid.

21. Ibid.

22. Marty, *The Noise of Conflict*, pp. 303–340; Dennis Voskuil, "Neo-Orthodoxy," in *Encyclopedia of the American Religious Experience*, ed. Charles H. Lippy and Peter W. Williams (New York: Charles Scribner's Sons, 1988), pp. 1147–1157. Moorhead, "Redefining Confessionalism," in *CM*, pp. 59–83; and Rogers and McKim, "Pluralism and Policy in Presbyterian Views of Scripture," in *CM*, pp. 37–58.

23. Moorhead, "Redefining Confessionalism," in *CM*, pp. 70–75; Mulder and Wyatt, "The Predicament of Pluralism," in *PV*, pp. 37–70.

24. Trotti and Ray, "Presbyterians and Their Publishing Houses," in *PV*, pp. 148–149; Dykstra and Wigger, "A Brief History of a Genre Problem," in *PV*, pp. 180–204; Hester, "The Use of the Bible in Presbyterian Curricula, 1923–1985," in *PV*, pp. 205–234; Overbeck, "The Rise and Fall of Presbyterian Official Journals," in *DD*, pp. 83–104; Marty, *The Noise of Conflict*, pp. 303–340; John McClure, "Changes in the Authority, Method, and Message of Presbyterian (UPCUSA) Preaching in the Twentieth Century," in *CM*, pp. 84–108; Beverly Ann Zink, "Themes in Southern Presbyterian Preaching, 1920 to 1983," in *CM*, pp. 109–133; Ronald P. Byars, "Challenging the Ethos: A History of Presbyterian Worship Resources in the Twentieth Century," in *CM*, pp. 134–161; Morgan F. Simmons, "Hymnody: Its Place in Twentieth-Century Presbyterianism," in *CM*, pp. 162–186.

25. Mulder and Wyatt, "The Predicament of Pluralism," in *PV*, pp. 49–52.

26. A. Roy Eckardt, *The Surge of Piety in America: An Appraisal* (New York: Association Press, 1958), p. 154.

27. Will Herberg, *Protestant, Catholic, Jew* (Garden City, N.Y.: Doubleday & Co., 1956); Peter L. Berger, *The Noise of Solemn Assemblies: Christian Commitment and Religious Establishment in America* (Garden City, N.Y.: Doubleday & Co., 1961); Gibson Winter, *The Suburban Captivity of the Churches* (Garden City, N.Y.: Doubleday & Co., 1961); and Martin E. Marty, *The New Shape of American Religion* (New York: Harper & Row, 1959).

28. William McGuire King, "The Reform Establishment and the Ambiguities of the Influence," in *Between the Times*, ed. William R. Hutchison (New York: Cambridge University Press, 1989), pp. 122–140.

29. Ahlstrom, *A Religious History of the American People*, pp. 947–48; and Moorhead, "Redefining Confessionalism," in *CM*, p. 66.

30. George Marsden, *Reforming Fundamentalism: Fuller Seminary and the New Evangelicalism* (Grand Rapids: Wm. B. Eerdmans Publishing Co., 1987), pp. 46–51, 153–171; and Marsden, *Understanding Fundamentalism and Evangelicalism*, pp. 62–82.

31. Ahlstrom, "The Radical Turn in Theology and Ethics: Why It Occurred in the 1960s," in *Religion in American History*, p. 446; and Ahlstrom, *A Religious History of the American People*, pp. 1079–1099.

32. Rogers and McKim, "Pluralism and Policy in Presbyterian Views of Scripture," in *CM*, pp. 40–41.

33. Moorhead, "Redefining Confessionalism," in *CM*, pp. 67–70; Rogers and McKim, "Pluralism and Policy in Presbyterian Views of Scripture," in *CM*, pp. 41–43.

34. Moorhead, "Redefining Confessionalism," in *CM*, pp. 68–69; and Arnold B. Come, "The Occasion and Contribution of the Confession of 1967," *Journal of Presbyterian History* 61 (1983): 24. Come's essay appears in an issue of the *Journal of Presbyterian History* devoted entirely (pp. 1–196) to the Confession of 1967.

35. Moorhead, "Redefining Confessionalism," in *CM*, p. 70.

36. *Union Theological Seminary in Virginia Catalogue* (1926–27), p. 52.

37. Rogers and McKim, "Pluralism and Policy in Presbyterian Views of Scripture," in *CM*, pp. 39–40, 44–45; and Moorhead, "Redefining Confessionalism," in *CM*, pp. 70–75.

38. Nutt, "The Tie That No Longer Binds," in *CM*, p. 256.

39. Mulder and Wyatt, "The Predicament of Pluralism," in *PV*, p. 60; Ahlstrom, *Religious History of the American People*, pp. 1009–1018, 1085. See also the fiftieth anniversary articles in *Theological Studies* 50 (1989), which surveyed the changes in twentieth-century Catholic biblical scholarship, and Gerald P. Fogarty, S.J., "American Catholic Biblical Scholarship," in *Altered Landscapes: Christianity in America, 1935–1985*, ed. David W.

Lotz, Donald W. Shriver, Jr., and John F. Wilson (Grand Rapids: Wm. B. Eerdmans Publishing Co., 1989), pp. 226–245.

40. Hugh T. Kerr, "Time for a Critical Theology," *Theology Today* 20 (1964): 461–466, reprinted in John M. Mulder, ed., *Our Life in God's Light: Essays by Hugh T. Kerr* (Philadelphia: Westminster Press, 1979), pp. 57–63. His italics.

41. Harvey Cox, *The Secular City: Secularization and Urbanization in Theological Perspective* (New York: Macmillan Co., 1965); and Dietrich Bonhoeffer, *Letters and Papers from Prison* (New York: Collier Books, 1953), p. 344; John A. T. Robinson, *Honest to God* (Philadelphia: Westminster Press, 1963); Joseph F. Fletcher, *Situation Ethics: The New Morality* (Philadelphia: Westminster Press, 1966); and Thomas J. J. Altizer, *The Gospel of Christian Atheism* (Philadelphia: Westminster Press, 1966).

42. James H. Cone, "Black Religious Thought," in *Encyclopedia of the American Religious Experience*, pp. 1173–1187. King's writings were widely read; see *Stride Toward Freedom* (New York: Harper & Row, 1958); *Strength to Love* (New York: Harper & Row, 1963); *Letter from Birmingham City Jail* (Philadelphia: American Friends Service Committee, 1963); *Where Do We Go from Here: Chaos or Community* (New York: Harper & Row, 1967). The best introduction to black theology of the 1960s and 1970s is Gayraud S. Wilmore and James H. Cone, eds., *Black Theology: Documentary History, 1966–1979* (Maryknoll, N.Y.: Orbis Books, 1979).

43. Arthur F. McGovern, *Liberation Theology and Its Critics* (Maryknoll, N.Y.: Orbis Books, 1989); Dean William Ferm, ed., *Third World Liberation Theologies: A Reader* (Maryknoll, N.Y.: Orbis Books, 1986); Alfred T. Hennelly, ed., *Liberation Theology: A Documentary History* (Maryknoll, N.Y.: Orbis, 1990); Susan Brooks Thistlewaite and Mary Potter Engel, eds., *Lift Every Voice: Constructing Christian Theologies from the Underside* (San Francisco: Harper & Row, 1990); and Dennis P. McCann, *Christian Realism and Liberation Theology* (Maryknoll, N.Y.: Orbis Books, 1981).

44. Nancy F. Cott, *The Bonds of Womanhood: "Woman's Sphere in New England, 1780–1835* (New Haven, Conn.: Yale University Press, 1977); Carl Degler, *At Odds: Women and the Family in America from the Revolution to the Present* (New York: Oxford University Press, 1981); Eleanor Flexner, *Century of Struggle* (Cambridge, Mass.: Harvard University Press, 1959); Elizabeth H. Verdesi, *In but Still Out: Women in the Church* (Philadelphia: Westminster Press, 1976); Aileen Kraditor, *The Ideas of*

the Women's Suffrage Movement, 1890–1920 (New York: Columbia University Press, 1967); Ann Douglas, *The Feminization of American Culture* (New York: Alfred A. Knopf, 1977); Barbara Welter, *Divinity Convictions: The American Woman in the Nineteenth Century* (Athens, Ohio: Ohio University Press, 1976); Mary P. Ryan, *Womanhood in America* (New York: Franklin Watts, 1983); and Epstein, *The Politics of Domesticity*.

45. See note 41 as well as Joan C. LaFollette, "Money and Power," in *OR*, pp. 198–231.

46. Lois A. Boyd and R. Douglas Brackenridge, "Presbyterian Women Ministers: A Historical Overview and Study of the Current Status of Women Pastors," in *PV*, pp. 289–307; Committee on Theological Education, Presbyterian Church (U.S.A.); Research Division, Support Agency, United Presbyterian Church U.S.A., *Comparative Statistics, 1976* (New York: UPCUSA, 1977), p. 10; and Research Services, Stewardship and Communication Development Unit, PC(USA), *Comparative Statistics, 1990* (Louisville, Ky.: PC(USA), 1990), p. 19.

47. Rosemary Radford Ruether, "The Feminist Critique in Religious Studies," *Soundings* 64 (1981): 388–402. For a typology of the development of feminist theology, see Barbara Brown Zikmund's "Theological Education as Advocate," *Theological Education* 25 (1988): 44–61. See also Katie G. Cannon et al. (The Mud Flower Collective), *God's Fierce Whimsy: Christian Feminism and Theological Education* (New York: Pilgrim Press, 1985); *The Cornball Collective, Your Daughters Shall Prophesy: Feminist Alternatives in Theological Education* (New York: Pilgrim Press, 1980); and Rosemary Radford Ruether, "The Future of Feminist Theology in the Academy," *Journal of the American Academy of Religion* 53 (1985): 703–713.

48. Mulder and Wyatt, "Predicament of Pluralism, in *PV*, pp. 37–70; and Van A. Harvey, "On the Intellectual Marginality of American Theology," in *Religion and Twentieth Century American Intellectual Life*, ed. Michael J. Lacey (Cambridge: Cambridge University Press, 1989), pp. 172–192.

49. Benton Johnson, "From Old to New Agendas: Presbyterians and Social Issues in the Twentieth Century," in *CM*, pp. 208–235.

50. Wuthnow, *Restructuring of American Religion*, pp. 133–172; Wuthnow, *The Struggle for America's Soul*, pp. 3–96; and Wuthnow, "The Restructuring of American Presbyterianism," in *PP*, pp. 27–48.

51. Marsden, *Reforming Fundamentalism*, pp. 104–107.

52. Vinson Synan, *The Holiness-Pentecostal Movement in the United States* (Grand Rapids: Wm. B. Eerdmans Publishing Co., 1971).

53. Sang Hyun Lee, "Korean American Presbyterians: A Need for Ethnic Particularity and the Challenge of Christian Pilgrimage," in *DD*, pp. 322–330; Barbara Brown Zikmund, "The Values and Limits of Representation and Pluralism in the Church," in *PV*, pp. 327–348.

54. Moorhead, "Redefining Confessionalism, in *CM*, pp. 82–83; and David B. McCarthy, "The Emerging Importance of Presbyterian Polity," in *OR*, p. 279.

55. Edward W. Farley, "The Presbyterian Heritage as Modernism: Reaffirming a Forgotten Past in Hard Times," in *PP*, pp. 49–66.

56. The PC(USA) Theology and Worship Unit has suggested a similar strategy as a first step to resolving the current struggles of theological pluralism in its report entitled *Is Christ Divided? Report of the Task Force on Theological Pluralism Within the Presbyterian Community of Faith* (Louisville, Ky.: Office of the General Assembly, PC(USA), 1988).

5: The Debate Over Evangelism

1. Clifford M. Drury, *Presbyterian Panorama: 150 Years of National Missions History* (Philadelphia: Board of Christian Education, PCUSA, 1952), p. 25.

2. Robert S. Paul, "Presbyterians and Evangelism: Historical Background," *Austin Seminary Bulletin* 100 (April 1985): 15–23; Norman Pettit, *The Heart Prepared: Grace and Conversion in Puritan Spiritual Life* (New Haven, Conn.: Yale University Press, 1966); Patricia Caldwell, *The Puritan Conversion Narrative* (Cambridge: Cambridge University Press, 1983); Alden T. Vaughan, *New England Frontier: Puritans and Indians, 1620–1675* (Boston: Little, Brown & Co., 1965).

3. Trinterud, *The Formation of an American Tradition* (Philadelphia: Westminster Press, 1949); Milton J Coalter, *Gilbert Tennent, Son of Thunder* (Westport, Conn.: Greenwood Press, 1986); and George M. Marsden, *The Evangelical Mind and the New School Presbyterian Experience* (New Haven, Conn.: Yale University Press, 1970).

4. Mathews, "The Second Great Awakening as an Organizing Process, 1780–1830," in John F. Wilson and John M. Mulder, eds., *Religion in American History* (Prentice-Hall, 1978), pp. 199–217.

5. Coalter, "Presbyterian Evangelism," in *DD*, pp. 34–35.

6. Ibid., pp. 35–37; PCUSA, G.A., *Minutes*, 1904, pt. I, pp. 30–31; PCUSA, G.A., *Minutes*, 1905, pt. I, pp. 30–31. The focus of the Simultaneous Movement on urban areas was in part a consequence of a territorial agreement between the Special Committee on Evangelistic Work and the Board of Home Missions in 1906. This compact assigned the special committee responsibility for larger towns and cities where evangelism would be conducted on an interdenominational basis. PCUSA, G.A., *Minutes*, 1906, pt. I, p. 24.

7. Coalter, "Presbyterian Evangelism," in *DD*, p. 36.

8. Ibid., p. 37.

9. Ibid., pp. 37–38.

10. Ibid.

11. George Marsden, *Fundamentalism and American Culture* (New York: Oxford University Press, 1980); and Charles G. Dennison, ed., *Orthodox Presbyterian Church* (Philadelphia: Committee for the Historian of the Orthodox Presbyterian Church, 1986).

12. Coalter, "Presbyterian Evangelism," in *DD*, pp. 38–41.

13. The official dates for the New Life Movement were January 1, 1947 to January 1, 1950. Ibid., pp. 41–43.

14. Ibid., p. 42.

15. Ibid.

16. Ibid., pp. 42–43.

17. Ibid.

18. Ibid., p. 44.

19. H. Richard Niebuhr, *The Social Sources of Denominationalism* (1929; reprint: Magnolia, Mass., Peter Smith, 1984), p. 6; Hudson, *Religion in America*, p. 358; and Coalter, "Presbyterian Evangelism," in *DD*, p. 48.

20. Reinhold Niebuhr, "Is There a Revival of Religion?" *New York Times Magazine*, Nov. 19, 1950, p. 13; *Christian Century* 75 (Sept. 17, 1958): 1046; *Christianity Today* 1 (Oct. 29, 1956): 22–23. The citations come from Dean R. Hoge, Benton Johnson, and Donald A. Luidens, *Vanishing Boundaries* (forthcoming). For a book-length assessment of the revival of the 1950s that captures this spirit, see A. Roy Eckhardt, *The Surge of Piety in America: An Appraisal* (New York: Association Press, 1958).

21. Coalter, "Presbyterian Evangelism," in *DD*, pp. 47–49.

22. Ibid., pp. 48–49.

23. Ibid., pp. 47–48; and UPCUSA, G.A., *Minutes*, 1967, pt. I, p. 221.

24. Coalter, "Presbyterian Evangelism," in *DD*, p. 49; and UPCUSA, G.A., *Minutes*, 1968, pt. I, pp. 293–294.

25. A fertile area for further research is the transformation of Protestant-sponsored community service organizations into independent agencies dependent on the goodwill and philanthropy of the entire population in a region. The play of external forces on this metamorphosis could be quite different in the case of hospitals, social service organizations, or colleges. The seeds for this insight, however, are embedded in Phillip E. Hammond, "The Extravasation of the Sacred and the Crisis of Liberal Protestantism," in Robert S. Michaelsen and Wade C. Roof, *Liberal Protestantism* (New York: Pilgrim Press, 1986), pp. 51–64; and Dorothy Bass, "Teaching with Authority?" in Dorothy C. Bass, Benton Johnson, and Wade Clark Roof, *Mainstream Protestantism in the Twentieth Century* (Louisville, Ky.: Committee on Theological Education, Presbyterian Church (U.S.A.), 1987) pp. 1–12.

26. Bullock, "Twentieth-Century Presbyterian New Church Development," in *DD*, pp. 56–60.

27. Ibid., p. 77.

28. Penny Long Marler and C. Kirk Hadaway, "New Church Development and Denominational Growth (1950–1988): Symptom or Cause?" (Unpublished ms.), pp. 16–17.

29. Robert Wuthnow, *The Restructuring of American Religion* (Princeton, N.J.: Princeton University Press, 1988), pp. 25–28.

30. Bullock, "Twentieth-Century Presbyterian New Church Development," in *DD*, pp. 67–69; and Brooks, "Reaching Out," in *MPD*, p. 191.

31. Ibid., pp. 59–64, 69, 71–73.

32. Ibid., p. 63.

33. Dorothy Bass, "Ministry on the Margin," in *Between the Times*, ed. William R. Hutchison (Cambridge: Cambridge University Press, 1989), pp. 57–61.

34. Ronald C. White, Jr., "Presbyterian Campus Ministries: Competing Loyalties and Changing Visions," in *PV*, pp. 126–147.

35. PCUSA, G.A., *Minutes*, 1904, pt. I, p. 31; PCUSA, G.A., *Minutes*, 1912, pt. I, p. 33; PCUSA, G.A., *Minutes*, 1913, pt. I, p. 27–29; PCUSA, G.A., *Minutes*, 1914, pt. I, p. 447; PCUSA,

G.A., *Minutes*, 1920, pt. I, pp. 395; PCUSA, G.A., *Minutes*, 1934, pt. I, p. 128; PCUSA, G.A., *Minutes*, 1939, pt. I, p. 132.

36. White, "Presbyterian Campus Ministries," in *PV*, pp. 133–134.

37. Ibid, pp. 127–147.

38. Ibid.

39. Wuthnow, *Restructuring of American Religion*, pp. 153–164; see also chapter 6 of this book.

40. White, "Presbyterian Campus Ministries," in *PV*, pp. 126–147; Bradley J. Longfield and George M. Marsden, "Presbyterian Colleges in Twentieth-Century America," in *PV*, pp. 111–112; John F. Wilson, "Introduction: The Background and Present Context of the Study of Religion in Colleges and Universities," in *The Study of Religion in Colleges and Universities*, ed. Paul Ramsey and John F. Wilson (Princeton, N.J.: Princeton University Press, 1970), pp. 3–21.

41. White, "Presbyterian Campus Ministries," in *PV*, p. 136.

42. Ibid., pp. 137–138; Dorothy C. Bass, "Revolutions, Quiet and Otherwise: Protestants and Higher Education During the 1960s," in *Caring for the Commonweal: Education for Religious and Public Life*, ed. Parker J. Palmer, Barbara G. Wheeler, and James W. Fowler (Macon, Ga.: Mercer University Press, 1990), pp. 207–226; Phillip E. Hammond, *The Campus Clergyman* (New York: Basic Books, 1966), p. 64.

43. White, "Presbyterian Campus Ministries," in *PV*, p. 140.

44. Quoted in ibid., p. 146; and Charles W. Doak, "History of the Association of Presbyterian University Pastors, 1930–1965: A Study of a Specialized Clergy Organization with Interpretations for the Future" (D.Min. diss., San Francisco Theological Seminary, 1985), p. 124.

45. Hadaway, "Denominational Defection," in *MPD*, p. 105.

46. J. W. Gregg Meister, "Presbyterians and Mass Media: A Case of Blurred Vision and Missed Mission," in *DD*, p. 184. For another excellent summary of mainstream Protestant involvement in mass media see Dennis N. Voskuil, "Reaching Out: Mainline Protestantism and the Media," in Hutchison, ed., *Between the Times*, pp. 72–92.

47. Meister, "Presbyterians and Mass Media," in *DD*, pp. 172, 175.

48. Voskuil, "Reaching Out," in Hutchison, ed., *Between the Times*, pp. 84–85; and Meister, "Presbyterians and Mass Media," in *DD*, pp. 174.

49. Meister, "Presbyterians and Mass Media," in *DD*, pp. 173–174, 184–185; and Voskuil, "Reaching Out," in Hutchison, ed., *Between the Times*, pp. 82–84.

50. Meister, "Presbyterians and Mass Media," in *DD*, pp. 177–178, 181–182.

51. Robert Kubey and Mihaly Csikszentmihalyi, *Television and the Quality of Life: How Viewing Shapes Everyday Experience* (Hillsdale, N.J.: Lawrence Erlbaum Associates, 1990), p. xi.

52. Report of the Department of Radio and Television to the Long-Range Planning Committee, 1960, vol. 1, p. 5. Archives, PC(USA), Department of History, Philadelphia.

53. Wuthnow, "The Restructuring of American Presbyterianism," in *PP*, pp. 35–48; and Coalter, "Presbyterian Evangelism," in *DD*, pp. 46–54.

54. "Denominational Perspectives, Personal Beliefs and Church Priorities," *Presbyterian Panel* (March 1989), 8.

6: The Diversities of Discipleship

1. John C. B. Webster, "American Presbyterian Global Mission Policy: An Overview of 150 Years," *American Presbyterians* 65 (1987): 72.

2. Loetscher, *A Brief History of the Presbyterians*, 4th ed. (Philadelphia: Westminster Press, 1983), pp. 86–87.

3. Ibid., pp. 99, 116–119, 123.

4. Kenneth Scott Latourette, *The Great Century*, vols. 4–6 in *A History of the Expansion of Christianity* (New York: Harper & Brothers, 1941).

5. William R. Hutchison, *Errand to the World: American Protestant Thought in Foreign Missions* (Chicago: University of Chicago Press, 1987), pp. 91–95.

6. LaFollette, "Money and Power," in *OR*, pp. 198–210; Hutchison, *Errand to the World*, pp. 101–102, 127; and Patricia R. Hill, *The World Their Household: The American Women's Foreign Mission Movement and Cultural Transformation, 1870–1920* (Ann Arbor, Mich.: University of Michigan Press, 1985).

7. Loetscher, *The Broadening Church* (Philadelphia: University of Pennsylvania Press, 1954), pp. 103–108, 149–155; and Marsden, *Fundamentalism and American Culture* (New York: Oxford University Press, 1980), pp. 192–193.

8. John R. Fitzmier and Randall Balmer, "A Poultice for the

Bite of the Cobra: The Hocking Report and Presbyterian Missions in the Middle Decades of the Twentieth Century," in *DD*, p. 105.

9. Ibid., pp. 106–109.

10. Ibid., pp. 106–107.

11. Ibid., p. 111.

12. Ibid., pp. 111–113.

13. Ibid., p. 123.

14. Ibid., p. 116.

15. Ibid., pp. 114–115.

16. Ibid., pp. 119–122.

17. Ibid.

18. Ibid., p. 124; PC(USA), Stewardship and Communication Development Unit, *Witness Offering 1990* (Louisville, Ky.: PC(USA), 1990), p. 1; William R. Hutchison, "Americans in World Mission: Revision and Realignment," in *Altered Landscapes: Christianity in America, 1935–1985*, ed. David W. Lotz et al. (Grand Rapids: Wm. B. Eerdmans Publishing Co., 1989), pp. 155–170; Joel A. Carpenter and Wilbert R. Shenk, eds., *Earthen Vessels: American Evangelicals and Foreign Missions, 1880–1980* (Grand Rapids: Wm. B. Eerdmans Publishing Co., 1990); Patricia R. Hill, "The Missionary Enterprise," in *Encyclopedia of the American Religious Experience*, ed. Charles H. Lippy and Peter W. Williams (New York: Charles Scribner's Sons, 1988), pp. 1683–1696.

19. PC(USA), G.A., *Minutes*, 1990, pt. II, p. 544.

20. Joel L. Alvis, Jr., "A Presbyterian Dilemma: Ecclesiastical and Social Racial Policy in the Twentieth-Century Presbyterian Communion," in *DD*, pp. 187–201; and Gayraud S. Wilmore, "Identity and Integration: Black Presbyterians and Their Allies in the Twentieth Century," in *DD*, pp. 214–218.

21. Alvis, "Presbyterian Dilemma," in *DD*, pp. 201–207; and Wilmore, "Identity and Integration," in *DD*, pp. 218–233.

22. Vincent Harding, "Black Power and the American Christ," in Floyd B. Barbour, ed., *The Black Power Revolt* (Boston: Porter E. Sargent, 1968), p. 86; quoted in Wilmore, "Identity and Integration," in *DD*, p. 209.

23. Albert J. Raboteau, *Slave Religion* (New York: Oxford University Press, 1978); Eugene Genovese, *Roll, Jordan, Roll* (New York: Vintage Books, 1974); Lawrence Levine, *Black Culture and Black Consciousness* (New York: Oxford University Press, 1977); Loetscher, *Brief History*, pp. 92–95.

24. Inez Parker Moore, *The Rise and Decline of the Program of Education for Black Presbyterians in the United Presbyterian Church U.S.A., 1865–1970* (San Antonio, Tex.: Trinity University Press, 1977).

25. Alvis, "Presbyterian Dilemma," in *DD*, pp. 200–201, 203–207; and Wilmore, "Identity and Integration," in *DD*, pp. 218–233.

26. Alvis, "Presbyterian Dilemma," in *DD*, pp. 206–207; and Wilmore, "Identity and Integration," in *DD*, pp. 226–233.

27. Alvis, "Presbyterian Dilemma," in *DD*, pp. 205–206; Wilmore, "Identity and Integration," in *DD*, pp. 226–233.

28. Ibid.

29. Francisco O. García-Treto and R. Douglas Brackenridge, "Hispanic Presbyterians: Life in Two Cultures," in *DD*, pp. 260–265.

30. Lee, "Korean American Presbyterians," in *DD*, pp. 321–325.

31. Henry Warner Bowden, "Native American Presbyterians: Assimilation, Leadership, and Future Challenges," in *DD*, pp. 234–256.

32. Lee, "Korean American Presbyterians," in *DD*, pp. 321–325.

33. Ibid., p. 321.

34. Ibid., 327; García-Treto and Brackenridge, "Hispanic Presbyterians," in *DD*, pp. 275–276.

35. Bowden, "Native American Presbyterians," in *DD*, p. 251; Lee, "Korean American Presbyterians," in *DD*, pp. 321–322; and García-Treto and Brackenridge, "Hispanic Presbyterians," in *DD*, p. 276.

36. García-Treto and Brackenridge, "Hispanic Presbyterians," in *DD*, pp. 275–276, 278–279; Lee, "Korean American Presbyterians," in *DD*, pp. 328–330.

37. William Temple, *The Church Looks Forward* (New York: Macmillan Co., 1944), p. 2.

38. Quoted in John T. McNeill and James Hastings Nichols, *Ecumenical Testimony: Concern for Christian Unity Within the Reformed and Presbyterian Churches* (Philadelphia: Westminster Press, 1974), p. 15.

39. Coalter, *Gilbert Tennent, Son of Thunder* (Westport, Conn.: Greenwood Press, 1986), pp. 12–25, 55–90, 108–112, 129–130, 147–148.

40. Erskine Clarke, "Presbyterian Ecumenical Activity in the United States," in *DD*, pp. 150–151.

41. Ibid.

42. Quoted in Webster, "American Presbyterian Global Mission Policy: An Overview of 150 Years," p. 72.

43. Clarke, "Presbyterian Ecumenical Activity," in *DD*, pp. 152–155.

44. James F. Findley, "Religion and Politics in the Sixties: The Churches and the Civil Rights Act of 1964," *Journal of American History* 77 (1990): 66–92.

45. Clarke, "Presbyterian Ecumenical Activity," in *DD*, pp. 157–158.

46. Paul A. Crow, Jr., "The Ecumenical Movement," in *Encyclopedia of the American Religious Experience*, pp. 977–993.

47. John M. Mulder, "The Long, Rocky Road to Reunion," *Presbyterian Survey*, November 1981, 14–17 (also in *A.D.*); John M. Mulder, "Road Signs on the Way to Reunion," *Presbyterian Survey*, June 1983, 15–17 (also in *A.D.*); and Robert H. Bullock, "Presbyterian Reunion and Union Negotiations, 1937–1955: The Political Dimensions," *Journal of Presbyterian History* 60 (1982): 145–160.

48. Crow, "The Ecumenical Movement," in *Encyclopedia of the American Religious Experience*, ed. Charles H. Lippy and Peter W. Williams (New York: Charles Scribner's Sons, 1988), p. 989.

49. Theodore A. Gill, Jr., "American Presbyterians in the Global Ecumenical Movement," in *DD*, pp. 129–130.

50. Ibid, pp. 130–131.

51. Ibid., pp. 139–145.

52. Ibid.

53. Ibid., p. 140.

54. Ibid., pp. 142–143.

55. Ibid., pp. 144–145.

56. *Presbyterian Survey*, September 1987, 12–15.

57. The statement from Henry P. Van Dusen is quoted in H. George Anderson, "Ecumenical Movements," in Lotz et al., eds., *Altered Landscapes*, p. 96.

58. Gill, "American Presbyterians in the Global Ecumenical Movement," in *DD*, pp. 163–164.

59. H. Richard Niebuhr, *Christ and Culture* (New York: Harper & Row, 1951), pp. 190–229.

60. David O. Moberg, *The Great Reversal: Evangelism and Social Concern,* rev. ed. (Philadelphia: J. B. Lippincott, 1977); inter-

estingly, the first edition in 1972 was entitled *The Great Reversal: Evangelism vs. Social Concern.* Also Walter Rauschenbusch, *A Theology for the Social Gospel* (New York: Macmillan Co., 1917), pp. 1, 2.

61. Henry F. May, *Protestant Churches and Industrial America* (New York: Harper & Row, 1967), pp. 192–193.

62. Wuthnow, *The Restructuring of American Religion* (Princeton, N.J.: Princeton University Press, 1988), pp. 241–267, 317–322.

63. Johnson, "From Old to New Agendas," in *CM*, pp. 208–235, 217.

64. See, for example, Donald W. Shriver, Jr., "The Biblical Life in America: Which Past Fits Us for the Future?" in Lotz et al., eds., *Altered Landscapes*, pp. 343–376. Shriver does not include the reexamination of gender roles and the family as part of his description of mainstream Protestantism social ethics.

65. Johnson, "From Old to New Agendas," in *CM*, pp. 220–232; Lyman A. Kellstedt and Mark A. Noll, "Religion, Voting for President, and Party Affiliation," in *Religion and American Politics: From the Colonial Period to the 1980s,* ed. Mark A. Noll (New York: Oxford University Press, 1990), pp. 355–379.

66. Johnson, "From Old to New Agendas," in *CM*, p. 234.

67. Anne Motley Hallum, "Presbyterians as Political Amateurs," in *Religion in American Politics,* ed. Charles W. Dunn (Washington, D.C.: Congressional Quarterly Press, 1989), pp. 63–73.

68. Johnson, "From Old to New Agendas," in *CM*, pp. 234–235.

7: The Ecology for Nurturing Faith

1. John Calvin, *Institutes of the Christian Religion,* ed. John T. McNeill, trans. Ford Lewis Battles (Philadelphia: Westminster Press, 1960), IV, i, 5.

2. Kenneth A. Lockridge, *Literacy in Colonial New England* (New York: W. W. Norton & Co., 1974), pp. 3–101.

3. "Second Helvetic Confession," in *The Book of Confessions* (Louisville: Presbyterian Church (U.S.A.), 1990), 5.220; and John T. McNeill, *The History and Character of Calvinism* (New York: Oxford University Press, 1960), pp. 53–89.

4. Calvin, *Institutes,* I, i, 1–3; and John T. McNeill, "John Calvin: Doctor Ecclesiae," in *The Heritage of John Calvin,* ed. John

W. Bratt (Grand Rapids: Wm. B. Eerdmans Publishing Co., 1973), p. 12.

5. Samuel Eliot Morison, *The Intellectual Life of Colonial New England* (Ithaca, N.Y.: Cornell University Press, 1956), pp. 31, 43, 68; and Louis Filler, ed., *Horace Mann and the Crisis in Education* (Yellow Springs, Ohio: Antioch Press, 1965), p. 103.

6. Lawrence Cremin, *American Education: The Colonial Experience, 1607–1783* (New York: Harper & Row, 1970); Bernard Bailyn, *Education in the Forming of American Society* (Chapel Hill, N.C.: University of North Carolina Press, 1960); Charles Hambrick-Stowe, *The Practice of Piety* (Chapel Hill, N.C.: University of North Carolina Press, 1982).

7. Lyman Beecher, *A Plea for the West* (Cincinnati, 1835; reprint, New York: Arno Press, 1977), p. 30.

8. *The Constitution of the Presbyterian Church in the United States of America* (Philadelphia: Presbyterian Board of Publication and Sabbath School Work, 1904), chapters XVI, I.

9. Quoted in Nancy F. Cott, *The Bonds of Womanhood* (New Haven, Conn.: Yale University Press, 1978), p. 199. See also Charles E. Hambrick-Stowe, "Reformed Spirituality: Dimensions of Puritan Devotional Practice," *Journal of Presbyterian History* 58 (1980): 17–33.

10. Barbara Welter, *Dimity Convictions: The American Woman in the Nineteenth Century* (Athens, Ohio: Ohio University Press, 1970), pp. 21–41; Cott, *The Bonds of Womanhood*, pp. 85–102.

11. Cott, *The Bonds of Womanhood*, pp. 126–206.

12. James H. Smylie, " 'Of Secret and Family Worship': Historical Meditations, 1875–1975," *Journal of Presbyterian History* 58 (1980): 95–115.

13. Barbara Dafoe Whitehead and David Blankenhorn, "Man, Woman and Public Policy," *First Things,* no. 15 (August-September 1991), p. 28. See Carl N. Degler, *At Odds: Women and the Family in America* (New York: Oxford University Press, 1980); Michael Gordon, *The American Family in Social-Historical Perspective* (New York: St. Martin's Press, 1973); J. E. Goldthorpe, *Family Life in Western Societies: A Historical Sociology of Family Relationships in Britain and North America* (Cambridge: Cambridge University Press, 1987); Edward L. Kain, *The Myth of Family Decline: Understanding Families in a World of Rapid Social Change* (Lexington, Mass.: Lexington Books, 1990); Steven Mintz and Susan Kellogg, *Domestic Revolutions: A Social History of American Family Life* (New York: Free Press, 1988); Robert V.

Wells, *Revolutions in Americans' Lives: A Demographic Perspective on the History of Americans, Their Families, and Their Society* (Westport, Conn.: Greenwood Press, 1982).

14. See PCUS, G.A., *Minutes*, 1902, Appendix, pp. 339–340, for one discussion of the Family Altar. Samples of the pledge cards are available at the Presbyterian Study Center, Montreat, N.C.; Presbyterian Church (U.S.A.), *Directory for Worship* (Louisville: Office of the General Assembly, 1990), W-5.7001.

15. Mulder and Wyatt, "The Predicament of Pluralism," in *PV*, pp. 55–56; E. Brooks Holifield, *A History of Pastoral Care* (Nashville: Abingdon Press, 1983), pp. 210–256; and E. Brooks Holifield, "Pastoral Care and Counseling," in *Encyclopedia of the American Religious Experience*, ed. Charles H. Lippy and Peter W. Williams (New York: Charles Scribner's Sons, 1988), pp. 1583–1594; Smylie, " 'Of Secret and Family Worship': Historical Meditations, 1875–1975," pp. 95–115; Christopher Lasch, *Haven in a Heartless World: The Family Besieged* (New York: Basic Books, 1977).

16. Mark A. Noll and Darryl G. Hart, "The Language(s) of Zion: Presbyterian Devotional Literature in the Twentieth Century," in *CM*, pp. 187–207.

17. Louis B. Weeks, "The Scriptures and Sabbath Observance in the South," *Journal of Presbyterian History* 59 (1981): 273.

18. Benton Johnson, "On Dropping the Subject: Presbyterians and Sabbath Observance in the Twentieth Century," in *PP*, pp. 90–108.

19. Thomas Walter Laqueur, *Religion and Respectability: Sunday Schools and Working Class Culture, 1780–1850* (New Haven, Conn.: Yale University Press, 1976), pp. 1–33.

20. PC(USA), G.A., *Minutes*, 1987, pt. I, pp. 75, 619.

21. Sunday school participation ratios are drawn from data compiled by Donald Luidens in an appendix for his article "Numbering the Presbyterian Branches," in *MPD*, pp. 29–65. This appendix with statistical tables is available from Donald Luidens at Hope College or from the series editors upon request. PC(USA), G.A., *Minutes*, 1990, pt. II, p. 529.

22. Dykstra and Wigger, "Brief History of a Genre Problem," in *PV*, pp. 187–188; and Paul W. Koper, "The United Presbyterian Church and Christian Education—an Historical Overview," *Journal of Presbyterian History* 59 (1981): 288–308.

23. Ibid.; and William B. Kennedy, "Neo-Orthodoxy Goes to

Sunday School: The Christian Faith and Life Curriculum," *Journal of Presbyterian History* 58 (1980): 326–370.

24. Hester, "The Use of the Bible in Presbyterian Curricula," in *PV*, pp. 205–234.

25. Robert W. Lynn and Eliott Wright, *The Big Little School* (Nashville: Abingdon Press, 1980), pp. 133–167.

26. Dykstra and Wigger, "Brief History of a Genre Problem," in *PV*, pp. 180–204.

27. James Hastings Nichols, *Corporative Worship in the Reformed Tradition* (Philadelphia: Westminster Press, 1968), pp. 11–51; and John H. Leith, *The Reformed Imperative: What the Church Has to Say That No One Else Can Say* (Philadelphia: Westminster Press, 1988), p. 21.

28. David A. Ramsay and Craig Koedel, "The Communion Season—An Eighteenth Century Model," *Journal of Presbyterian History* 54 (1976): 203–216. See the letter from Ashbel Green to W. B. Sprague in William B. Sprague, *Lectures on Revivals of Religion* (Albany, N.Y.: Webster & Skinners, 1832), pp. 124–145, for one recollection of the continuity and the change.

29. Clifford M. Drury, *Presbyterian Panorama* (Philadelphia, Board of Christian Education, PCUSA, 1952), pp. 21–41.

30. See chapter 15, "Pastors and Preachers," in E. T. Thompson, *Presbyterians in the South*, vol. 2 (Richmond: John Knox Press, 1972), pp. 377–413, for one helpful summary of style and content.

31. John McClure, "Changes in the Authority, Method, and Message of Presbyterian (UPCUSA) Preaching in the Twentieth Century," in *CM*, pp. 86, 87.

32. Ibid., pp. 104–108; see also Moore, "Secularization: Religion and the Social Sciences," in *Between The Times*, ed. William R. Hutchison (New York: Cambridge University Press, 1989), pp. 233–252.

33. Zink, "Themes in Southern Presbyterian Preaching," in *CM*, pp. 109–133.

34. Loetscher, *A Brief History of the Presbyterians*, 4th ed. (Philadelphia: Westminster Press, 1983), p. 136.

35. Byars, "Challenging the Ethos," in *CM*, pp. 134–161.

36. Simmons, "Hymnody," in *CM*, pp. 162–186.

37. Ibid.

38. John M. Mulder, *Woodrow Wilson: The Years of Preparation* (Princeton, N.J.: Princeton University Press, 1978), p. 177; John W. Kuykendall, "The Presbyterian Heritage and Higher Ed-

ucation," *Presbyterian Outlook* 166 (April 23, 1984): 8–13; Donald G. Tewksbury, *The Founding of American Colleges and Universities Before the Civil War* (Hamden, Conn.: Archon Books, 1965), pp. 91–95; James Findley, "Agency, Denominations and the Western Colleges, 1830–1860: Some Connections Between Evangelicalism and American Higher Education," *Church History* 50 (1981): 64–80; and Leonard I. Sweet, "The Female Seminary Movement and Woman's Mission in Antebellum America," *Church History* 54 (1985): 41–55.

39. Longfield and Marsden, "Presbyterian Colleges in Twentieth-Century America," in *PV*, pp. 99–125; Bass, "Teaching With Authority," in *Mainstream Protestantism in the Twentieth Century*, p. 5; and The Task Force on Higher Education, "The Church's Mission in Higher Education," *Journal of Presbyterian History* 59 (1981): 440–465.

40. Bass, "Ministry on the Margins," in Hutchison, ed., *Between the Times*, pp. 48–57; and Longfield and Marsden, "Presbyterian Colleges in Twentieth-Century America," in *PV*, pp. 99–125.

41. Virginia Lieson Brereton, *Training God's Army: The American Bible School, 1880–1940* (Bloomington, Ind.: Indiana University Press, 1990).

42. Quoted in Longfield and Marsden, "Presbyterian Colleges in Twentieth-Century America," in *PV*, pp. 115.

43. Ibid.; also White, "Presbyterian Campus Ministries," in *PV*, pp. 126–147; D. Keith Naylor, "Campus Ministry and the Liberal Protestant Dilemma," in *Liberal Protestantism*, ed. Robert S. Michaelsen and Wade Clark Roof, pp. 115–128.

44. Bass, "Ministry in the Margin," in Hutchison, ed., *Between the Times*, pp. 48–71.

45. Quoted in Longfield and Marsden, "Presbyterian Colleges in Twentieth-Century America," in *PV*, p. 99.

46. Robert Wood Lynn, "A Ministry on the Margin," *The Church, the University, and Social Policy*, ed. Kenneth Underwood II (Middletown, Conn.: Wesleyan University Press, 1969), pp. 19–24.

47. Lefferts A. Loetscher, *The Broadening Church* (Philadelphia: University of Pennsylvania Press, 1954), p. 75.

48. Mark A. Noll, ed., *The Princeton Theology, 1812–1921* (Grand Rapids: Baker Book House, 1983), p. 56. Italics in the original.

49. John W. Hart, "Princeton Theological Seminary: The Reor-

ganization of 1929," *Journal of Presbyterian History* 58 (1980): 124–140.

50. Mulder and Wyatt, "The Predicament of Pluralism," in *PV*, p. 43.

51. The same shift can be detected at other seminaries; ibid., n. 23.

52. Quoted in ibid., p. 46.

53. Ibid., pp. 37–70.

54. Ibid.

55. Steve Hancock, "Nurseries of Piety? Spiritual Formation at Four Presbyterian Seminaries," in *PV*, pp. 71–98.

56. Mulder and Wyatt, "The Predicament of Pluralism," in *PV*, p. 63.

57. John B. Trotti and Richard A. Ray, "Presbyterians and Their Publishing Houses," in *PV*, p. 152.

58. Ibid., pp. 155–160.

59. Ibid., pp. 172–179.

60. James A. Overbeck, "The Rise and Fall of Presbyterian Official Journals," in *DD*, pp. 83–104.

61. Meister, "Presbyterians and Mass Media," in *DD*, pp. 170–186.

62. LaFollette, "Money and Power," in *OR*, pp. 198–231; and R. Douglas Brackenridge and Lois A. Boyd, "United Presbyterian Policy on Women and the Church—An Historical Overview," *Journal of Presbyterian History* 59 (1981): 383–407.

63. Ibid. Also see Lois A. Boyd and R. Douglas Brackenridge, "Presbyterian Women Ministers: A Historical Overview and Study of the Current Status of Women Pastors," in *PV*, pp. 289–307.

64. LaFollette, "Money and Power," in *OR*, pp. 198–231.

65. Dale E. Soden, "Men and Mission: The Shifting Fortunes of Presbyterian Men's Organizations in the Twentieth Century," in *OR*, pp. 232–252; and Daniel W. Martin, "The United Presbyterian Church Policy on the Men's Movement—an Historical Overview," *Journal of Presbyterian History* 59 (1981): 408–439.

8: A Case of Conflicting Allegiances

1. George M. Marsden, *Fundamentalism and American Culture* (New York: Oxford University Press, 1980), pp. 118–123.

2. Loetscher, *The Broadening Church* (Philadelphia: University of Pennsylvania Press, 1954), p. 135.

3. Rogers and McKim, "Pluralism and Policy," in *CM*, pp. 57–58.

4. For differing views on this important question, see Dean M. Kelley, "Religion and Justice: The Volcano and the Terrace," *Review of Religious Research* 26 (September 1984): 3–14; Arthur F. McGovern, *Liberation Theology and Its Critics* (Maryknoll, N.Y.: Orbis Books, 1989); Deane W. Ferm, ed., *Third World Liberation Theologies* (Maryknoll, N.Y.: Orbis Books, 1986); Alfred Hennelley, *Liberation Theology* (Maryknoll, N.Y.: Orbis Books, 1989).

5. The image of the Cheshire cat is borrowed from Os Guinness; see the chapter on the "Cheshire Cat Factor" in his *The Gravedigger File: Papers on the Subversion of the Modern Church* (Downers Grove, Ill.: InterVarsity Press, 1983), pp. 49–70.

6. Bryan F. LeBeau, "Subscription Controversy and Jonathan Dickinson," *Journal of Presbyterian History* 54 (Fall 1976): 317–335; Milton J Coalter, *Gilbert Tennent* (Westport, Conn.: Greenwood Press, 1986), pp. 27–28; Leonard J. Trinterud, *The Formation of an American Tradition* (Philadelphia: Westminster Press, 1949), pp. 61–66.

7. Edward A. Dowey, Jr., *A Commentary on the Confession of 1967 and an Introduction to the "Book of Confessions"* (Philadelphia: Westminster Press, 1968), pp. 28–31; and James H. Moorhead, "Redefining Confessionalism," in *CM*, p. 67.

8. Reifsnyder, "Managing the Mission," in *OR*, pp. 65–70, 78–83.

9. Eller, "Special-Interest Groups and American Presbyterianism," in *OR*, pp. 253–277.

10. UPCUSA, *Book of Order*, 1981–82, 47.016.

11. Reifsnyder, "Managing the Mission," in *OR*, pp. 65–75.

12. *The Constitution of the Presbyterian Church (U.S.A.)*, Part II, *Book of Order* (Louisville, Ky.: Office of the General Assembly, PC(USA), 1990), section G-9.0105.

13. PC(USA) Research Services, "The Presbyterian Congregation Profile Study," [1989], Report. No. 1.

14. Calvin, *Institutes*, IV, i, 9; John Stevenson McEwen, *The Faith of John Knox* (London: Lutterworth Press, 1961), pp. 59–60; and John H. Leith, *An Introduction to the Reformed Tradition* (Atlanta: John Knox Press, 1977), p. 140.

15. Dykstra and Hudnut-Beumler, "The National Organiza-

tional Structures of Protestant Denominations," in *OR*, pp. 317–330.

16. The one exceptional case was the United Church of Christ, which has a more congregationalist structure. It too has lost members.

17. For example, in 1963 $10.9 million was given for synod and presbytery causes in the United Presbyterian Church (U.S.A.) while $29.9 million went to the General Assembly. By 1983, $36.4 million was donated to synod and presbytery causes but $24.7 million to the General Assembly. Brunger and Klay, "A Financial History of American Presbyterian Giving, 1923–1983," in *OR*, pp. 122–131; Klay, "Changing Priorities," in *OR*, pp. 132–152; Brunger, "Global and Local Mission," in *OR*, pp. 153–169.

Similarly, the Major Mission Fund campaign of the 1970s determined a policy that 40 percent of its proceeds would go to either synods or presbyteries and 60 percent would go to General Assembly causes. But the current Bicentennial Fund campaign reversed these figures so that 60 percent or more of its proceeds will be received by presbyteries or synods while only 40 percent or less will go to assist the General Assembly. UPCUSA, G.A., *Minutes*, 1977, pt. I, p. 390.

18. Wulff and Marcum, "Cleavage or Consensus? A New Look at the Clergy-Laity Gap," in *PV*, pp. 308–326.

19. Cormode, "A Financial History of Presbyterian Congregations Since World War II," in *OR*, pp. 170–197; and Dykstra and Hudnut-Beumler, "The National Organizational Structures of Protestant Denominations," in *OR*, pp. 317–330.

20. Robert Wuthnow, *The Restructuring of American Religion* (Princeton, N.J.: Princeton University Press, 1988), pp. 133–240; Wuthnow, *The Struggle for America's Soul*, pp. 68–94; and Wuthnow, "The Restructuring of American Presbyterianism," in *PP*, pp. 27–48.

21. William R. Hutchison, ed., *Between the Times* (New York: Cambridge University Press, 1989), pp. 3–13; Jon Butler, *Awash in a Sea of Faith: Christianizing the American People* (Cambridge, Mass.: Harvard University Press, 1990). Catherine Albanese represents another school of thought that rejects the idea of a mainstream or establishment Protestant tradition altogether. See Catherine Albanese, *American Religions and Religion* (Belmont, Calif.: Wadsworth Publishing Co., 1981).

9: An Agenda for Reform

1. UPCUSA, G.A., *Minutes*, pt. I, pp. 336–397; John M. Mulder, "Brubaker Report Discusses Trends in Church Membership," *A.D.* 6 (June 1977): 50–51; Letter, *A.D.* 6 (September 1977): 5.

2. Erling Jorstad, *Holding Fast/Pressing On: Religion in America in the 1980s* (New York: Praeger Publishers, 1990), pp. 49–50.

3. Ferdinand Pharr, Conference at Hilton Head, N.C., Feb. 28—March 2, 1991; Gene and Nancy Preston, "A Friendly Church Is Hard to Find," *Christian Century* 108 (Jan. 30, 1991): 102–103.

4. "Denominational Perspectives, Personal Beliefs and Church Priorities," *Presbyterian Panel,* March 1989, 12; Gallup Organization, Inc., *The Spiritual Health of the Episcopal Church* (Washington, D.C.: n.p., 1990), p. 11; "Evangelism," *Presbyterian Panel*, June 1986, A4; and Roy M. Oswald and Speed B. Leas, *The Inviting Church: A Study of New Member Assimilation* (New York: Alban Institute, 1987), p. 44.

5. Donald P. Smith, "Closing the Back Door: Toward the Retention of Church Members," in *MPD*, pp. 86–101.

6. Coalter, "Presbyterian Evangelism," in *DD*, pp. 46–54.

7. Bullock, "Twentieth-Century Presbyterian New Church Development," in *DD*, pp. 55–82; and Brooks, "Reaching Out," in *MPD*, pp. 177–197.

8. See chapter 2.

9. Ibid.; Hadaway, "Denominational Defection," in *MPD*, pp. 102–121. See also Tex Sample, *U.S. Lifestyles and Mainline Churches.*

10. Dean R. Hoge, Benton Johnson, and Donald A. Luidens, *Vanishing Boundaries* (forthcoming); see also Sample, *U.S. Lifestyles and Mainline Churches* (Louisville, Ky.: Westminster/John Knox Press, 1990); and Franklin B. Gillespie, "Youth Programs of the United Presbyterian Church—an Historical Overview," *Journal of Presbyterian History* 59 (1981): 309–382.

11. Data provided by Research Services, PC(USA).

12. Wade Clark Roof and William McKinney, *American Mainline Religion* (New Brunswick, N.J.: Rutgers University Press, 1987), pp. 168, 172.

13. PCUSA, Board of Home Missions, *One Hundred Twenty-First Annual Report* (New York, 1923), p. 13.

14. A study coordinated at Louisville Presbyterian Theological Seminary and funded by the Pew Charitable Trust is currently under way which will investigate the history, theology, and practice of American Presbyterians in evangelism.

15. William Tyndale, *Prologue to the New Testament*, quoted in Hugh T. Kerr, *The Simple Gospel* (Louisville, Ky.: Westminster/John Knox Press, 1991), p. 72.

16. Calvin, *Institutes*, III, ii, 7.

17. Robert Booth Fowler, *Unconventional Partners: Religion and Liberal Culture in the United States* (Grand Rapids: Wm. B. Eerdmans Publishing Co., 1989), pp. 4, 32–47.

18. Darrell Guder, *Be My Witnesses: The Church's Mission, Message and Messengers* (Grand Rapids: Wm. B. Eerdmans Publishing Co., 1985), pp. 99–174.

19. Grayson L. Tucker, "Enhancing Church Vitality Through Congregational Identity Change," in *MPD*, p. 73.

20. Phillip Barron Jones, "An Examination of the Statistical Growth of the Southern Baptist Convention," in *Understanding Church Growth and Decline*, ed. Dean R. Hoge and David A. Roozen (New York: Pilgrim Press, 1979), pp. 160–178.

21. Robert Bullock, "A Thousand Points of Light," *Presbyterian Outlook* 172 (Oct. 8, 1990): 8.

22. Robert Wuthnow, *The Restructuring of American Religion* (Princeton, N.J.: Princeton University Press, 1988), pp. 170–171.

23. Hoge, Johnson, and Luidens, *Vanishing Boundaries*.

24. White, "Presbyterian Campus Ministries," in *PV*, pp. 126–147.

25. Conversations with Warner Darnell, Associate Synod Executive for the Synod of Living Waters; conversation with Professor Bill Leonard, Southern Baptist Theological Seminary, Louisville, Ky.

26. Meister, "Presbyterians and Mass Media," in *DD*, pp. 170–186; Voskuil, "Reaching Out: Mainline Protestantism and the Media," in *Between the Times,* ed. William R. Hutchison (New York: Cambridge University Press, 1989), pp. 72–92.

27. Johnson, "From Old to New Agendas," in *CM*, pp. 208–235; Don S. and Carol Browning, "The Church and the Family Crisis: A New Love Ethic," *Christian Century* 108 (August 7–14, 1991): 747; David Harrington Watt, "The Private Hopes of American Fundamentalists and Evangelicals, 1925–1975," *Religion and American Culture* 1 (1991): 155–176.

28. Ibid., pp. 746–749.

29. PC(USA) Research Services, *The Presbyterian Panel: 1991–93 Background Report*, pp. 20–22.

30. Peter L. Benson and Carolyn H. Eklin, *Effective Christian Education: A National Study of Protestant Congregations: A Summary Report on Faith, Loyalty and Congregational Life* (Minneapolis: Search Institute, 1990), p. 38.

31. *Directory for Worship*, W-5.7000–7003.

32. Barbara G. Wheeler, "Uncharted Territory: Congregational Identity and Mainline Protestantism," in *PP*, p. 68. See also David Heim, "Thinking About Congregations," *Christian Century* 108 (Oct. 2, 1991): 867–868.

33. Tucker, "Enhancing Church Vitality Through Congregational Identity Change," in *MPD*, pp. 66–85; Smith, "Closing the Back Door: Toward the Retention of Church Members," in *MPD*, pp. 86–101; Stone, "The New Voluntarism and Presbyterian Affiliation," in *MPD*, pp. 122–149; Wilhelm, "Membership Decline and Congregational Identity in Yonkers, New York: A Case Study in the Presbyterian Church (U.S.A.)," in *MPD*, pp. 150–176; Warner, "Mirror for American Protestantism: Mendocino Presbyterian Church in the Sixties and Seventies," in *MPD*, pp. 198–224.

34. Johnson, "On Dropping the Subject: Presbyterians and Sabbath Observance in the Twentieth Century," in *PP*, p. 107.

35. Stephen P. McCutchan, "Breaking the Tyranny of Time," *Journal for Preachers* 14 (1991): 3–6.

36. Dykstra and Wigger, "A Brief History of a Genre Problem," in *PV*, pp. 180–204; and Hester, "The Use of the Bible in Presbyterian Curricula," in *PV*, pp. 205–234.

37. Robert W. Lynn, *Protestant Strategies in Education* (New York: Association Press, 1964), p. 49; C. Ellis Nelson, "Congregations' Educational Strategy," in *Carriers of Faith: Lessons from Congregational Studies*, ed. Carl S. Dudley, Jackson W. Carroll, and James P. Wind (Louisville: Westminster/John Knox Press, 1991), pp. 163–164.

38. C. Ellis Nelson, *How Faith Matures* (Louisville, Ky.: Westminster/John Knox Press, 1989); C. Ellis Nelson, "Congregations' Educational Strategy," in Dudley et al., eds., *Carriers of Faith*, p. 169.

39. Bellah et al., *Habits of the Heart*, pp. 56–65.

40. Dykstra and Hudnut-Beumler, "The National Organizational Structures of Protestant Denominations," in *OR*, pp. 306–330; McCarthy, "The Emerging Importance of Presbyterian

Polity," in *OR*, pp. 278–305; and Moorhead, "Redefining Confessionalism," in *CM*, pp. 75–83.

41. Weeks and Fogleman, "A 'Two Church' Hypothesis," pp. 8–10.

42. "Denominational Perspectives, Personal Beliefs and Church Priorities," *Presbyterian Panel*, March 1989, 5, A-3.

43. Paul Wilkes, "The Hands That Would Shape Our Souls," *Atlantic Monthly*, December 1990: 59–88.

44. Calvin, *Institutes*, IV, iii, 11.

45. Ahlstrom, "The Ministry from the Placid Decade to the Present, 1950–1980," in *The Ministry in Historical Perspectives*, ed. H. Richard Niebuhr and Daniel D. Williams, rev. ed. (San Francisco: Harper & Row, 1983), pp. 303–304.

46. Harvey, "On the Intellectual Marginality of American Theology," in *Religion and Twentieth-Century American Intellectual Life*, ed. Michael J. Lacey (New York: Cambridge University Press, 1989), pp. 172–192.

47. Benton Johnson, "Winning Lost Sheep: A Recovery Course for Liberal Protestantism," in *Liberal Protestantism*, ed. Robert S. Michaelsen and Wade Clark Roof (New York: Pilgrim Press, 1986), p. 229.

48. Hutchison, "Discovering America," in idem, ed., *Between the Times*, pp. 303–338.

49. Paul Tillich, *The Protestant Era* (Chicago: University of Chicago Press, 1948), pp. 161–181; *Book of Order*, G-1.0301, 1.0307.

50. Zikmund, "Ministry of Word and Sacrament," in *PP*, pp. 134–158.

51. Farley, "The Presbyterian Heritage as Modernism," in *PP*, pp. 49–66.

52. Zikmund, "The Values and Limits of Representation and Pluralism in the Church," in *PV*, pp. 327–348; and Dorothy C. Bass, "Faith and Pluralism in the United States," *On the Way* 3 (1985): 12–22.

53. Hoge, *Division in the Protestant House*, p. 126.

54. Bill Leonard, *God's Last and Only Hope: The Fragmentation of the Southern Baptist Convention* (Grand Rapids: Wm. B. Eerdmans Publishing Co., 1990) and Nancy Tatom Ammerman, *Baptist Battles: Social and Religious Conflict in the Southern Baptist Convention* (New Brunswick, N.J.: Rutgers University Press, 1990).

55. Kellstedt and Noll, "Religion, Voting for President, and

Party Affiliation," in *Religion and American Politics*, ed. Mark A. Noll (New York: Oxford University Press, 1989), pp. 369–370.

56. Rogers and McKim, "Pluralism and Policy in Presbyterian Views of Scripture," in *CM*, pp. 56–58.

57. Martin E. Marty, "The Sacred and the Secular in American History," in *Transforming Faith: The Sacred and the Secular in Modern American History*, ed. M. L. Bradbury and James B. Gilberts (Westport, Conn.: Greenwood Press, 1989), pp. 8–9.

58. Hoge, Johnson, and Luidens, *Vanishing Boundaries*.

59. Lesslie Newbigin, *Foolishness to the Greeks* (Grand Rapids: Wm. B. Eerdmans Publishing Co., 1989), pp. 1–20; Wuthnow, *Restructuring of American Religion*, pp. 268–296.

60. Wuthnow, "The Restructuring of American Presbyterianism," in *PP*, pp. 46–48.

61. Reinhold Niebuhr, *The Irony of American History* (New York: Charles Scribner's Sons, 1952; Joseph C. Hough, Jr., "The Loss of Optimism as a Problem for Liberal Christian Faith," in Michaelsen and Roof, eds., *Liberal Protestantism*, pp. 145–166.

62. Presbyterian Church (U.S.A.), *The Constitution of the Presbyterian Church (U.S.A.):* Part II, *Book of Order* (Louisville, Ky.: Office of the General Assembly, PC(USA), 1990), G-2.0500.

63. *Book of Order*, G-2.0300–0500.

64. Barbara Cross, ed., *The Autobiography of Lyman Beecher*, 2 vols. (Cambridge: Harvard University Press, 1961), I, 252–253.

65. Ibid.

66. Ibid. The italics are Beecher's.

Selected Readings

Bass, Dorothy C., Benton Johnson, and Wade Clark Roof. *Mainstream Protestantism in the Twentieth Century: Its Problems and Prospects.* 1986; Louisville, Ky.: Committee on Theological Education, Presbyterian Church (U.S.A.).

Bellah, Robert N., et al. *Habits of the Heart.* New York: Harper & Row, 1985.

Boyd, Lois A., and R. Douglas Brackenridge. *Presbyterian Women in America: Two Centuries of a Quest for Status.* Westport, Conn.: Greenwood, 1983.

Bromley, David G., ed. *Falling from the Faith: Causes and Consequences of Religious Apostasy.* Newbury Park, Calif.: Sage Publications, 1988.

Gallup, George, Jr., and Jim Castelli. *The People's Religion: American Faith in the 90s.* New York: Macmillan Publishing Co., 1989.

Hale, J. Russell. *Who Are the Unchurched? An Exploratory Study.* Washington, D.C.: Glenmary Research Center, 1977.

Handy, Robert T. *A Christian America: Protestant Hopes and Historical Realities.* 2nd ed., rev. and enlarged. New York: Oxford University Press, 1984.

Hoge, Dean R., Benton Johnson, and Donald A. Luidens. *Vanishing Boundaries: The Religion of Protestant Baby Boomers* (forthcoming).

Hoge, Dean R., and David A. Roozen, eds. *Understanding Church Growth and Decline: 1950–1978.* New York: Pilgrim Press, 1979.

Hunter, James Davison. *Culture Wars: The Struggle to Define America.* New York: Basic Books, 1991.

Hutchison, William R., ed. *Between the Times: The Travail of the Protestant Establishment in America, 1900–1960.* New York: Cambridge University Press, 1989.

Lincoln, C. Eric, and Lawrence Mamiya. *The Black Church in the African American Experience.* Durham, N.C.: Duke University Press, 1990.

Loetscher, Lefferts A. *A Brief History of the Presbyterians.* 4th ed. Philadelphia: Westminster Press, 1983.

———. *The Broadening Church: A Study of Theological Issues in the Presbyterian Church Since 1869.* Philadelphia: University of Pennsylvania Press, 1954.

Longfield, Bradley J. *The Presbyterian Controversy: Fundamentalists, Modernists, and Moderates.* New York: Oxford University Press, 1991.

Lotz, David W., ed. *Altered Landscapes: Christianity in America, 1935–1985.* Grand Rapids: Wm. B. Eerdmans Publishing Co., 1989.

Lyon, David. *The Steeple's Shadow: On the Myths and Realities of Secularization.* Grand Rapids: Wm. B. Eerdmans Publishing Co., 1985.

Marsden, George M. *Fundamentalism and American Culture.* New York: Oxford University Press, 1980.

———. *Reforming Fundamentalism: Fuller Seminary and the New Evangelicalism.* Grand Rapids: Wm. B. Eerdmans Publishing Co., 1987.

———. *Understanding Fundamentalism and Evangelicalism.* Grand Rapids: Wm. B. Eerdmans Publishing Co., 1991.

Marty, Martin E. *The Noise of Conflict, 1919–1941*, vol. 2. *Modern American Religion.* Chicago: University of Chicago Press, 1991.

Michaelsen, Robert S., and Wade Clark Roof, eds. *Liberal Protestantism: Realities and Possibilities.* New York: Pilgrim Press, 1986.

Neuhaus, Richard John, ed. *The Believable Futures of American Protestantism.* Grand Rapids: Wm. B. Eerdmans Publishing Co., 1988.

Newbigin, Lesslie. *Foolishness to the Greeks: The Gospel and Western Culture.* Grand Rapids: Wm. B. Eerdmans Publishing Co., 1986.

————. *The Gospel in a Pluralist Society.* Grand Rapids: Wm. B. Eerdmans Publishing Co., 1989.

Palmer, Parker J., Barbara G. Wheeler, and James W. Fowler, eds. *Caring for the Commonweal: Education for Religious and Public Life.* Macon, Ga.: Mercer University Press, 1990.

Roof, Wade Clark, and William McKinney. *American Mainline Religion: Its Changing Shape and Future.* New Brunswick, N.J.: Rutgers University Press, 1987.

Sample, Tex. *U.S. Lifestyles and Mainline Churches: A Key to Reaching People in the 90s.* Louisville, Ky.: Westminster/John Knox Press, 1990.

Wuthnow, Robert. *The Struggle for America's Soul: Evangelicals, Liberals, and Secularism.* Grand Rapids: Wm. B. Eerdmans Publishing Co., 1989.

————. *The Restructuring of American Religion: Society and Faith Since World War II.* Princeton, N.J.: Princeton University Press, 1988.

The Presbyterian Presence:
The Twentieth-Century Experience

Series Contents

Index